Laying *the* Foundation

By
Dr. Michael Elliott

Laying
the
Foundation

By
Dr. Michael Elliott

River City Press, Inc.
Life Changing Books.

Laying the Foundation

Copyright 2006 by Dr. Michael Elliott

ISBN: 0-9706962-9-9
EAN: 978-0-970696298

Unless otherwise indicated, all Scripture quotations are from the New King James Version, copyright 1979, 1980, 1982 by Thomas Nelson, Inc.

Cover Design: Sandra Jeltema

Editor: Ann Elliott

Published by:
River City Press, Inc.
Life Changing Books.
4301 Emerson Avenue North
Minneapolis, MN 54412

Printed in the United States of America

Dedication

To my wonderful grandchildren: Ashley, Austin, Jacob, Alexis, Makenzie and Michael. May you fall in love with God's Word and determine in your hearts to know Him. Choose daily to live in all of His promised fullness. Study hard; walk straight; trust His grace; and enjoy the journey.

Papa

Acknowledgments

My deepest gratitude goes to my wife, Ann, for her countless hours of editing this book. Her thoughts and wisdom melt into mine throughout each chapter. I constantly relied on her quiet strength and encouragement as this book was taking shape and becoming a reality. She is truly a gift of God to my life, which just proves once more ... the amazing grace of our Lord.

Laying the Foundation
Table of Contents

Laying the Foundation
Preface

Every construction project begins with diligently laying a proper foundation. The foundation establishes the potential strength and the weight that the building can support. The more elaborate the structure, the more critical the foundation becomes as the building would be at great risk of collapse if not properly anchored.

Just as a proper foundation is crucial for a construction project, it is even more imperative to have a solid foundation upon which to anchor our beliefs. Tragically, far too many Christians attempt to build their spiritual lives without first laying a proper foundation for their faith in God. The end result is often the collapse of their belief system, leaving them confused and discouraged.

In this study, we will examine seventeen fundamental truths of Christianity of which every Christian needs to have a working knowledge. While none of these studies are exhaustive, they do provide an overview of the subject. There are several practical applications for this study:

1. If you are a new Christian, this study will help you start on the journey of becoming a disciplined follower of Jesus Christ by laying a proper spiritual foundation to which your beliefs can be anchored;

2. If you are a seasoned Christian, this study will help reinforce the foundation of your beliefs, as well as, provide a resource tool that will enable you to explore each of these truths in order to gain a deeper understanding;

3. If you are a pastor or teacher of the Word of God, this study will be an invaluable tool to help you ground your congregation, or Bible study group, in the fundamental truths of God's Word.

Jesus spent a great deal of time teaching His disciples the fundamental truths of living in the Kingdom of God; in doing so, He laid the foundation upon which the early church was to be built. This must have been an important concept as the Apostle Paul also continually reminded the churches to adhere to the principles of Christianity. There are several reasons that each of us, as individual believers, must lay this important foundation:

1. Laying a proper foundation will enable a believer to establish what they believe and why they believe it. For many, their belief system is a product of how they were raised: "My grandparents and parents were good people and they believed it this way; if it was good enough for them it is good enough for me." Tragically, they have taken the opinion of their family, denomination, or their pastor, to be the truth without searching the Scriptures for themselves. While the traditions and beliefs of those close to us may enhance our understanding, the Holy Spirit must be our mentor in the discovery of God's principles. Peter tells us that we need to be ready to give an answer to everyone concerning our beliefs.

   But sanctify the Lord God in your hearts, and always be ready to give a defense to everyone who asks you a reason for the hope that is in you, with meekness and fear (I Peter 3:15).

2. Laying a proper foundation will eliminate doubts and misconceptions that have been formed regarding God's Word. The prophet, Hosea, warned that men would perish without the knowledge of God's will as revealed and expressed in His Word.

   My people are destroyed for lack of knowledge. Because you have rejected knowledge, I also will reject you from being priest for Me; Because you have forgotten the law of your God, I also will forget your children (Hosea 4:6).

2

Jesus rebuked the religious leaders of His day because they spoke their opinions. Their lack of knowledge and understanding of the Scriptures caused them to live and minister under deception and misconceptions.

Jesus answered and said to them, "You are mistaken, not knowing the Scriptures nor the power of God" (Matthew 22:29).

3. Laying a proper foundation will enable you to build a strong Christian walk with the Lord. When you are confronted with a different or strange doctrine, you will not be swayed; but rather, you will remain rooted and grounded in the truth of the Word of God.

    That we should no longer be children, tossed to and fro and carried about with every wind of doctrine, by the trickery of men, in the cunning craftiness of deceitful plotting, but, speaking the truth in love, may grow up in all things into Him who is the head—Christ (Ephesians 4:14-15).

4. Laying a proper foundation will give you an anchor in the trials of life. You will have a place of refuge, security, and stability. You will be able to use your knowledge of God's Word as an effective weapon in waging spiritual warfare.

    In the Lord I put my trust; how can you say to my soul, "Flee as a bird to your mountain"? For look! The wicked bend their bow, they make ready their arrow on the string, that they may shoot secretly at the upright in heart. If the foundations are destroyed, what can the righteous do (Psalm 11:1-3)?

5. Finally, laying a proper foundation will promote unity and will bridge the gaps in our differences. While we may not agree on every aspect of interpretation and the application of Scripture, we can find common ground in the fundamental principles of Christianity. As we unite in love, we can then join in the common cause of reaching our world with the gospel of Jesus.

Therefore if there is any consolation in Christ, if any comfort of love, if any fellowship of the Spirit, if any affection and mercy, fulfill my joy by being like-minded, having the same love, being of one accord, of one mind (Philippians 2:1-2).

God is never going to change His mind about His Word; *"The Word of God is forever settled"* **(Psalm 119:89). We can anchor our lives upon the authority of His principles. We never have to fear that the Word will fail us; and we can chart the course of our lives according to the timeless precepts found within its pages. Jesus prayed that God would set us apart from the ways of the world by establishing us in the truth of His Word.**

I have given them Your word; and the world has hated them because they are not of the world, just as I am not of the world. I do not pray that You should take them out of the world, but that You should keep them from the evil one. They are not of the world, just as I am not of the world. Sanctify them by Your truth. Your word is truth (John 17:14-17).

As you embark on your study of these principles, ask the Holy Spirit to teach you the practical application of each truth.

Open my eyes, that I may see wondrous things from Your law (Psalm 119:18).

May the prayers of the Apostle Paul become a living reality in your life as you study the foundational precepts of the Word.

For this reason we also, since the day we heard it, do not cease to pray for you, and to ask that you may be filled with the knowledge of His will in all wisdom and spiritual understanding; that you may walk worthy of the Lord, fully pleasing Him, being fruitful in every good work and increasing in the knowledge of God; strengthened with all might, according to His glorious power, for all patience and longsuffering with joy; giving thanks to the Father who has qualified us to be partakers of the inheritance of the saints in the light. He has delivered us from the power of darkness and conveyed us into the kingdom of the Son of His love, in whom we have redemption through His blood, the forgiveness of sins (Colossians 1:9-14).

For this reason I bow my knees to the Father of our Lord Jesus Christ, from whom the whole family in heaven and earth is named, that He would grant you, according to the riches of His glory, to be strengthened with might through His Spirit in the inner man, that Christ may dwell in your hearts through faith; that you, being rooted and grounded in love, may be able to comprehend with all the saints what is the width and length and depth and height— to know the love of Christ which passes knowledge; that you may be filled with all the fullness of God. Now to Him who is able to do exceedingly abundantly above all that we ask or think, according to the power that works in us, to Him be glory in the church by Christ Jesus to all generations, forever and ever. Amen (Ephesians 3:14-21).

May you grow in the grace and knowledge of our Lord and Savior, Jesus Christ. To Him be the glory both now and forevermore. Amen.

(The Apostle Paul)

Chapter One

The Gift of Salvation

I. Our Spiritual New Birth.

A. We must be born again in order to have a relationship with God and gain entrance into His eternal kingdom.

Jesus answered and said to him, "Most assuredly, I say to you, unless one is born again, he cannot see the kingdom of God" (John 3:3).

B. The reason we must be born again is that by our very nature we are at war with God.

Because the carnal mind is enmity against God; for it is not subject to the law of God, nor indeed can be (Romans 8:7).

C. It is impossible for the natural man to receive things from God, because things received from God are spiritually discerned.

But the natural man does not receive the things of the Spirit of God, for they are foolishness to him; nor can he know them, because they are spiritually discerned (I Corinthians 2:14).

D. We must also be born again because our sin has separated us from God.

For all have sinned and fall short of the glory of God (Romans 3:23).

E. The penalty for our sin is death.

For the wages of sin is death, but the gift of God is eternal life in Christ Jesus our Lord (Romans 6:23).

F. No man has escaped the touch of sin. All of us have been born with the fallen and sinful nature of the first man, Adam.

Therefore, just as through one man sin entered the world, and death through sin, and thus death spread to all men, because all sinned (Romans 5:12).

G. **It is not God's desire, nor is it His will, for any man to perish under the penalty of sin.**

The Lord is not slack concerning His promise, as some count slackness, but is longsuffering toward us, not willing that any should perish but that all should come to repentance (II Peter 3:9).

H. **God desires for every man to believe in Him and turn from their sin, so that they can enjoy His great love.**

For God so loved the world that He gave His only begotten Son, that whoever believes in Him should not perish but have everlasting life (John 3:16).

I. **God did far more than just declare His love for mankind; He proved it conclusively through Christ's death on the cross. Through His death, Jesus paid man's sin penalty in full.**

But God demonstrates His own love toward us, in that while we were still sinners, Christ died for us (Romans 5:8).

In this is love, not that we loved God, but that He loved us and sent His Son to be the propitiation for our sins (I John 4:10).

J. **In order to receive God's free gift of salvation by faith, we must believe in our hearts that Jesus died for our sins. Then, we must confess with our mouths what we have believed in our hearts … Jesus is our Savior.**

But what does it say? "The word is near you, in your mouth and in your heart" (that is, the word of faith which we preach): that if you confess with your mouth the Lord Jesus and believe in your heart that God has raised Him from the dead, you will be saved. For with the heart one believes unto righteousness, and with the mouth confession is made unto salvation. For the Scripture says, "Whoever believes on Him will not be put to shame." For there is no distinction between Jew and Greek, for the same Lord over all is rich to all who call upon Him. For "whoever calls on the name of the Lord shall be saved" (Romans 10:8-13).

K. It is impossible for anyone to earn their salvation; for salvation is a gift from God and a work of His grace.

For by grace you have been saved through faith, and that not of yourselves; it is the gift of God, not of works, lest anyone should boast (Ephesians 2:8-9).

II. Our New Position in Christ.

A. When we receive Christ as our personal Savior, we then become a member of God's family.

But as many as received Him, to them He gave the right to become children of God, to those who believe in His name (John 1:12).

For as many as are led by the Spirit of God, these are sons of God (Romans 8:14).

Beloved, now we are children of God; and it has not yet been revealed what we shall be, but we know that when He is revealed, we shall be like Him, for we shall see Him as He is (I John 3:2).

B. Every day the Holy Spirit confirms to our hearts that God is our Father and we His children.

The Spirit Himself bears witness with our spirit that we are children of God (Romans 8:16).

C. As a member of God's family we are now positioned and entitled to share in the family inheritance.

If children, then heirs—heirs of God and joint heirs with Christ if indeed we suffer with Him, that we may also be glorified together (Romans 8:17).

D. We are made new in Christ; literally, we are His new creation and our old natures and ways are gone.

Therefore, if anyone is in Christ, he is a new creation; old things have passed away; behold, all things have become new (II Corinthians 5:17).

E. **We are justified in God's eyes when we accept Christ's sacrifice for our sins. The word justified means that God sees us "just-as-if-we-had-never-sinned."**

Therefore, having been justified by faith, we have peace with God through our Lord Jesus Christ (Romans 5:1).

F. **As we grow in Christ we become partakers of His divine nature.**

His divine power has given to us all things that pertain to life and Godliness, through the knowledge of Him who called us by glory and virtue, by which have been given to us exceedingly great and precious promises, that through these you may be partakers of the divine nature, having escaped the corruption that is in the world through lust (II Peter 1:3-4).

G. **Jesus suffered the full wrath of God's judgment for our sins on the cross. He suffered and died on our behalf so that when we receive Him as our Savior, we can stand before God as righteous because He has clothed us in His righteousness.**

For He made Him who knew no sin to be sin for us, that we might become the righteousness of God in Him (II Corinthians 5:21).

H. **As a result of Christ's victory on the cross over Satan, hell's agenda has been defeated. Now, regardless of our circumstances, He will deliver us from being victims and will make us victorious conquerors.**

Who shall separate us from the love of Christ? Shall tribulation, or distress, or persecution, or famine, or nakedness, or peril, or sword? As it is written: "For Your sake we are killed all day long; We are accounted as sheep for the slaughter." Yet in all these things we are more than conquerors through Him who loved us. For I am persuaded that neither death nor life, nor angels nor principalities nor powers, nor things present nor things to come, nor height nor depth, nor any other created thing, shall be able to separate us from the love of God which is in Christ Jesus our Lord (Romans 8:35-39).

I.   **No matter what the devil tries to do, we can overcome hell's agenda through the blood of Jesus and with the confession of our faith in God's Word.**

And they overcame him by the blood of the Lamb and by the word of their testimony, and they did not love their lives to the death (Revelation 12:11).

J.   **Jesus has made us to be royal priests unto God.**

1.   **Royalty speaks of our new position in Christ as a king. We are to exercise our God-given authority in every area of our lives and bring it in line with the Word.**

2.   **Priesthood speaks of our ministry to the Lord. As a priest, we are to daily offer our praise for His faithfulness and we are to release the adoration of our hearts to Him in worship.**

But you are a chosen generation, a royal priesthood, a holy nation, His own special people, that you may proclaim the praises of Him who called you out of darkness into His marvelous light (I Peter 2:9).

And from Jesus Christ the faithful witness, the firstborn from the dead, and the ruler over the kings of the earth. To Him who loved us and washed us from our sins in His own blood, and has made us kings and priests to His God and Father, to Him be glory and dominion forever and ever. Amen (Revelation 1:5-6).

And have made us kings and priests to our God; And we shall reign on the earth (Revelation 5:10).

K.   **We have been appointed as ambassadors of God's kingdom. We have been given the full authority to represent the government of heaven through our actions and our words.**

Now then, we are ambassadors for Christ, as though God were pleading through us: we implore you on Christ's behalf, be reconciled to God (II Corinthians 5:20).

L.   We have special gifts and talents given to us by God. We are to use these gifts and talents to serve Him and His church.

For as we have many members in one body, but all the members do not have the same function, so we, being many, are one body in Christ, and individually members of one another. Having then gifts differing according to the grace that is given to us, let us use them: if prophecy, let us prophesy in proportion to our faith; or ministry, let us use it in our ministering; he who teaches, in teaching; he who exhorts, in exhortation; he who gives, with liberality; he who leads, with diligence; he who shows mercy, with cheerfulness (Romans 12:4-8).

But one and the same Spirit works all these things, distributing to each one individually as He wills. But now God has set the members, each one of them, in the body just as He pleased (I Corinthians 12:11, 18).

M.   We must accept the fact that we are here on earth to serve Christ and His Church; we are not here to be served. We are to offer our service to God whenever, and wherever, He calls us.

Let a man so consider us, as servants of Christ and stewards of the mysteries of God (I Corinthians 4:1).

N.   We, as Christians, are called to be a living witness to the reality of a living God.

But you shall receive power when the Holy Spirit has come upon you; and you shall be witnesses to Me in Jerusalem, and in all Judea and Samaria, and to the end of the earth (Acts1:8).

That which was from the beginning, which we have heard, which we have seen with our eyes, which we have looked upon, and our hands have handled, concerning the Word of life— the life was manifested, and we have seen, and bear witness, and declare to you that eternal life which was with the Father and was manifested to us— that which we have seen and heard we declare to you, that you also may have fellowship with us; and truly our fellowship is with the Father and with His Son Jesus Christ (I John 1:1-3).

14

a. **Realizing that we are God's servants and witnesses on the earth, we must not live our lives by the world's standards; rather, we are to present ourselves as a living sacrifice before God. We are to live according to God's standards.**

I beseech you therefore, brethren, by the mercies of God, that you present your bodies a living sacrifice, holy, acceptable to God, which is your reasonable service. And do not be conformed to this world, but be transformed by the renewing of your mind, that you may prove what is that good and acceptable and perfect will of God (Romans 12:1-2).

b. **It matters how we conduct our lives. We need to daily ask ourselves if we are living in such a way that people will be able to see Jesus in us.**

You are the light of the world. A city that is set on a hill cannot be hidden (Matthew 5:14).

O. **We are to live with the awareness that the Holy Spirit lives in us. Consequently, we make Him a party to our every thought, word, and action.**

Having been built on the foundation of the apostles and prophets, Jesus Christ Himself being the chief cornerstone in whom the whole building, being joined together, grows into a holy temple in the Lord, in whom you also are being built together for a dwelling place of God in the Spirit (Ephesians 2:20-22).

Do you not know that you are the temple of God and that the Spirit of God dwells in you (I Corinthians 3:16).

P. **Christ has positioned us to live a victorious Christian life. However, in order to live in Christ's victory, we must daily discipline ourselves to embrace the mandates of God's Word with absolute obedience.**

And the Lord will make you the head and not the tail; you shall be above only, and not be beneath, if you heed the commandments of the Lord your God, which I command you today, and are careful to observe them (Deuteronomy 28:13).

Q. **We will never understand, nor fully grasp on this side of heaven, the scope of God's amazing love for us.**

   1. **He watches over our lives and never allows anyone, or anything, to separate us from His love.**

   2. **We are not only the object of His love; we are the apple of His eye.**

   He found him in a desert land and in the wasteland, a howling wilderness; He encircled him, He instructed him, He kept him as the apple of His eye (Deuteronomy 32:10).

   For thus says the Lord of hosts: "He sent Me after glory, to the nations which plunder you; for he who touches you touches the apple of His eye" (Zechariah 2:8).

III. Our New Benefits.

A. **Jesus has redeemed us from the hand of our enemy and has spoiled hell's agenda against us.**

Let the redeemed of the Lord say so, whom He has redeemed from the hand of the enemy (Psalm 107:2).

B. **Jesus has redeemed us and delivered us from the curse of the law.**

   1. **The curse of the law impacted three areas of our life: poverty; sickness; and death.**

   2. **The Bible tells us we have been delivered from the curse of the law and instructs us on how to be successful and prosperous in every area of life.**

   Christ has redeemed us from the curse of the law, having become a curse for us (for it is written, "Cursed is everyone who hangs on a tree"), that the blessing of Abraham might come upon the Gentiles in Christ Jesus, that we might receive the promise of the Spirit through faith (Galatians 3:13-14).

16

Now Abraham was old, well advanced in age; and the Lord had blessed Abraham in all things (Genesis 24:1).

He who did not spare His own Son, but delivered Him up for us all, how shall He not with Him also freely give us all things (Romans 8:32).

This Book of the Law shall not depart from your mouth, but you shall meditate in it day and night, that you may observe to do according to all that is written in it. For then you will make your way prosperous, and then you will have good success (Joshua 1:8).

C. **Jesus has delivered us from the power and control of the devil; we are under His influence and command.**

He has delivered us from the power of darkness and conveyed us into the kingdom of the Son of His love (Colossians 1:13).

D. **Jesus has abundantly blessed our lives with all of His spiritual blessings.**

Blessed be the God and Father of our Lord Jesus Christ, who has blessed us with every spiritual blessing in the heavenly places in Christ (Ephesians 1:3).

Blessed shall you be when you come in, and blessed shall you be when you go out (Deuteronomy 28:6).

E. **The blood of Jesus cleanses our lives from each and every one of our sins. This cleansing gives us the confidence to enjoy our relationship with God.**

But if we walk in the light as He is in the light, we have fellowship with one another, and the blood of Jesus Christ His Son cleanses us from all sin (I John 1:7).

F. **Jesus has completely set us free from sin's control and dominion over our lives.**

But God be thanked that though you were slaves of sin, yet you obeyed from the heart that form of doctrine to which you were delivered. And having been set free from sin, you became slaves of righteousness (Romans 6:17-18).

G. **Once we have placed our sins under the blood of Jesus and have received God's forgiveness, we will never be confronted with our sins again.**

   1. **God has chosen to never again remember our sins, or to hold our past mistakes against us.**

   2. **Jesus has not only forgiven our sins, but He has set us free from the guilt and penalty of them.**

   Then He adds, "Their sins and their lawless deeds I will remember no more" (Hebrews 10:17).

H. **When God forgives us, He removes our sins from us as far as the east is from the west. This distance cannot be measured and therefore we are assured our sins are forever gone. However, if He had said our sins were removed as far as the north is from the south, then we would not have the confidence, or assurance, that our sins were forever gone as the distance between the North Pole and the South Pole can be measured.**

   As far as the east is from the west, so far has He removed our transgressions from us (Psalm 103:12).

I. **God promises us that anytime we fail and sin, He will forgive us if we will repent of our sin.**

   If we confess our sins, He is faithful and just to forgive us our sins and to cleanse us from all unrighteousness (I John 1:9).

J. **Through the sacrifice of Christ on the cross we are no longer the enemies of God.**

   For it pleased the Father that in Him all the fullness should dwell, and by Him to reconcile all things to Himself, by Him, whether things on earth or things in heaven, having made peace through the blood of His cross. And you, who once were alienated and enemies in your mind by wicked works, yet now He has reconciled in the body of His flesh through death, to present you holy, and blameless, and above reproach in His sight (Colossians 1:19-22).

K. **The Holy Spirit promises to lead us in every decision and direction that we take in our lives.**

For as many as are led by the Spirit of God, these are sons of God (Romans 8:14).

L. **The Holy Spirit has been assigned to reveal the plans of God for our lives and to help us understand the mysteries of God's Word.**

But as it is written: "Eye has not seen, nor ear heard, nor have entered into the heart of man the things which God has prepared for those who love Him" But God has revealed them to us through His Spirit. For the Spirit searches all things, yes, the deep things of God. For what man knows the things of a man except the spirit of the man which is in him? Even so no one knows the things of God except the Spirit of God. Now we have received, not the spirit of the world, but the Spirit who is from God, that we might know the things that have been freely given to us by God (I Corinthians 2:9-12).

M. **God grants us His peace which guards our hearts and minds in every circumstance; therefore, we focus our thoughts on God's promises and not on our problems.**

Be anxious for nothing, but in everything by prayer and supplication, with thanksgiving, let your requests be made known to God; and the peace of God, which surpasses all understanding, will guard your hearts and minds through Christ Jesus (Philippians 4:6-7).

Finally, brethren, whatever things are true, whatever things are noble, whatever things are just, whatever things are pure, whatever things are lovely, whatever things are of good report, if there is any virtue and if there is anything praiseworthy— meditate on these things. The things which you learned and received and heard and saw in me, these do, and the God of peace will be with you (Philippians 4:8-9).

N. **Regardless of how vile our past sins and lifestyles may have been, we now live free from condemnation because of God's forgiveness; through the blood of Jesus.**

There is therefore now no condemnation to those who are in Christ Jesus, who do not walk according to the flesh, but according to the Spirit (Romans 8:1).

O. **Jesus not only paid our sin penalty on the cross, He also purchased our healing. He desires that we live in divine health and prosper in all areas of our lives.**

Who Himself bore our sins in His own body on the tree, that we, having died to sins, might live for righteousness—by whose stripes you were healed (I Peter 2:24).

Beloved, I pray that you may prosper in all things and be in health, just as your soul prospers (III John 2).

P. **Christ's death and resurrection defeated the devil. His victory frees us from the fear of death because we have placed our faith in Him.**

But thanks be to God, who gives us the victory through our Lord Jesus Christ (I Corinthians 15:57).

But has now been revealed by the appearing of our Savior Jesus Christ, who has abolished death and brought life and immortality to light through the gospel (II Timothy 1:10).

Inasmuch then as the children have partaken of flesh and blood, He Himself likewise shared in the same, that through death He might destroy him who had the power of death, that is, the devil, and release those who through fear of death were all their lifetime subject to bondage (Hebrews 2:14-15).

Q. **We have the assurance from God's Word, that when we pray, Jesus promises to meet our needs when we place our trust in Him. He feels what we are feeling and He truly cares for us.**

My God shall supply all your need according to His riches in glory by Christ Jesus (Philippians 4:19).

For we do not have a High Priest who cannot sympathize with our weaknesses, but was in all points tempted as we are, yet without sin (Hebrews 4:15).

Casting all your care upon Him, for He cares for you (I Peter 5:7).

R.   We have been given the mind of Christ; therefore, His thoughts must dominate ours. We must let heaven's perspective dominate every circumstance of life.

Let this mind be in you which was also in Christ Jesus (Philippians 2:5).

S.   Our relationship with God is secure because He has hidden our lives in Christ and has sealed us with the Holy Spirit. The Holy Spirit guarantees the fulfillment of all the promises of God to us as we live by faith.

In Him you also trusted after you heard the word of truth, the gospel of your salvation; in whom also, having believed, you were sealed with the Holy Spirit of promise, who is the guarantee of our inheritance until the redemption of the purchased possession, to the praise of His glory (Ephesians 1:13-14).

T.   Even though our natural bodies are dying with each passing day; our spirits are being renewed daily with the very life of God.

Therefore we do not lose heart. Even though our outward man is perishing, yet the inward man is being renewed day by day. For our light affliction, which is but for a moment, is working for us a far more exceeding and eternal weight of glory, while we do not look at the things which are seen, but at the things which are not seen. For the things which are seen are temporary, but the things which are not seen are eternal (II Corinthians 4:16-18).

U.   We have been given the strength of Christ to face any situation or circumstance; therefore, we live with an absolute confidence of victory.

I can do all things through Christ who strengthens me (Philippians 4:13).

V.   Jesus has given us His faith.

1.   The same faith He used to work miracles in His earthly ministry now resides in us.

2. **There will never be an adverse circumstance that will transcend the ability of faith to conquer.**

I have been crucified with Christ; it is no longer I who live, but Christ lives in me; and the life which I now live in the flesh I live by faith in the Son of God, who loved me and gave Himself for me (Galatians 2:20).

W. **Wherever we go, and whatever we do, our lives are kept in safety because God has assigned His angels to watch over us.**

For He shall give His angels charge over you, to keep you in all your ways (Psalm 91:11).

But to which of the angels has He ever said: "Sit at My right hand, till I make Your enemies Your footstool"? Are they not all ministering spirits sent forth to minister for those who will inherit salvation (Hebrews 1:13-14)?

Chapter Two

The Eternal Godhead

I. Understanding the Trinity.

A. The Bible does not attempt to prove the existence of God; it simply declares it.

In the beginning God created the heavens and the earth (Genesis 1:1).

B. Our faith is rooted in our belief that God exists. We must believe that He is who He says He is, and that He can, and will, do all He says He will do.

But without faith it is impossible to please Him, for he who comes to God must believe that He is, and that He is a rewarder of those who diligently seek Him (Hebrews 11:6).

C. It is impossible for anyone to discover God, or even to know God, apart from God revealing Himself.

Can you search out the deep things of God? Can you find out the limits of the Almighty (Job 11:7)?

At that time Jesus answered and said, "I thank You, Father, Lord of heaven and earth, that You have hidden these things from the wise and prudent and have revealed them to babes. Even so, Father, for so it seemed good in Your sight. All things have been delivered to Me by My Father, and no one knows the Son except the Father. Nor does anyone know the Father except the Son, and the one to whom the Son wills to reveal Him" (Matthew 11:25-27).

D. Primarily, God reveals Himself through His Word.

Then the Lord appeared again in Shiloh. For the Lord revealed Himself to Samuel in Shiloh by the word of the Lord (I Samuel 3:21).

Now to Him who is able to establish you according to my gospel and the preaching of Jesus Christ, according to the revelation of the mystery kept secret since the world began but now made manifest, and by the prophetic Scriptures made known to all nations, according to the commandment of the everlasting God, for obedience to the faith (Romans 16:25-26).

25

E. **The Bible reveals that God is located in heaven and also on the earth. He inhabits the whole of His creation.**

Therefore know this day, and consider it in your heart, that the Lord Himself is God in heaven above and on the earth beneath; there is no other (Deuteronomy 4:39).

Thus says the Lord: "Heaven is My throne, and earth is My footstool" (Isaiah 66:1).

F. **The Godhead (referred to as the Trinity) is comprised of the Father, the Son, and the Holy Spirit.**

Go therefore and make disciples of all the nations, baptizing them in the name of the Father and of the Son and of the Holy Spirit (Matthew 28:19).

G. **God is revealed in the Scriptures as triune in His nature and being. God is one, in that His unity is indivisible: yet, God is three, in that His tri-unity is distinguishable. God is one God, who is manifested to us in three distinct persons.**

Hear, O Israel: The Lord our God, the Lord is one (Deuteronomy 6:4)!

H. **We must come to a conclusion regarding what we believe concerning the Trinity:**

> **"We believe in the eternal Godhead, who has revealed Himself as one God existing in three persons, even the Father, Son, and Holy Spirit; distinguishable, but indivisible in essence; co-eternal; co-equal; and co-existent in attributes, power, nature, and glory."**

II. Discovering the Father.

A. **The Bible reveals to us the nature of God the Father.**

1. **God the Father is Spirit.**

   a. **He is a person with a will, feelings, self-consciousness, self-determination, and intelligence.**

   b. **God the Father is essentially a spiritual being, rather than a physical being.**

   God is Spirit, and those who worship Him must worship in spirit and truth (John 4:24).

2. **God the Father is light.**

   a. **Light is a reference to the majesty and the glory of God the Father. Light is absolutely pure and impossible to defile.**

   b. **God the Father, whom no man has ever seen, dwells in unapproachable light.**

   This is the message which we have heard from Him and declare to you, that God is light and in Him is no darkness at all (I John 1:5).

3. **God the Father is love.**

   a. **We must understand that love is not just an action of God: love is His very nature.**

   b. **Love involves the goodness, mercy, kindness, grace, and the benevolence of God toward all of His creation.**

   And we have known and believed the love that God has for us. God is love, and he who abides in love abides in God, and God in him (I John 4:16).

4. **God the Father is a consuming fire.**

   a. **Fire is not God; but God is a consuming fire.**

b. Fire is significant in light of His holiness and righteousness; as seen in His judgment of sin.

For our God is a consuming fire (Hebrews 12:29).

B. **The Bible reveals the attributes of God the Father.**

1. **God the Father is eternal.**

   a. The Word eternal, when applied to God the Father, signifies that He had no beginning, nor will He have an end, and He has no equal.

   b. Literally, there has never been a time when God did not exist.

   Before the mountains were brought forth, or ever You had formed the earth and the world, even from everlasting to everlasting, You are God (Psalm 90:2).

   Before Me there was no God formed, nor shall there be after Me (Isaiah 43:10).

   Thus says the Lord, the King of Israel, and his Redeemer, the Lord of hosts: "I am the First and I am the Last; besides Me there is no God" (Isaiah 44:6).

2. **God the Father is self-existent.**

   a. God exists in and of Himself. He is the reason for His own existence. He does not owe His existence to any other; nor does He depend on any other to sustain Himself.

   b. God is source of all life and His life is un-derived and inexhaustible. He is absolutely independent of all outside of Himself.

   And God said to Moses, "I AM WHO I AM." And He said, "Thus you shall say to the children of Israel, 'I AM has sent me to you'" (Exodus 3:14).

   For as the Father has life in Himself, so He has granted the Son to have life in Himself (John 5:26).

3. **God the Father is immutable.**

   a. **He is unchangeable in character and being.**

   b. **He is eternally the same.**

   For I am the Lord, I do not change (Malachi 3:6).

   Jesus Christ is the same yesterday, today, and forever (Hebrews 13:8).

   Every good gift and every perfect gift is from above, and comes down from the Father of lights, with whom there is no variation or shadow of turning (James 1:17).

4. **God the Father is omnipotent.**

   a. **He is all-powerful; therefore, there is absolutely nothing that is impossible to Him.**

   b. **He is sovereign; therefore, He has the absolute right to govern His creation as He pleases.**

   And I heard, as it were, the voice of a great multitude, as the sound of many waters and as the sound of mighty thunderings, saying, "Alleluia! For the Lord God Omnipotent reigns" (Revelation 19:6)!

   You are worthy, O Lord, to receive glory and honor and power; for You created all things, and by Your will they exist and were created (Revelation 4:11).

   All the inhabitants of the earth are reputed as nothing; He does according to His will in the army of heaven and among the inhabitants of the earth. No one can restrain His hand or say, "What have You done?" (Daniel 4:35).

5. **God the Father is omniscient.**

   a. **He is all-knowing and has perfect knowledge of all things; whether past, present, or future.**

   b. **Omniscience makes Him infallible; He is incapable of error in His judgments.**

    c.   **Omniscience involves perfect knowledge, which is the accurate possession of all facts.**

    d.   **Omniscience involves perfect understanding, which is the full perception and interpretation of all facts.**

    e.   **Omniscience involves perfect wisdom, which is the proper application of the facts.**

The eyes of the Lord are in every place, keeping watch on the evil and the good (Proverbs 15:3).

Great is our Lord, and mighty in power; His understanding is infinite (Psalm 147:5).

Oh, the depth of the riches both of the wisdom and knowledge of God! How unsearchable are His judgments and His ways past finding out (Romans 11:33)!

6.   **God the Father is omnipresent.**

    a.   **He is present everywhere at all times.**

    b.   **He is not limited to time or space. He fills all things and is above and beyond finite space.**

And one cried to another, and said, "Holy, holy, holy is the Lord of hosts; the whole earth is full of His glory" (Isaiah 6:3)!

"Can anyone hide himself in secret places, so I shall not see him?" says the Lord. "Do I not fill heaven and earth?" says the Lord (Jeremiah 23:24).

But will God indeed dwell with men on the earth? Behold, heaven and the heaven of heavens cannot contain You (II Chronicles 6:18).

Where can I go from Your Spirit? Or where can I flee from Your presence? If I ascend into heaven, You are there; if I make my bed in hell, behold, You are there. If I take the wings of the morning, and dwell in the uttermost parts of the sea, even there Your hand shall lead me, and Your right hand shall hold me (Psalm 139:7-10).

III. Discovering the Son.

A. **The Bible reveals that the life of Christ was both significant and unique.**

1. **Jesus is the Son of God.**

   For God so loved the world that He gave His only begotten Son, that whoever believes in Him should not perish but have everlasting life (John 3:16).

2. **Jesus was conceived of the Holy Spirit and was born of a virgin.**

   Now the birth of Jesus Christ was as follows: After His mother Mary was betrothed to Joseph, before they came together, she was found with child of the Holy Spirit (Matthew 1:18).

   Behold, the virgin shall be with child, and bear a Son, and they shall call His name Immanuel, which is translated, "God with us" (Matthew 1:23).

3. **Jesus lived a perfect, sinless life.**

   For such a High Priest was fitting for us, who is holy, harmless, undefiled, separate from sinners, and has become higher than the heavens (Hebrews 7:26).

4. **Jesus' death on the cross provided the full payment for our sins.**

   For I delivered to you first of all that which I also received: that Christ died for our sins according to the Scriptures (I Corinthians 15:3).

5. **Jesus physically rose from the dead.**

   And that He was buried, and that He rose again the third day according to the Scriptures (I Corinthians 15:4).

6. **Jesus ascended into heaven after His resurrection.**

   After the Lord had spoken to them, He was received up into heaven, and sat down at the right hand of God (Mark 16:19).

7. Jesus is in heaven interceding on our behalf.

Therefore He is also able to save to the uttermost those who come to God through Him, since He always lives to make intercession for them (Hebrews 7:25).

8. Jesus will return one day to earth as both Lord and Judge.

And behold, I am coming quickly, and My reward is with Me, to give to every one according to his work (Revelation 22:12).

B. Jesus clearly established His Deity while on earth.

1. Jesus acknowledged His own Deity.

And Thomas answered and said to Him, "My Lord and my God!" Jesus said to him, "Thomas, because you have seen Me, you have believed. Blessed are those who have not seen and yet have believed" (John 20:28-29).

2. Jesus claimed to be the Christ, the Son of God.

But He kept silent and answered nothing. Again the high priest asked Him, saying to Him, "Are You the Christ, the Son of the Blessed?" Jesus said, "I am. And you will see the Son of Man sitting at the right hand of the Power, and coming with the clouds of heaven" (Mark 14:61-62).

3. Jesus claimed equality with God.

But Jesus answered them, "My Father has been working until now, and I have been working." Therefore the Jews sought all the more to kill Him, because He not only broke the Sabbath, but also said that God was His Father, making Himself equal with God (John 5:17-18).

C. Jesus clearly established His humanity.

1. Jesus was born in the form and flesh of a man.

And the Word became flesh and dwelt among us, and we beheld His glory, the glory as of the only begotten of the Father, full of grace and truth (John 1:14).

Let this mind be in you which was also in Christ Jesus, who, being in the form of God, did not consider it robbery to be equal with God, but made Himself of no reputation, taking the form of a bondservant, and coming in the likeness of men. And being found in appearance as a man, He humbled Himself and became obedient to the point of death, even the death of the cross (Philippians 2:5-8).

2. Jesus was born of a woman's seed as was foretold.

And I will put enmity between you and the woman, and between your seed and her Seed (Genesis 3:15).

But when the fullness of the time had come, God sent forth His Son, born of a woman, born under the law (Galatians 4:4).

D. The character of Christ is revealed in the manner by which He lived life on earth. He demonstrated God's nature; which validated He was the Son of God.

1. Jesus lived a holy life.

And the angel answered and said to her, "The Holy Spirit will come upon you, and the power of the Highest will overshadow you; therefore, also, that Holy One who is to be born will be called the Son of God" (Luke 1:35).

2. Jesus lived a sinless life.

Who committed no sin, nor was deceit found in His mouth (I Peter 2:22).

3. Jesus lived His life full of mercy and was faithful to God in all things.

Therefore, in all things He had to be made like His brethren, that He might be a merciful and faithful High Priest in things pertaining to God, to make propitiation for the sins of the people (Hebrews 2:17).

4. Jesus' life was marked by His open humility.

And being found in appearance as a man, He humbled Himself and became obedient to the point of death, even the death of the cross (Philippians 2:8).

5. Jesus offered everyone forgiveness, regardless of the offense.

Then Jesus said, "Father, forgive them, for they do not know what they do" (Luke 23:34).

6. Jesus proved to be righteous in all of His ways.

My little children, these things I write to you so that you may not sin. And if anyone sins, we have an Advocate with the Father, Jesus Christ the righteous (I John 2:1).

7. Jesus was the greatest example of love in action the world has even seen.

I have been crucified with Christ; it is no longer I who live, but Christ lives in me; and the life which I now live in the flesh I live by faith in the Son of God, who loved me and gave Himself for me (Galatians 2:20).

8. The character of Christ is manifested in our lives through the fruit of the Spirit.

But the fruit of the Spirit is love, joy, peace, longsuffering, kindness, goodness, faithfulness, gentleness, self-control. Against such there is no law (Galatians 5:22-23).

E. The purpose of Jesus' life was fulfilled in His earthly ministry.

1. Jesus revealed the Father and thereby, removed man's fear of God.

Philip said to Him, "Lord, show us the Father, and it is sufficient for us." Jesus said to him, "Have I been with you so long, and yet you have not known Me, Philip? He who has seen Me has seen the Father; so how can you say, 'Show us the Father?'" (John 14:8-9).

2. Jesus opened the way for man to come to God.

Jesus said to him, "I am the way, the truth, and the life. No one comes to the Father except through Me" (John 14:6).

3. Jesus came to seek and save the lost.

For the Son of Man has come to save that which was lost
(Matthew 18:11).

4. Jesus paid man's sin penalty through His death on the cross.

But God demonstrates His own love toward us, in that while we were still sinners, Christ died for us (Romans 5:8).

In this is love, not that we loved God, but that He loved us and sent His Son to be the propitiation for our sins (I John 4:10).

5. Jesus purchased our healing through His scourging and subsequent death on the Cross.

But He was wounded for our transgressions, He was bruised for our iniquities; The chastisement for our peace was upon Him, and by His stripes we are healed (Isaiah 53:5).

6. Jesus destroyed the works of the devil through His death and resurrection. In doing so, He released man from the bondage of the fear of death.

He who sins is of the devil, for the devil has sinned from the beginning. For this purpose the Son of God was manifested, that He might destroy the works of the devil (I John 3:8).

Inasmuch then as the children have partaken of flesh and blood, He Himself likewise shared in the same, that through death He might destroy him who had the power of death, that is, the devil, and release those who through fear of death were all their lifetime subject to bondage (Hebrews 2:14-15).

7. Jesus came to give the free gift of eternal life to all who will place their faith in Him.

And I give them eternal life, and they shall never perish; neither shall anyone snatch them out of My hand (John 10:28).

The thief does not come except to steal, and to kill, and to destroy. I have come that they may have life, and that they may have it more abundantly (John 10:10).

IV. Discovering the Holy Spirit.

A. We must understand that the Holy Spirit is a person.

1. The Holy Spirit has a mind.

Now He who searches the hearts knows what the mind of the Spirit is, because He makes intercession for the saints according to the will of God (Romans 8:27).

2. The Holy Spirit has a will.

But one and the same Spirit works all these things, distributing to each one individually as He wills (I Corinthians 12:11).

3. The Holy Spirit has emotions.

Now I beg you, brethren, through the Lord Jesus Christ, and through the love of the Spirit, that you strive together with me in prayers to God for me (Romans 15:30).

Or do you think that the Scripture says in vain, "The Spirit who dwells in us yearns jealously" (James 4:5)?

And you became followers of us and of the Lord, having received the word in much affliction, with joy of the Holy Spirit (I Thessalonians 1:6).

B. The Holy Spirit performs personal acts.

1. The Holy Spirit searches out the things of God and reveals them to us.

But God has revealed them to us through His Spirit. For the Spirit searches all things, yes, the deep things of God (I Corinthians 2:10).

2. The Holy Spirit bears witness to our hearts in all matters regarding the truths of Jesus Christ.

This is He who came by water and blood—Jesus Christ; not only by water, but by water and blood. And it is the Spirit who bears witness, because the Spirit is truth (I John 5:6).

3. The Holy Spirit is our mentor. He personally instructs us in the Word and in the ways of God.

But the Helper, the Holy Spirit, whom the Father will send in My name, He will teach you all things, and bring to your remembrance all things that I said to you (John 14:26).

4. The Holy Spirit intercedes for us in prayer.

Likewise the Spirit also helps in our weaknesses. For we do not know what we should pray for as we ought, but the Spirit Himself makes intercession for us with groanings which cannot be uttered (Romans 8:26).

5. The Holy Spirit guides us into all truth and will glorify Jesus.

However, when He, the Spirit of truth, has come, He will guide you into all truth; for He will not speak on His own authority, but whatever He hears He will speak; and He will tell you things to come. He will glorify Me, for He will take of what is Mine and declare it to you (John 16:13-14).

6. The Holy Spirit convicts men of sin and is the agent of regeneration.

And when He has come, He will convict the world of sin, and of righteousness, and of judgment (John 16:8).

Jesus answered, "Most assuredly, I say to you, unless one is born of water and the Spirit, he cannot enter the kingdom of God" (John 3:5).

C. The Holy Sprit has personal feelings.

1. The Holy Spirit can be insulted.

Of how much worse punishment, do you suppose, will he be thought worthy who has trampled the Son of God underfoot, counted the blood of the covenant by which he was sanctified a common thing, and insulted the Spirit of grace (Hebrews 10:29)?

2. The Holy Spirit can be grieved.

And do not grieve the Holy Spirit of God, by whom you were sealed for the day of redemption (Ephesians 4:30).

3. The Holy Spirit can be lied to.

But Peter said, "Ananias, why has Satan filled your heart to lie to the Holy Spirit and keep back part of the price of the land for yourself" (Acts 5:3)?

4. The Holy Spirit can be vexed. In other words, He can become disturbed, irritated, provoked, angered, and annoyed.

But they rebelled, and vexed his Holy Spirit: so he turned against them as an enemy, and he fought against them (Isaiah 63:10).

5. The Holy Spirit's presence and activity can be quenched.

Do not quench the Spirit (I Thessalonians 5:19).

D. The Holy Spirit does a profound work within the lives and hearts of everyone who believes in Jesus Christ as their Savior.

1. The Holy Sprit indwells us as believers and gives us the assurance of our salvation.

But you are not in the flesh but in the Spirit, if indeed the Spirit of God dwells in you. Now if anyone does not have the Spirit of Christ, he is not His (Romans 8:9).

The Spirit Himself bears witness with our spirit that we are children of God (Romans 8:16).

2. The Holy Spirit helps us to understand the Word and the ways of God.

Now we have received, not the spirit of the world, but the Spirit who is from God, that we might know the things that have been freely given to us by God (I Corinthians 2:12).

3. **The Holy Spirit assists and enables us as believers to worship the Lord.**

But the hour is coming, and now is, when the true worshipers will worship the Father in spirit and truth; for the Father is seeking such to worship Him. God is Spirit, and those who worship Him must worship in spirit and truth (John 4:23-24).

4. **The Holy Spirit gives us the strength to face the challenges of life and to hold to our convictions.**

That He would grant you, according to the riches of His glory, to be strengthened with might through His Spirit in the inner man (Ephesians 3:16).

5. **The Holy Spirit empowers us as believers to be bold and effective in sharing our faith.**

But you shall receive power when the Holy Spirit has come upon you; and you shall be witnesses to Me in Jerusalem, and in all Judea and Samaria, and to the end of the earth (Acts 1:8).

6. **The Holy Spirit is the agent of our resurrection and immortality.**

But if the Spirit of Him who raised Jesus from the dead dwells in you, He who raised Christ from the dead will also give life to your mortal bodies through His Spirit who dwells in you (Romans 8:11).

Chapter Three

The Person and Work of the Holy Spirit

I. The Promised Coming of the Holy Spirit.

A. **The Holy Spirit revealed Himself at various times in the Old Testament to certain people to inform and empower them for a specific task.**

1. **The Holy Spirit was not available to everyone.**

2. **The activity of the Holy Spirit was usually confined to: judges; kings; prophets; and priests.**

B. **The prophets spoke of a day coming when God would pour out the Holy Spirit on those who would believe Him and receive Him.**

1. **Prophets prophesied of the Holy Spirit's coming.**

It shall come to pass afterward that I will pour out My Spirit on all flesh; Your sons and your daughters shall prophesy, your old men shall dream dreams, your young men shall see visions. And also on My menservants and on My maidservants I will pour out My Spirit in those days (Joel 2:28-29).

I will give you a new heart and put a new spirit within you; I will take the heart of stone out of your flesh and give you a heart of flesh. I will put My Spirit within you and cause you to walk in My statutes, and you will keep My judgments and do them (Ezekiel 36:26-27).

2. **John the Baptist spoke of the Holy Spirit's work.**

I indeed baptize you with water unto repentance, but He who is coming after me is mightier than I, whose sandals I am not worthy to carry. He will baptize you with the Holy Spirit and fire (Matthew 3:11).

3. **Jesus promised the gift of the Holy Spirit.**

I will pray the Father, and He will give you another Helper, that He may abide with you forever— the Spirit of truth, whom the world cannot receive, because it neither sees Him nor knows Him; but you know Him, for He dwells with you and will be in you (John 14:16-17).

But the Helper, the Holy Spirit, whom the Father will send in My name, He will teach you all things, and bring to your remembrance all things that I said to you (John 14:26).

And being assembled together with them, He commanded them not to depart from Jerusalem, but to wait for the Promise of the Father, "which," He said, "you have heard from Me; for John truly baptized with water, but you shall be baptized with the Holy Spirit not many days from now." Therefore, when they had come together, they asked Him, saying, "Lord, will You at this time restore the kingdom to Israel?" And He said to them, "It is not for you to know times or seasons which the Father has put in His own authority. But you shall receive power when the Holy Spirit has come upon you; and you shall be witnesses to Me in Jerusalem, and in all Judea and Samaria, and to the end of the earth" (Acts 1:4-8).

C. **There are three levels of relationship that we as believers enjoy with the Holy Spirit.**

1. **The Holy Spirit is "with us" convicting us of sin and drawing us to God.**

And when He has come, He will convict the world of sin, and of righteousness, and of judgment: of sin, because they do not believe in Me; of righteousness, because I go to My Father and you see Me no more; of judgment, because the ruler of this world is judged (John 16:8-11).

2. **The Holy Spirit is "inside us" as a result of our new birth.**

The Spirit of truth, whom the world cannot receive, because it neither sees Him nor knows Him; but you know Him, for He dwells with you and will be in you (John 14:17).

Then I will sprinkle clean water on you, and you shall be clean; I will cleanse you from all filthiness and from all your idols. I will give you a new heart and put a new spirit within you; I will take the heart of stone out of your flesh and give you a heart of flesh. I will put My Spirit within you and cause you to walk in My statutes, and you will keep My judgments and do them. Then you shall dwell in the land that I gave to your fathers; you shall be My people, and I will be your God (Ezekiel 36:25-28).

3.   **The Holy Spirit is "upon us" to give us divine power to fulfill the work of ministry that has been entrusted to us.**

You shall receive power when the Holy Spirit has come upon you; and you shall be witnesses to Me in Jerusalem, and in all Judea and Samaria, and to the end of the earth (Acts 1:8).

II.   The Pattern by Which the Holy Spirit Came.

A.   **The Book of Acts records the Holy Spirit's entrance not only into the lives of the Jewish believers, but the Gentile believers as well.**

1.   **The Holy Spirit was present on the Day of Pentecost.**

When the Day of Pentecost had fully come, they were all with one accord in one place. And suddenly there came a sound from heaven, as of a rushing mighty wind, and it filled the whole house where they were sitting. Then there appeared to them divided tongues, as of fire, and one sat upon each of them. And they were all filled with the Holy Spirit and began to speak with other tongues, as the Spirit gave them utterance (Acts 2:1-4).

2.   **The Holy Spirit was present at Samaria.**

Now when the apostles who were at Jerusalem heard that Samaria had received the word of God, they sent Peter and John to them, who, when they had come down, prayed for them that they might receive the Holy Spirit. For as yet He had fallen upon none of them. They had only been baptized in the name of the Lord Jesus. Then they laid hands on them, and they received the Holy Spirit. And when Simon saw that through the laying on of the apostles' hands the Holy Spirit was given, he offered them money, saying, "Give me this power also, that anyone on whom I lay hands may receive the Holy Spirit" (Acts 8:15-19).

3.   **The Holy Spirit was present in Paul's life.**

And Ananias went his way and entered the house; and laying his hands on him he said, "Brother Saul, the Lord Jesus, who appeared to you on the road as you came, has sent me that you may receive your sight and be filled with the Holy Spirit" (Acts 9:17).

4.   The Holy Spirit was present at Cornelius' home.

While Peter was still speaking these words, the Holy Spirit fell upon all those who heard the word. And those of the circumcision who believed were astonished, as many as came with Peter, because the gift of the Holy Spirit had been poured out on the Gentiles also (Acts 10:44-45).

5.   The Holy Spirit was present with the believers at Ephesus.

And it happened, while Apollos was at Corinth, that Paul, having passed through the upper regions, came to Ephesus. And finding some disciples he said to them, "Did you receive the Holy Spirit when you believed?" So they said to him, "We have not so much as heard whether there is a Holy Spirit." And he said to them, "Into what then were you baptized?" So they said, "Into John's baptism." Then Paul said, "John indeed baptized with a baptism of repentance, saying to the people that they should believe on Him who would come after him, that is, on Christ Jesus." When they heard this, they were baptized in the name of the Lord Jesus. And when Paul had laid hands on them, the Holy Spirit came upon them, and they spoke with tongues and prophesied (Acts 19:1-6).

B.   Two things are consistent as we read of the Holy Spirit's activities in the Book of Acts:

1.   The experience of the Holy Spirit was received as a secondary experience to salvation; in each case, they were already believers in Jesus Christ.

2.   The experience was marked by great joy and open praise to God. In some cases, heaven's language of prayer and praise was released through them as they celebrated and prophesied.

III. The Purpose of the Holy Spirits' Coming.

A. The Holy Spirit is the Spirit of life.

For the law of the Spirit of life in Christ Jesus has made me free from the law of sin and death. And if Christ is in you, the body is dead because of sin, but the Spirit is life because of righteousness. But if the Spirit of Him who raised Jesus from the dead dwells in you, He who raised Christ from the dead will also give life to your mortal bodies through His Spirit who dwells in you (Romans 8:2, 10-11).

1. The Holy Spirit, as the Spirit of life, makes us alive to God by creating the life of Jesus within us.

2. The Holy Spirit is assigned to give us all things that pertain to the divine qualities of the life of Christ; His peace, His joy, His righteousness, His grace, and His love.

B. The Holy Spirit is the Spirit of holiness.

Concerning His Son Jesus Christ our Lord, who was born of the seed of David according to the flesh, and declared to be the Son of God with power according to the Spirit of holiness, by the resurrection from the dead (Romans 1:3-4).

1. True holiness is a work of the Holy Spirit within us. Holiness will manifest the character of Christ in us and will be evidenced in our lifestyle.

2. Operating as the Spirit of holiness, the Holy Spirit will produce God's nature in us. He will do so by the workings of His grace; thereby, He frees us from the failure of our feeble attempts to be holy.

C. The Holy Spirit is the Spirit of adoption.

For you did not receive the spirit of bondage again to fear, but you received the Spirit of adoption by whom we cry out, "Abba, Father." The Spirit Himself bears witness with our spirit that we are children of God (Romans 8:15-16).

1. Our Western concept of adoption is taking the child of another by choice and raising them as our own. However, in Biblical culture, adoption involved a family taking their own son by birth, and upon his reaching maturity, he was adopted as an heir. He was then vested with joint ownership in the family name and enterprise.

2. As children of God we are born into the family of God. The Holy Spirit, the Spirit of adoption, teaches and trains us. He enables us to mature and prepares us to one day rule with Christ.

D. The Holy Spirit is the Spirit of grace.

Anyone who has rejected Moses' law dies without mercy on the testimony of two or three witnesses. Of how much worse punishment, do you suppose, will he be thought worthy who has trampled the Son of God underfoot, counted the blood of the covenant by which he was sanctified a common thing, and insulted the Spirit of grace (Hebrews 10:28, 29)?

1. The Holy Spirit operating in us as the Spirit of grace will govern our attitudes and actions as we live out our Christian lives.

2. As the Spirit of grace the Holy Spirit will divinely enable us to fully obey God; which will fulfill the requirements of Scripture.

E. The Holy Spirit is the Spirit of supplication.

And I will pour on the house of David and on the inhabitants of Jerusalem the Spirit of grace and supplication; then they will look on Me whom they have pierced; they will mourn for Him as one mourns for his only son, and grieve for Him as one grieves for a firstborn (Zechariah 12:10).

1. As the Spirit of supplication the Holy Spirit develops in us a desire and the discipline to pray.

2. The Holy Spirit establishes us in a prayer relationship with God so that we are not only comfortable in His presence; we are confident.

F. The Holy Spirit is the Spirit of glory.

If you are reproached for the name of Christ, blessed are you, for the Spirit of glory and of God rests upon you. On their part He is blasphemed, but on your part He is glorified (I Peter 4:14).

1. The Holy Spirit operating as the Spirit of glory will challenge our motives as we offer our service to God. His duty is to ensure that our service is for the Lord's glory, and not for our own.

2. The Spirit of glory will rest upon us in times of adversity. He will change our character into the character of Christ and will reveal the glory of God through our suffering.

G. The Holy Spirit is the Spirit of truth.

But when the Helper comes, whom I shall send to you from the Father, the Spirit of truth who proceeds from the Father, He will testify of Me (John 15:26).

However, when He, the Spirit of truth, has come, He will guide you into all truth; for He will not speak on His own authority, but whatever He hears He will speak; and He will tell you things to come (John 16:13).

1. It is impossible for us to know God apart from the Holy Spirit operating as the Spirit of truth. He reveals God to us through the Word and through His indwelling presence.

2. Our understanding of God is born out of a progressive revelation from the Spirit of truth as we daily commune with Him and yield to His instructions.

IV. The Passion of the Holy Spirit.

A. **The New Testament places an emphasis on believers receiving the Holy Spirit and continually living in His fullness.**

Do not be drunk with wine, in which is dissipation; but be filled with the Spirit (Ephesians 5:18).

B. **A study of the different Greek verbs in the Book of Acts will help us understand the various ways the Holy Spirit seeks to bring us into His fullness.**

1. ***Bapto* means "baptized."**

For John truly baptized with water, but you shall be baptized with the Holy Spirit not many days from now (Acts 1:5).

   a. **This verb describes being immersed; much like a sunken ship, or dipping bread into a drink, or even like the dying of a garment.**

   b. **The word *bapto* is used to describe our entry into the dynamic of the Holy Spirit's fullness, which gives us two points of understanding:**

      (1) **It describes the flooding of His love and power into the compartments of our lives;**

      (2) **Also it describes change. Just as a garment that has been dyed takes on a new beauty, so the Holy Spirit's fullness brings new qualities to our character.**

2. ***Eperchomai* means "to come upon."**

But you shall receive power when the Holy Spirit has come upon you; and you shall be witnesses to Me in Jerusalem, and in all Judea and Samaria, and to the end of the earth (Acts 1:8).

a. This is the same verb used in Luke 24:49 when Jesus instructed His disciples to ... "wait until you are endued with power." Jesus wanted His disciples to fulfill His great commission to evangelize the world and tell them of His great love and sacrifice for them.

b. Jesus instructed them to wait until they were clothed in the enabling power of the Holy Spirit.

3. *Ekcheo* means "to be poured out."

And it shall come to pass in the last days, says God, that I will pour out of My Spirit on all flesh (Acts 2:17).

a. This verb describes the release of the Holy Spirit in abundance; like unto water behind a dam which is suddenly released.

b. Just as water released from a dam generates power and electricity to light a city, so the Holy Spirit's release in our lives will be a source of power and light; not only to us, but to those around us.

4. *Pleroo* means "to be filled."

And they were all filled with the Holy Spirit and began to speak with other tongues, as the Spirit gave them utterance (Acts 2:4).

a. This verb is only used to describe an overflow of something.

b. The fullness of the Holy Spirit means that there is more than enough of His power and resources resident in us to address any need we may have.

c.   **The evidence of the Holy Spirit's overflow in our life will be joy, praise, and thanksgiving.**

Speaking to one another in psalms and hymns and spiritual songs, singing and making melody in your heart to the Lord, giving thanks always for all things to God the Father in the name of our Lord Jesus Christ (Ephesians 5:19-20).

5.   *Epipipto* means "to fall upon."

While Peter was still speaking these words, the Holy Spirit fell upon all those who heard the word (Acts 10:44).

a.   **Jesus used this verb as He told the story of the prodigal son; the verb describes the father's gracious embrace of his wayward son.**

b.   **The Holy Spirit has the desire to wrap us in the embrace of heaven's love and grace as He bring us into the fullness of God's intended purposes for our lives.**

6.   *Lambano* means "to receive."

Then they laid hands on them, and they received the Holy Spirit (Acts 8:17).

a.   **This verb describes the "giving" and the "receiving" process by which we interact with the Holy Spirit.**

b.   **Ultimately, everything relates to our willingness to be open. We must allow the Holy Spirit to release His abundant fullness through us.**

c.   **Living in the fullness of the Holy Spirit is more than just an experience; it is a lifestyle that is determined by an act of our will to receive His work in our lives.**

V. The Provision of the Holy Spirit.

A. **The goal of the Spirit-filled life is to live in the fullness of Christ and to have His fullness expressed in our ministries; which will bring about a unity of the faith.**

Till we all come to the unity of the faith and of the knowledge of the Son of God, to a perfect man, to the measure of the stature of the fullness of Christ (Ephesians 4:13).

1. **The unity of the faith will not be evidenced by a interdenominational agreement on all facets of doctrine, or a unified acceptance of one method of worship, evangelism, and church government.**

2. **In order to attain the unity of the faith, we must embrace the goal of such unity; that being, to be filled with the fullness of Christ.**

3. **The unity of the faith will be realized when with open hearts and minds we lay down our differences of interpretation and methodology. We must embrace with grace the common goal of taking the message of Christ to the nations.**

B. **The Book of Acts portrays the ministry of the church as being the continued ministry of Jesus.**

The former account I made, O Theophilus, of all that Jesus began both to do and teach (Acts 1:1).

1. **Jesus' ministry was a teaching and preaching ministry, as well as, a miracle healing ministry.**

And Jesus went about all Galilee, teaching in their synagogues, preaching the gospel of the kingdom, and healing all kinds of sickness and all kinds of disease among the people. Then His fame went throughout all Syria; and they brought to Him all sick people who were afflicted with various diseases and torments, and those who were demon-possessed, epileptics, and paralytics; and He healed them (Matthew 4:23-24).

53

2. **Jesus further defined the ministry of the church as being characterized by the miracle workings of the Holy Spirit.**

Most assuredly, I say to you, he who believes in Me, the works that I do he will do also; and greater works than these he will do, because I go to My Father (John 14:12).

C. **We should expect the supernatural signs of Jesus to be in our lives and ministries as we allow Him to do through our ministries, what He did in His.**

1. **We must declare the message of His love and saving grace as we welcome the Holy Spirit's power to work through us to bring wholeness to broken humanity.**

2. **If Christ's continued ministry is to flow through us, then we must have His continuing power in us.**

D. **Jesus gave us the promise by which we may receive the fullness of His power.**

And being assembled together with them, He commanded them not to depart from Jerusalem, but to wait for the Promise of the Father, "which," He said, "you have heard from Me; for John truly baptized with water, but you shall be baptized with the Holy Spirit not many days from now. But you shall receive power when the Holy Spirit has come upon you; and you shall be witnesses to Me in Jerusalem, and in all Judea and Samaria, and to the end of the earth" (Acts 1:4-5, 8).

1. **"Whatever 'the baptism with the Spirit' may mean to us, whenever we may feel it is experienced, or however it may be evidenced, this much is sure: Jesus said that baptism is to provide us with power to minister everything Jesus has and is to the world He died to redeem and touch with His fullness"** (*A Passion for Fullness* by Jack Hayford).

2. When we desire the Holy Spirit's fullness, it will open us to the constant overflow of His gifts and abilities, which transcend our limitations.

E. Jesus taught that the Holy Spirit would be the channel through which His divine life would flow and present His truth to the world.

On the last day, that great day of the feast, Jesus stood and cried out, saying, "If anyone thirsts, let him come to Me and drink. He who believes in Me, as the Scripture has said, out of his heart will flow rivers of living water" (John 7:37-38).

1. Our desire for the fullness of Jesus is actually a quest for Jesus Himself.

2. It should be our desire to live before God in the fullness of His promises; to find the fullness of His purposes; and live without placing any restrictions on how He expresses His ministry through us.

F. The Apostle Paul prayed for the church to be filled with all the fullness of God.

For this reason I bow my knees to the Father of our Lord Jesus Christ, from whom the whole family in heaven and earth is named, that He would grant you, according to the riches of His glory, to be strengthened with might through His Spirit in the inner man, that Christ may dwell in your hearts through faith; that you, being rooted and grounded in love, may be able to comprehend with all the saints what is the width and length and depth and height— to know the love of Christ which passes knowledge; that you may be filled with all the fullness of God (Ephesians 3:14-19).

1. The Greek word for "fullness" that Paul used is *pleroma,* which means ... "the full content, entirety and whole sum."

2. The most frequent use of this word in the New Testament is a direct reference to Jesus Christ.

3. Paul prayed that our lives would be filled with the fullness of Christ; and as we invite the Holy Spirit to fill every facet of our lives with His presence and power, that fullness will be realized.

G. We would be wise to recognize that God works in many different ways; therein, His church is a diverse organism. Our way is not the only way that God has worked, or will ever work.

1. When we claim God only works in certain ways, it is harmful and shows we are full of pride; not to mention, Biblically inaccurate.

But now indeed there are many members, yet one body. And the eye cannot say to the hand, "I have no need of you"; nor again the head to the feet, "I have no need of you." No, much rather, those members of the body which seem to be weaker are necessary. And those members of the body which we think to be less honorable, on these we bestow greater honor; and our unpresentable parts have greater modesty, but our presentable parts have no need. But God composed the body, having given greater honor to that part which lacks it, that there should be no schism in the body, but that the members should have the same care for one another. And if one member suffers, all the members suffer with it; or if one member is honored, all the members rejoice with it. Now you are the body of Christ, and members individually (I Corinthians 12:20-27).

2. The identifying hallmark of genuine ministry that is inspired and empowered by the Holy Spirit according to the Bible, is that Jesus Christ will be central in all its worship, disciplines, and witness.

H. When it comes to the evidence of the Holy Spirit's fullness in our lives, we most likely will look to our traditions to set the defining standard.

1. Pentecostals point to speaking in tongues as the initial evidence of the Holy Spirit's entrance.

2. Non-Pentecostals point to the fruit of the Spirit in the life of the believer as the initial evidence of the Holy Spirit's entrance.

3. However, a strong Scriptural case can be built for both opinions and it would be inaccurate to make one or the other the only evidence of the Holy Spirit's entrance and abiding presence.

I. The fullness of the Holy Spirit is evidenced by a broad scope of manifestations. This includes, but is not limited too the following:

1. An unquenchable thirst for God, His Word, and His ways; which will be expressed in our lifestyle and evidenced by the sincerity of our praise and worship;

2. A burning desire to reach out to people with the love of Jesus, and through the power of the Holy Spirit working in us, bring them to a saving knowledge of Christ;

3. A yielded heart and life through which the Holy Spirit produces the nature and character of Christ in us, as can be seen in the fruit of the Spirit;

4. A desire and openness for the Holy Spirit to release His supernatural gifts through us; thereby, enabling us to successfully take Christ's love to the nations of the world and to fulfill our ministry assignments;

5. And a heart that is completely at rest in His calming peace and tempered with His abiding joy. We can, with confidence, release our faith to trust the Lord to keep all of His promises.

J. Just as the Holy Spirit calls us to be open to new and fresh expressions of worship, He also confronts our temptation to insist on our way of receiving and living in His fullness as being the only way.

    1. The Old Testament priest Eli pronounced his judgment on Hannah for her silence before God as she poured out her soul before the Lord—she asked God to fill her womb with a son.

And it happened, as she continued praying before the Lord, that Eli watched her mouth. Now Hannah spoke in her heart; only her lips moved, but her voice was not heard. Therefore Eli thought she was drunk. So Eli said to her, "How long will you be drunk? Put your wine away from you!" And Hannah answered and said, "No, my lord, I am a woman of sorrowful spirit. I have drunk neither wine nor intoxicating drink, but have poured out my soul before the Lord" (I Samuel 1:12-15).

    2. The 120 disciples responded to the outpouring of the Holy Spirit on the Day of Pentecost by praising God with the gift of tongues. There were some that accused them of being drunk with wine.

So they were all amazed and perplexed, saying to one another, "Whatever could this mean?" Others mocking said, "They are full of new wine" (Acts 2:12-13).

    3. Formulas will not bring fullness—only our driving desire to be full of Christ.

        a. When the expressions of God's holiness and power begin to flow in the hearts of those thirsty for the Holy Spirit, we must be careful not to quench His moving by any of our personal prejudices or restrictions of form.

        b. We would be wise to remain open to the various ways Jesus works through His people; whether through Hannah's tears, or in an expression such as Pentecost's tongues.

VI. Receiving the Promise of the Holy Spirit.

A. **Receiving the Baptism with the Holy Spirit from Jesus requires us to agree to His terms.**

1. **We must prepare our hearts through repentance and remove all areas of compromise in order to receive His purity.**

Then Peter said to them, "Repent, and let every one of you be baptized in the name of Jesus Christ for the remission of sins; and you shall receive the gift of the Holy Spirit" (Acts 2:38).

2. **We must purpose in our hearts to obey God and desire His way above our own. We must choose to live according to the mandates of His Word.**

And we are His witnesses to these things, and so also is the Holy Spirit whom God has given to those who obey Him (Acts 5:32).

3. **We must deeply desire all that God has made available to us through the promises of His Word. We must remove all restrictions and conditions to His entrance and activity in our lives, now, and in the future.**

Blessed are those who hunger and thirst for righteousness, for they shall be filled (Matthew 5:6).

4. **We must ask Jesus to baptize us with the Holy Spirit by faith; and by that same faith, we must expect to receive His fullness. We should not be seeking an experience evidenced by an outward sign, but we should be hungering for His fullness in our life.**

If you then, being evil, know how to give good gifts to your children, how much more will your heavenly Father give the Holy Spirit to those who ask Him (Luke 11:13)!

B. Perhaps you have never asked Jesus to baptize you
    with the Holy Spirit since you became a Christian. I
    encourage you to lay aside your traditions and with
    an open heart seek all that Jesus has promised you in
    His Word. Let me offer this simple prayer to help you
    reach out and receive what you desire from the Lord.
    Pray with me, from a sincere heart, and then expect
    Jesus to fill you with the fullness of the Holy Spirit.

    *"Lord Jesus, I want to follow You as a disciple. I want to
    know the power of the Holy Spirit in my life enabling me
    to become all that You have called me to be. I want to
    grow in every dynamic of my relationship with You. I
    want to receive the Holy Spirit's fullness and I humbly
    ask You to fill me now and let my life overflow with His
    power. As I lift my voice in praise, by faith, I expect You
    to express Your grace in my life. Accomplish in me the
    desire of Your heart towards me, and let the evidence of
    the Holy Spirit's presence in my life be pleasing in Your
    eyes. Thank You for filling me with Your Holy Spirit."*

Chapter Four

Maintaining the Integrity of the Heart

I. The Importance of the Heart.

A. The Bible warns us to guard our heart because the issues of life flow out of it.

Keep your heart with all diligence, for out of it spring the issues of life (Proverbs 4:23).

B. We must be aware of how important our heart is as we develop a relationship with God.

1. Without your heart embracing the fact that God raised His only Son, Jesus, from the dead; you cannot be saved.

That if you confess with your mouth the Lord Jesus and believe in your heart that God has raised Him from the dead, you will be saved. For with the heart one believes unto righteousness, and with the mouth confession is made unto salvation (Romans 10:9-10).

2. Without your heart responding in love to God; you cannot truly worship God.

And you shall love the Lord your God with all your heart, with all your soul, with all your mind, and with all your strength. This is the first commandment (Mark 12:30).

Therefore the Lord said: "Inasmuch as these people draw near with their mouths and honor Me with their lips, but have removed their hearts far from Me, and their fear toward Me is taught by the commandment of men" (Isaiah 29:13).

3. Without your heart believing in God's power; you cannot operate your faith.

Jesus answered and said to them, "Have faith in God. For assuredly, I say to you, whoever says to this mountain, 'Be removed and be cast into the sea' and does not doubt in his heart, but believes that those things he says will be done, he will have whatever he says" (Mark 11:22-23).

4. Without your heart being totally surrendered to God; you cannot find Him.

You will seek Me and find Me, when you search for Me with all your heart (Jeremiah 29:13).

5. Without your heart's involvement; you cannot give God an acceptable offering.

So let each one give as he purposes in his heart, not grudgingly or of necessity; for God loves a cheerful giver (II Corinthians 9:7).

C. We must realize the danger of an un-guarded heart.

1. Our heart will expose who we really are.

As in water face reflects face, so a man's heart reveals the man (Proverbs 27:19).

2. Our heart will tell our deepest secrets.

For out of the abundance of the heart his mouth speaks (Luke 6:45).

3. Our heart will rebel against God.

Your word I have hidden in my heart that I might not sin against You (Psalm 119:11).

4. Our heart will doubt the Word of God.

Then He said to them, "O foolish ones, and slow of heart to believe in all that the prophets have spoken" (Luke 24:25)!

5. Our heart will tire of right things while waiting.

And let us not grow weary while doing good, for in due season we shall reap if we do not lose heart (Galatians 6:9).

6. Our heart will desire to do all the wrong things.

For from within, out of the heart of men, proceed evil thoughts, adulteries, fornications, murders, thefts, covetousness, wickedness, deceit, lewdness, an evil eye, blasphemy, pride, foolishness (Mark 7:21).

II. Allowing Integrity to Rule Our Hearts.

A. Living our life with a heart full of integrity will encompass three dynamics:

   1. We will live completely and unreservedly honest before God in all matters of life.

   2. We will live with an open and immediate response to every dealing and prompting of the Holy Spirit.

   3. We will live totally submitted to the Holy Spirit's correction without offering excuses or attempting to justify our actions.

B. Abraham and Sarah had an agreement between them in their nomadic travels; if a territorial king wanted to add her to his harem, Sarah would spare Abraham's life by claiming to be his sister.

   1. Abimelech, the King of Gerar, noticed Sarah and decided to take her for himself.

   Now Abraham said of Sarah his wife, "She is my sister." And Abimelech king of Gerar sent and took Sarah (Genesis 20:2).

   2. God steps in to protect Abraham and Sarah from their fear and lack of faith; He visits Abimelech in a dream.

      a. God quickly gets King Abimelech's attention in a dream by referring to him as a "dead man."

      But God came to Abimelech in a dream by night, and said to him, "Indeed you are a dead man because of the woman whom you have taken, for she is a man's wife" (Genesis 20:3).

b.   **Abimelech appeals to God concerning the intent of his actions; he claims integrity of heart.**

But Abimelech had not come near her; and he said, "Lord, will You slay a righteous nation also? Did he not say to me, 'She is my sister'? And she, even she herself said, 'He is my brother.' In the integrity of my heart and innocence of my hands I have done this" (Genesis 20:4-5).

3.   **As with Abimelech, God will protect and deliver anyone who possesses a heart of integrity; He will deliver those innocently entangled in evil schemes.**

And God said to him in a dream, "Yes, I know that you did this in the integrity of your heart. For I also withheld you from sinning against Me; therefore I did not let you touch her" (Genesis 20:6).

a.   **King David knew this to be true in his life. Based on the integrity of His heart before God, David requested that God be his defender when he did not have enough troops to protect his borders.**

Let integrity and uprightness preserve me, for I wait for You (Psalm 25:21).

b.   **King Solomon also knew this to be true in his life. God promised him the perpetuation of his kingdom if he would maintain the integrity of his heart.**

Now if you walk before Me as your father David walked, in integrity of heart and in uprightness, to do according to all that I have commanded you, and if you keep My statutes and My judgments, then I will establish the throne of your kingdom over Israel forever, as I promised David your father, saying, "You shall not fail to have a man on the throne of Israel" (I Kings 9:4-5).

C.   **The word "integrity" is derived from the foundational idea found in the following two words:**

1. The first word is *integer* which means a "whole number," such as the numbers 1, 2, 3 … etc., as opposed to a "fraction." This presents us with the idea of "completeness and entirety";

2. The second word is *integration* which means that parts are fitted together to bring about "wholeness and completeness."

D. Living with a heart of integrity will require us to bring the pieces of our hearts before the Lord. Our heart must be maintained in wholeness so we can remain honest, open, and pure before God in all matters of life.

1. King David asked God to bind the pieces of his heart together. He promised that he would perpetually keep his life aligned with God's ways.

Teach me Your way, O Lord; I will walk in Your truth; Unite my heart to fear Your name. I will praise You, O Lord my God, with all my heart and I will glorify Your name forevermore (Psalm 86:11-12).

2. King David also asked God to keep his heart from becoming divided. He did not want to yield to the temptation to concentrate on the negativity of the circumstances of His life.

With my whole heart I have sought You; Oh, let me not wander from Your commandments! Your word I have hidden in my heart, that I might not sin against You (Psalm 119:10-11)!

E. As believers we have been made priests unto God and are charged with the responsibility of maintaining our hearts with integrity.

To Him who loved us and washed us from our sins in His own blood, and has made us kings and priests to His God and Father, to Him be glory and dominion forever and ever (Revelation 1:5-6).

1. The Old Testament word for "integrity" is the Hebrew word *tom*, and it finds it's counterpart in the New Testament Greek work *eirene*, which is translated as "peace."

2. As priests before God we are to let peace be the ruling factor in all of our decisions; thoughts; and actions.

And let the peace of God rule in your hearts, to which also you were called in one body; and be thankful (Colossians 3:15).

F. Whenever we exercise our own will and employ our human reasoning, our heart can become fragmented; the Holy Spirit will alert us that we are grieving Him.

Do not grieve the Holy Spirit of God, by whom you were sealed for the day of redemption (Ephesians 4:30).

1. The Holy Spirit promises to direct our steps as we seek to follow His will for our lives.

Your ears shall hear a word behind you, saying, "This is the way, walk in it," whenever you turn to the right hand or whenever you turn to the left (Isaiah 30:21).

2. The Holy Spirit will confirm His leading in our lives with His peace; or He will convict us of our error by removing His peace from our hearts.

III. Integrity of the Heart and Repentance.

A. Repentance involves us changing our minds and our attitudes toward sin. This change of mind and attitude will bring about a change of our behavior.

B. Repentance is a command of God; it is not an option. Repentance is the first step in our walk as a believer.

Truly, these times of ignorance God overlooked, but now commands all men everywhere to repent (Acts 17:30).

C. Repentance is the first major emphasis of the Gospel.

1. Repentance was the message of John the Baptist.

In those days John the Baptist came preaching in the wilderness of Judea, and saying, "Repent, for the kingdom of heaven is at hand" (Matthew 3:1-2)!

2. Repentance was the message of Jesus Christ.

From that time Jesus began to preach and to say, "Repent, for the kingdom of heaven is at hand" (Matthew 4:17).

3. Repentance was the message of the apostles.

So they went out and preached that people should repent (Mark 6:12).

4. Repentance was the message of Peter.

Then Peter said to them, "Repent, and let every one of you be baptized in the name of Jesus Christ for the remission of sins; and you shall receive the gift of the Holy Spirit" (Acts 2:38).

D. There are two Hebrew words for "repentance:"

1. The first word is *naham* which means to "feel sorry, to lament, and to grieve."

2. The second word is *shubh* which means to "turn back, to make a radical change in one's attitude towards sin."

E. There are two Greek words for "repentance:"

1. The first word is *metanoia* which means to "change one's mind and attitude, to repent of wrong thinking."

2. The second word is *epistrepho* which means to "change one's actions; thereby, resulting in a change in one's relationship."

F. **There are three areas that are affected by repentance:**

    1. **First of all, repentance will impact our emotions. We will feel differently about sin and about ourselves as sinners. Repentance causes us to see God as both, holy, and merciful.**

        a. **Repentance produces a Godly sorrow for sin.**

        The sacrifices of God are a broken spirit, a broken and a contrite heart—These, O God, You will not despise (Psalm 51:17).

        b. **Repentance produces a sense of shame for our sinfulness.**

        And I said, "O my God, I am too ashamed and humiliated to lift up my face to You, my God; for our iniquities have risen higher than our heads, and our guilt has grown up to the heavens" (Ezra 9:6).

        c. **Repentance produces a hatred for sin.**

        You who love the Lord, hate evil! He preserves the souls of His saints; He delivers them out of the hand of the wicked (Psalm 97:10).

    2. **Secondly, our intellect is impacted by repentance. Repentance involves a complete change of mind regarding how we previously thought about sin.**

        a. **We must acknowledge our sin for what it really is … sin. We cannot relegate our sin to merely a lifestyle, or an unfortunate choice, or a habit that is out of control.**

        b. **We must confess our sin as sin. God will not forgive what we will not confess.**

        For I acknowledge my transgressions, and my sin is always before me (Psalm 51:3).

c.   **We must acknowledge that God's judgment of our sin is right and justified.**

Against You, You only, have I sinned, and done this evil in Your sight—That You may be found just when You speak, and blameless when You judge (Psalm 51:4).

3.   **Thirdly, our will is impacted by repentance. Repentance is a decision of our will to deliberately turn away from sin, and turn to God.**

a.   **We must accept the moral responsibility for our sin.**

But each one is tempted when he is drawn away by his own desires and enticed. Then, when desire has conceived, it gives birth to sin; and sin, when it is full-grown, brings forth death (James 1:14-15).

b.   **We must embrace God's provision for change.**

If we confess our sins, He is faithful and just to forgive us our sins and to cleanse us from all unrighteousness (I John 1:9).

c.   **We must repent of old habits and establish new patterns of living as set forth in God's Word.**

The night is far spent, the day is at hand. Therefore let us cast off the works of darkness, and let us put on the armor of light. Let us walk properly, as in the day, not in revelry and drunkenness, not in lewdness and lust, not in strife and envy. But put on the Lord Jesus Christ, and make no provision for the flesh, to fulfill its lusts (Romans 13:12-14).

G.   **We must be reconciled to God through repentance because sin breaks our fellowship with God.**

You are of purer eyes than to behold evil, and cannot look on wickedness (Habakkuk 1:13).

IV. Repentance, Versus Remorse.

A. **There is a tremendous difference between repentance and remorse. Remorse is a deep feeling of regret, despair and hopelessness, but it does not lead to a constructive change.**

   1. **Judas was full of sorrow, but his sorrow caused him to commit suicide.**

   2. **King David was full of sorrow, but his sorrow was a Godly sorrow which led him to repent and resulted in his life being changed.**

   For Godly sorrow produces repentance leading to salvation, not to be regretted; but the sorrow of the world produces death (II Corinthians 7:10).

B. **God makes every effort to encourage us to repent and live with our hearts in right relationship with Him.**

   1. **God reveals His goodness to us.**

   Or do you despise the riches of His goodness, forbearance, and longsuffering, not knowing that the goodness of God leads you to repentance (Romans 2:4)?

   2. **God speaks to our hearts concerning His desire for us to repent.**

   But go and learn what this means: "I desire mercy and not sacrifice." For I did not come to call the righteous, but sinners, to repentance (Matthew 9:13).

   3. **God convicts our hearts creating in us a desire to repent and be right with Him.**

   Now when they heard this, they were cut to the heart, and said to Peter and the rest of the apostles, "Men and brethren, what shall we do?" (Acts 2:37).

4. **God rebukes and chastens us in order to motivate us to repent.**

As many as I love, I rebuke and chasten. Therefore be zealous and repent (Revelation 3:19).

5. **God hears our prayers when we choose to repent and we ask for His forgiveness.**

I have surely heard Ephraim bemoaning himself: You have chastised me, and I was chastised, like an untrained bull; Restore me, and I will return, for You are the Lord my God. Surely, after my turning, I repented; and after I was instructed, I struck myself on the thigh; I was ashamed, yes, even humiliated, because I bore the reproach of my youth. Is Ephraim My dear son? Is he a pleasant child? For though I spoke against him, I earnestly remember him still; Therefore My heart yearns for him; I will surely have mercy on him, says the Lord (Jeremiah 31:18-20).

C. **The fruit of our repentance is seen in three ways:**

1. **We will confess our sin and seek His forgiveness.**

When I kept silent, my bones grew old through my groaning all the day long. For day and night Your hand was heavy upon me; My vitality was turned into the drought of summer. I acknowledged my sin to You, and my iniquity I have not hidden. I said, "I will confess my transgressions to the Lord," and You forgave the iniquity of my sin (Psalm 32:3-5).

2. **We will have renewed power and confidence in prayer as we reach out to help others in need.**

Confess your trespasses to one another, and pray for one another, that you may be healed. The effective, fervent prayer of a righteous man avails much (James 5:16).

3. **We will not tolerate, excuse, or attempt to justify, our sins. We will confess and forsake our sins; thereby, enjoying the mercy of God's forgiveness.**

He who covers his sins will not prosper, but whoever confesses and forsakes them will have mercy (Proverbs 28:13).

D. When we choose to repent of our sins and posture
    ourselves within the boundaries of God's desire for us,
    we will be the recipient of a number of benefits given
    to us as a result of His grace.

    1. Repentance produces joy in heaven, as well as, in
        our hearts.

    *And when she has found it, she calls her friends and neighbors
    together, saying, "Rejoice with me, for I have found the piece
    which I lost!" Likewise, I say to you, there is joy in the
    presence of the angels of God over one sinner who repents*
    (Luke 15:9-10).

    2. Repentance produces forgiveness.

    *Repent therefore and be converted, that your sins may be
    blotted out, so that times of refreshing may come from the
    presence of the Lord* (Acts 3:19).

    3. Repentance brings us into a sweet fellowship with
        the Holy Spirit, Who in turn, will open our
        understanding of the Word of God.

    *Turn at my reproof; Surely I will pour out my spirit on you; I
    will make my words known to you* (Proverbs 1:23).

V. Repentance Releases Us to Trust God.

A. We must repent of placing our trust in our own
    abilities to deal with the issues of our everyday lives.
    We must place the full weight of our trust in God to
    help us.

    *Yes, we had the sentence of death in ourselves, that we should
    not trust in ourselves but in God who raises the dead, who
    delivered us from so great a death, and does deliver us; in
    whom we trust that He will still deliver us*
    (II Corinthians 1:9-10).

B. There is a vast difference between the activity of God's grace that is resident in our lives and our individual effort to deal with the issues before us.

    1. God's grace is the opposite of our own efforts.

And if by grace, then it is no longer of works; otherwise grace is no longer grace. But if it is of works, it is no longer grace; otherwise work is no longer work (Romans 11:6).

    2. Only grace can justify us in the eyes of God; no effort of our own will ever justify us before Him.

Having been justified by His grace we should become heirs according to the hope of eternal life (Titus 3:7).

Knowing that a man is not justified by the works of the law but by faith in Jesus Christ, even we have believed in Christ Jesus, that we might be justified by faith in Christ and not by the works of the law; for by the works of the law no flesh shall be justified (Galatians 2:16).

    3. Our efforts to be right with God will never be accomplished, for even our best efforts will leave us short of God's standard for relationship.

For all have sinned and fall short of the glory of God (Romans 3:23).

    4. Our efforts to be righteous before God will bring failure; God's grace is freely given as His gift.

Being justified freely by His grace through the redemption that is in Christ Jesus (Romans 3:24).

    5. God's grace working in us will produce humility in us and build our faith. On the other hand, our individual effort will fill us with pride which will make us boastful and resistant to God's mercy.

For by grace you have been saved through faith, and that not of yourselves; it is the gift of God, not of works, lest anyone should boast (Ephesians 2:8-9).

6. **The grace of God in our lives will cause us to glorify God in all that we do in life.**

    To the praise of the glory of His grace, by which He has made us accepted in the Beloved (Ephesians 1:6).

C. **Through the blood of Jesus our conscience is cleansed from dead works and we will desire to serve God from a pure heart.**

    How much more shall the blood of Christ, who through the eternal Spirit offered Himself without spot to God, purge your conscience from dead works to serve the living God (Hebrews 9:14)?

D. **Serving God in our individual effort will make us weary; however, when we turn to Him and trust His grace we find His perfect rest from our labors.**

    For he who has entered His rest has himself also ceased from his works as God did from His (Hebrews 4:10).

E. **Repentance is an on-going, daily activity in our lives as believers; not just a one-time event at our conversion.**

    If we confess our sins, He is faithful and just to forgive us our sins and to cleanse us from all unrighteousness (I John 1:9).

    1. **To confess our sins does not mean to merely make a list of our sins...God already has the list.**

    2. **To confess our sins means that we come into agreement with God concerning our sins and that we offer no excuse or justification for our sins.**

    3. **When we confess our sins, He promises not only to forgive us, but He will also cleanse our lives from the ravages of sin, and the pollution that sin leaves in our hearts and lives.**

Chapter Five

Releasing Our Praise and Worship

I. The Purpose of Man.

A. People spend a lifetime seeking answers to life's most puzzling questions: "Who am I?"; "Why am I here?"; and "What is my purpose in life?"

B. The answer to these questions will be discovered as we understand and participate in the offering of our praise and worship to God.

C. The prevalent misconception regarding the purpose of man is that he was created by God for fellowship with God.

   1. While it is true that we enjoy fellowship with God, we need to remember that God is not a lonely deity looking for a playmate.

   2. God immensely enjoys our fellowship; but He craves our praise and worship.

D. Man was created for the pleasure of God.

   For by Him all things were created that are in heaven and that are on earth, visible and invisible, whether thrones or dominions or principalities or powers. All things were created through Him and for Him (Colossians 1:16).

   You are worthy, O Lord, to receive glory and honor and power; for You have created all things, and by Your will they exist (Revelation 4:11).

E. Man was created to be a true worshiper of God.

   But the hour is coming, and now is, when the true worshipers will worship the Father in spirit and truth; for the Father is seeking such to worship Him (John 4:23).

   That we who first trusted in Christ should be to the praise of His glory (Ephesians 1:12).

F. Man was created by God with a two-fold purpose on the earth:

1. The first purpose of man is to have a relationship with God; this relationship is maintained through worship.

2. The second purpose of man is to exercise his God-given dominion in ruler-ship over all of God's creation.

G. Our effectiveness in ruler-ship under God is linked to the depth of our relationship with God.

1. Worship is the key to developing a strong relationship with God.

2. The ability to be effective in our ruler-ship will increase as our relationship with God grows.

H. Lucifer, the worship leader of heaven, led one-third of the angels in a rebellious attempt to overthrow God in eternity past.

1. The issue at the heart of this rebellion was ruler-ship and worship.

    a. Lucifer wanted to set his throne above God's and be the supreme ruler of heaven; as well as, rule over all of God's creation.

    b. Lucifer wanted to be the object and recipient of heaven's worship.

2. Lucifer was cast out of heaven, along with the angels who followed his leadership.

I.   Satan has now set his eyes on man and his objectives haven't changed in regards to worship and ruler-ship.

    1.   He still wants to be the recipient of man's worship; and if that isn't possible, he tries to get man to worship anything but God.

    2.   He wants to rule over man; but if he can't gain that ruler-ship, he will seek to weaken man's ability to rule under God.

J.   There are many who operate under the misconception that praise and worship is an activity which occurs in a Sunday church service. Praise and worship is a life-style of daily offering our heart's acknowledgement of God's greatness and pouring out our hearts' affections to the Lord.

From the rising of the sun to its going down the Lord's name is to be praised (Psalm 113:3).

K.   God has appointed every believer to be a priest.

My sons, do not be negligent now, for the Lord has chosen you to stand before Him, to serve Him, and that you should minister to Him and burn incense (II Chronicles 29:11).

You also, as living stones, are being built up a spiritual house, a holy priesthood, to offer up spiritual sacrifices acceptable to God through Jesus Christ (I Peter 2:5).

But you are a chosen generation, a royal priesthood, a holy nation, His own special people, that you may proclaim the praises of Him who called you out of darkness into His marvelous light (I Peter 2:9).

And has made us kings and priests to His God and Father, to Him be glory and dominion forever and ever. Amen (Revelation 1:6).

L.   God dwells in the midst of our praise and worship.

But You are holy, enthroned in the praises of Israel (Psalm 22:3).

M. When we offer our praise and worship to God, His power is released on our behalf.

But at midnight Paul and Silas were praying and singing hymns to God, and the prisoners were listening to them. Suddenly there was a great earthquake, so that the foundations of the prison were shaken; and immediately all the doors were opened and everyone's chains were loosed (Acts 16:25-26).

N. The Holy Spirit has been assigned to assist us in fulfilling our purpose of being true worshipers of God.

God is Spirit, and those who worship Him must worship in spirit and truth (John 4:24).

He will glorify Me, for He will take of what is Mine and declare it to you (John 16:14).

O. The Holy Spirit will transform us into the image of Jesus as we offer our praise and worship to God.

1. We are to set our affections upon Jesus and spend time nurturing our relationship with Him.

2. Time spent becoming acquainted with Jesus will close the gap in our differences. We will love what He loves; see what He sees; and hear what He hears.

If then you were raised with Christ, seek those things which are above, where Christ is, sitting at the right hand of God. Set your mind on things above, not on things on the earth. For you died, and your life is hidden with Christ in God. When Christ who is our life appears, then you also will appear with Him in glory (Colossians 3:1-4).

3. The rate of our transformation is determined by the time we spend in God's presence. As we spend time with Him, we will become more like Jesus.

But we all, with unveiled face, beholding as in a mirror the glory of the Lord, are being transformed into the same image from glory to glory, just as by the Spirit of the Lord (II Corinthians 3:18).

II. The Ministry of Praise.

A. Praise is the acknowledgement of the works of God's hands on the earth. Praise also expresses our thanks, gratitude, adoration, and applause for His goodness.

Praise Him for His mighty acts; praise Him according to His excellent greatness (Psalm 150:2)!

Oh, give thanks to the Lord, for He is good! For His mercy endures forever (Psalm 136:1).

B. Praise is a command, not an option.

Let everything that has breath praise the Lord. Praise the Lord (Psalm 150:6)!

Praise the Lord! Praise, O servants of the Lord, praise the name of the Lord! Blessed be the name of the Lord from this time forth and forevermore! From the rising of the sun to its going down the Lord's name is to be praised (Psalm 113:1-3).

C. Our conversations and actions are to be tempered with praise.

Therefore by Him let us continually offer the sacrifice of praise to God, that is, the fruit of our lips, giving thanks to His name (Hebrews 13:15).

D. We are to offer God our praise with our whole heart.

Praise the Lord! I will praise the Lord with my whole heart, in the assembly of the upright and in the congregation (Psalm 111:1).

I will praise You with my whole heart; before the gods I will sing praises to You (Psalm 138:1).

E. The offering of our praise to God will always be an act of our will.

I will praise You, O Lord, with my whole heart; I will tell of all Your marvelous works. I will be glad and rejoice in You; I will sing praise to Your name, O Most High (Psalm 9:1-2).

F.   We are to offer God our praise because He is worthy.

I will call upon the Lord, who is worthy to be praised; so shall I be saved from my enemies (Psalm 18:3).

G.   When we offer God our praise, we glorify Him.

Whoever offers praise glorifies Me; and to him who orders his conduct aright I will show the salvation of God (Psalm 50:23).

H.   When we offer our praise and thanksgiving to God, we fulfill the will of God.

In everything give thanks; for this is the will of God in Christ Jesus for you (I Thessalonians 5:18).

I.   The offering of our praise to God is to be a lifestyle: each day should be marked by the offering of praise.

While I live I will praise the Lord; I will sing praises to my God while I have my being (Psalm 146:2).

J.   We are to offer our praise to God, regardless of our circumstances: our circumstances do not change His worthiness to receive our praise.

I will bless the Lord at all times; His praise shall continually be in my mouth (Psalm 34:1).

K.   The offering of our praise is to be in the public arena, as well as in our private devotions.

I will declare Your name to My brethren; in the midst of the assembly I will praise You (Psalm 22:22).

L.   Our open praise to God will become a ministry to the hearts of unbelievers.

He has put a new song in my mouth—Praise to our God; many will see it and fear, and will trust in the Lord (Psalm 40:3).

Then our mouth was filled with laughter, and our tongue with singing. Then they said among the nations, "The Lord has done great things for them." The Lord has done great things for us, and we are glad (Psalm 126:2-3).

III. The Ministry of Worship.

A. There is no one single verse or passage of Scripture that defines worship. Our understanding of worship must be derived from the various verbs used in the Biblical examples of worship.

B. Perhaps, the most definitive verse in Scripture that explains worship to us came from Jesus, Himself.

"And you shall love the Lord your God with all your heart, with all your soul, with all your mind, and with all your strength." This is the first commandment (Mark 12:30).

C. Worship involves the unconditional commitment of our hearts to God.

   1. Worship flows out of a relationship in which love responds to love.

   2. Worship is progressive, in that it flows out of relationship. With each passing day, our worship should become increasingly more intimate.

   3. The depth and the warmth of our worship will be directly proportionate to the depth and warmth of our relationship with God.

D. The activity of worship requires the presence of God.

   1. Worship is an inter-personal action between an individual and God.

   2. Worship occurs when we embrace the presence of God and allow the Holy Spirit to help us release our deepest, heartfelt emotions and attitudes.

   3. The end result of true worship will always be a renewal of commitment to both love and serve the Lord.

E. **Worship is the pursuit of God for who He is rather than just for what He does. In worship we seek His face, not just the works of His hands.**

When You said, "Seek My face," my heart said to You, "Your face, Lord, I will seek" (Psalm 27:8).

F. **Redemption from sin is the foundation of worship in the Old and in the New Testament.**

1. **The Old Testament saints worshiped God from a distance because their sins separated them from God.**

2. **Now, in the New Testament, the blood of Jesus removes our sins and opens the way for us to have a relationship with God.**

3. **The expression of our love and gratitude in worship to God for the sacrifice of His Son (this sacrifice brought about our redemption), becomes the foundation from which all our worship will flow, both now, and for all of eternity.**

But if we walk in the light as He is in the light, we have fellowship with one another, and the blood of Jesus Christ His Son cleanses us from all sin (I John 1:7).

But now in Christ Jesus you who once were far off have been brought near by the blood of Christ (Ephesians 2:13).

Therefore, brethren, having boldness to enter the Holiest by the blood of Jesus (Hebrews 10:19).

G. **The Holy Spirit is assigned to help us enter into worship as we offer ourselves to God.**

1. **The Holy Spirit enables us to communicate with God by our spirits.**

86

2. God is the one who initiates worship within us through the agency of the Holy Spirit. The Holy Spirit enables us to respond to God's love.

But the hour is coming, and now is, when the true worshipers will worship the Father in spirit and truth; for the Father is seeking such to worship Him. God is Spirit, and those who worship Him must worship in spirit and truth (John 4:23-24).

H. Worship is to be characterized by brokenness.

1. Brokenness before the Lord has always been an acknowledgment that we are in need of the Holy Spirit's work in our lives to shape us for God's purposes.

    a. When we come into God's holy presence through our worship, we will recognize our imperfections in the light of His perfection. This should result in our brokenness before the Lord.

    The sacrifices of God are a broken spirit, a broken and a contrite heart—These, O God, You will not despise (Psalm 51:17).

    b. Worship lays bare our motives, integrity, purity, priorities, and the status of our relationship with God. This exposure should convict us of our inconsistencies, and bring us to repentance.

    c. We cannot truly worship God while we are complacent within ourselves.

    The Lord is near to those who have a broken heart, and saves such as have a contrite spirit (Psalm 34:17).

2. In the Old Testament brokenness was physically required when animals were slain as a sacrificial expression of worship.

3. Broken sacrifices represented several things:

   a. The atonement for the sins of the worshiper;

   b. It was symbolic of the sacrifice of one's self;

   c. The gift of life showed that the worshiper was giving up their personal interest in the animal by sacrificing it in an act of worship to God.

4. The requirement for a spotless or perfect sacrifice was due to the fact that the condition of the sacrifice reflected the perception of the worshiper as to the worthiness of God.

   a. A crippled or blemished animal was worthless to the owner.

   b. Offering a blemished animal as a sacrifice would reveal the insincerity of the worshiper's heart and would be a dishonor to God.

5. The Psalmist David understood both the desire of God for worship and the attitude of the worshiper in worship.

For You do not desire sacrifice, or else I would give it; You do not delight in burnt offering. The sacrifices of God are a broken spirit, a broken and a contrite heart—These, O God, You will not despise (Psalm 51:16-17).

6. Today, God is not looking for broken animal sacrifices on His altar of worship; but rather, He is looking for a surrendered heart.

   a. He is looking for hearts that are sensitive to the pain caused by sin.

   b. He is looking for hearts that are tender towards Him in the expressions of worship.

I. Worship is to be characterized by humility.

   1. Humility in worship is the ability to worship freely without thought of our reputations or what anyone around us may think of our expressions.

   2. Humility approaches God from the position of His grace; not from our own self-righteousness.

   For thus says the High and Lofty One Who inhabits eternity, whose name is Holy: "I dwell in the high and holy place, with him who has a contrite and humble spirit, to revive the spirit of the humble, and to revive the heart of the contrite one" (Isaiah 57:15).

   3. Humility is the absence of pride. Our pride repels the presence of God and will keep us from freely expressing ourselves to God. Pride always makes us self-conscience instead of God-conscience.

   Likewise you younger people, submit yourselves to your elders. Yes, all of you be submissive to one another, and be clothed with humility, for "God resists the proud, but gives grace to the humble" (I Peter 5:5).

J. Our worship is characterized by our spiritual hunger and thirst for the presence of God.

   1. We must realize that our spirit literally craves fellowship with God.

   2. There is nothing known to man that is more satisfying than to be in God's presence.

   You will show me the path of life; in Your presence is fullness of joy; at Your right hand are pleasures forevermore (Psalm 16:11).

   For a day in Your courts is better than a thousand. I would rather be a doorkeeper in the house of my God than dwell in the tents of wickedness (Psalm 84:10).

3. **Just as our appetite stimulates eating, so our hunger for God stimulates our worship.**

O God, You are my God; early will I seek You; my soul thirsts for You; my flesh longs for You in a dry and thirsty land where there is no water. So I have looked for You in the sanctuary, to see Your power and Your glory. Because Your loving-kindness is better than life, my lips shall praise You. Thus I will bless You while I live; I will lift up my hands in Your name. My soul shall be satisfied as with marrow and fatness, and my mouth shall praise You with joyful lips. When I remember You on my bed, I meditate on You in the night watches. Because You have been my help, therefore in the shadow of Your wings I will rejoice. My soul follows close behind You; Your right hand upholds me (Psalm 63:1-8).

IV. The Protocol for Entrance to His Presence.

A. **Most of the time, we fail to honor the protocol for entering into God's presence.**

1. **Far too often we rush right in and take our place at the "complaint window." We then proceed to lodge our complaint concerning His faithfulness and perceived lack of emotional involvement with us.**

2. **After filing our complaint we give the Lord His marching orders. We tell Him to whom He should report when He accomplishes His assignment.**

3. **We make sure He knows how important His task is; what will happen to us if He fails; and the time frame in which we need Him to finish the task.**

4. **Our venting at the "complaint window" leaves us angry and bitter. Is it any wonder that we are not all that excited about spending time in the Lord's presence and offering our praise and worship?**

B. The Bible clearly spells out for us the protocol that we are to observe as we enter into the Lord's presence.

1. We are to approach Him full of joy.

Make a joyful shout to the Lord, all you lands (Psalm 100:1)!

2. We are to come before the Lord with singing.

Serve the Lord with gladness; come before His presence with singing (Psalm 100:2).

3. We are to approach Him with our focus on Him.

Know that the Lord, He is God; it is He who has made us, and not we ourselves; we are His people and the sheep of His pasture (Psalm 100:3).

4. We are to come before Him with thanksgiving and praise as we lift our voices to bless His name.

Enter into His gates with thanksgiving, and into His courts with praise. Be thankful to Him, and bless His name (Psalm 100:4).

5. We are to know the reason for the protocol: the Lord is good; merciful; and is the source of truth.

For the Lord is good; His mercy is everlasting, and His truth endures to all generations (Psalm 100:5).

C. We gravitate to tradition as we express ourselves to God. We fail to understand the diversity of God's vast creation; we falsely assume our way is the only way.

1. We approach Him from learned methods; comfort zones; preferences; personalities; and experiences.

2. We judge different expressions as lacking spiritual substance; fanatical; insincere; and emotional.

D. We fail to consider the diversity of God's vast creation; we falsely assume our way is the only way.

E. The various expressions in and of themselves cannot produce worship. It is not the performance that makes worship; it is our worship that motivates performance.

1. The intensity of our expression does not determine the intensity of our worship.

2. Sighing and silence are as valid and intense in their expression as singing and shouting.

F. We would be wise to search the Scriptures and observe the variety of expressions that the Lord enjoys.

1. Singing is a form of our expression.

Sing praise to the Lord, you saints of His, and give thanks at the remembrance of His holy name (Psalm 30:4).

Speaking to one another in psalms and hymns and spiritual songs, singing and making melody in your heart to the Lord (Ephesians 5:19).

Let the word of Christ dwell in you richly in all wisdom, teaching and admonishing one another in psalms and hymns and spiritual songs, singing with grace in your hearts to the Lord (Colossians 3:16).

2. Singing in the Spirit is a form of our expression.

Oh, sing to the Lord a new song! For He has done marvelous things; His right hand and His holy arm have gained Him the victory (Psalm 98:1).

What is the conclusion then? I will pray with the spirit, and I will also pray with the understanding. I will sing with the spirit, and I will also sing with the understanding (I Corinthians 14:15).

They sang as it were a new song before the throne, before the four living creatures, and the elders; and no one could learn that song except the hundred and forty-four thousand who were redeemed from the earth (Revelation 14:3).

3. Shouting is a form of our expression.

Let them shout for joy and be glad, who favor my righteous cause; and let them say continually, "Let the Lord be magnified, who has pleasure in the prosperity of His servant" (Psalm 35:27).

Be glad in the Lord and rejoice, you righteous; and shout for joy, all you upright in heart (Psalm 32:11)!

Shout joyfully to the Lord, all the earth; break forth in song, rejoice, and sing praises (Psalm 98:4).

4. Clapping is a form of our expression.

Oh, clap your hands, all you peoples! Shout to God with the voice of triumph (Psalm 47:1)!

For you shall go out with joy, and be led out with peace; the mountains and the hills shall break forth into singing before you, and all the trees of the field shall clap their hands (Isaiah 55:12).

5. Lifting our hands is a form of our expression.

Lift up your hands in the sanctuary, and bless the Lord (Psalm 134:2).

I desire therefore that the men pray everywhere, lifting up holy hands, without wrath and doubting (I Timothy 2:8).

Thus I will bless You while I live; I will lift up my hands in Your name (Psalm 63:4).

6. Standing is a form of our expression.

Behold, bless the Lord, all you servants of the Lord, who by night stand in the house of the Lord (Psalm 134:1)!

You who stand in the house of the Lord, in the courts of the house of our God, praise the Lord, for the Lord is good; sing praises to His name, for it is pleasant (Psalm 135:2-3).

At that time the Lord separated the tribe of Levi to bear the ark of the covenant of the Lord, to stand before the Lord to minister to Him and to bless in His name, to this day (Deuteronomy 10:8).

7.   Kneeling and bowing is a form of our expression.

Oh come, let us worship and bow down; let us kneel before the Lord our Maker (Psalm 95:6).

For Solomon had made a bronze platform five cubits long, five cubits wide, and three cubits high, and had set it in the midst of the court; and he stood on it, knelt down on his knees before all the assembly of Israel, and spread out his hands toward heaven (II Chronicles 6:13).

And when he had said these things, he knelt down and prayed with them all (Acts 20:36).

8.   Dancing is a form of our expression.

Let them praise His name with the dance; let them sing praises to Him with the timbrel and harp (Psalm 149:3).

You have turned for me my mourning into dancing; you have put off my sackcloth and clothed me with gladness (Psalm 30:11).

Then Miriam the prophetess, the sister of Aaron, took the timbrel in her hand; and all the women went out after her with timbrels and with dances (Exodus 15:20).

9.   Playing musical instruments is a form of our expression.

The Lord was ready to save me; therefore we will sing my songs with stringed instruments all the days of our life, in the house of the Lord (Isaiah 38:20).

Praise Him with the sound of the trumpet; praise Him with the lute and harp! Praise Him with the timbrel and dance; praise Him with stringed instruments and flutes! Praise Him with loud cymbals (Psalm 150:3-5).

Thus all Israel brought up the ark of the covenant of the Lord with shouting and with the sound of the horn, with trumpets and with cymbals, making music with stringed instruments and harps (I Chronicles 15:28).

Chapter Six

Learning
to Pray

I. The Call to Prayer.

A. **God has given us a standing invitation to fellowship with Him in prayer.**

    1. **God requires us to humble ourselves before Him, seek His face, and turn from our sinful ways.**

    2. **If we will meet the afore-mentioned criteria, God promises to answer our prayers.**

If My people who are called by My name will humble themselves, and pray and seek My face, and turn from their wicked ways, then I will hear from heaven, and will forgive their sin and heal their land. Now My eyes will be open and My ears attentive to prayer made in this place (II Chronicles 7:14-15).

B. **Prayer is a command, not an option. When we pray, God releases His peace into our hearts and minds.**

Be anxious for nothing, but in everything by prayer and supplication, with thanksgiving, let your requests be made known to God; and the peace of God, which surpasses all understanding, will guard your hearts and minds through Christ Jesus (Philippians 4:6-7).

Pray without ceasing (I Thessalonians 5:17).

C. **Prayer, in its purest form, is communion with God; it is an open, verbal exchange which will enhance our companionship with Him.**

Give ear to my words, O Lord, consider my meditation. Give heed to the voice of my cry, my King and my God, for to You I will pray. My voice You shall hear in the morning, O Lord; in the morning I will direct it to You, and I will look up (Psalm 5:1-3).

D. **God is not only willing, but anxious to answer us.**

It shall come to pass that before they call, I will answer; and while they are still speaking, I will hear (Isaiah 65:24).

E. **Prayer brings us into God's presence and there, in His presence, the desires of our heart is satisfied.**

The Lord is near to all who call upon Him, to all who call upon Him in truth. He will fulfill the desire of those who fear Him; He also will hear their cry and save them (Psalm 145:18-19).

F. **God takes great delight in our fellowship with Him.**

He shall pray to God, and He will delight in him, he shall see His face with joy, for He restores to man His righteousness (Job 33:26).

G. **Through prayer we receive instructions and direction.**

Therefore, as the Holy Spirit says: "Today, if you will hear His voice" (Hebrews 3:7).

H. **We are to pray with boldness and confidence. Our boldness is not born out of presumption; it flows out of our confidence in God and the promises of His Word.**

Seeing then that we have a great High Priest who has passed through the heavens, Jesus the Son of God, let us hold fast our confession. For we do not have a High Priest who cannot sympathize with our weaknesses, but was in all points tempted as we are, yet without sin. Let us therefore come boldly to the throne of grace, that we may obtain mercy and find grace to help in time of need (Hebrews 4:14-16).

I. **When we pray, we are to pray in earnest.**

Arise, cry out in the night, at the beginning of the watches; pour out your heart like water before the face of the Lord. Lift your hands toward Him for the life of your young children, who faint from hunger at the head of every street (Lamentations 2:19).

J. **When we fail to discipline ourselves in prayer, we rob ourselves of God's blessings.**

You lust and do not have. You murder and covet and cannot obtain. You fight and war. Yet you do not have because you do not ask (James 4:2).

II. The Power of Prayer.

A. **God promises to reveal things to us in prayer that we couldn't get from any other source but Him.**

Call to Me, and I will answer you, and show you great and mighty things, which you do not know (Jeremiah 33:3).

B. **Jesus has made us righteous in God's eyes.**

    1. **We are assured our prayer will bring results.**

    2. **The words "avails much," as found in James 5:16, literally means "to prevail with great power."**

Confess your trespasses to one another, and pray for one another, that you may be healed. The effective, fervent prayer of a righteous man avails much (James 5:16).

C. **Prayer allows us to release our cares to the Lord.**

    1. **Prayer allows us to release the negative emotions of fear; unbelief; worry; and anger.**

    2. **We are invited to shift the heavy weight of our cares onto the strong shoulders of our Lord.**

Casting all your care upon Him, for He cares for you (I Peter 5:7).

Come to Me, all you who labor and are heavy laden, and I will give you rest. Take My yoke upon you and learn from Me, for I am gentle and lowly in heart, and you will find rest for your souls. For My yoke is easy and My burden is light (Matthew 11:28-30).

D. **Jesus has granted us His "power of attorney" to use His name in prayer.**

And whatever you ask in My name, that I will do, that the Father may be glorified in the Son. If you ask anything in My name, I will do it (John 14:13-14).

E. **The Holy Spirit has been assigned to assist us in offering our prayers to God.**

Likewise the Spirit also helps in our weaknesses. For we do not know what we should pray for as we ought, but the Spirit Himself makes intercession for us with groanings which cannot be uttered. Now He who searches the hearts knows what the mind of the Spirit is, because He makes intercession for the saints according to the will of God (Romans 8:26-27).

F. **Our obedience to God's Word positions us to receive God's answers to our prayers.**

And whatever we ask we receive from Him, because we keep His commandments and do those things that are pleasing in His sight (I John 3:22).

G. **God desires to release His abundant supply into our lives. His answer to our prayers will always exceed our requests and even our expectations.**

Now to Him who is able to do exceedingly abundantly above all that we ask or think, according to the power that works in us (Ephesians 3:20).

H. **When we commune with God in prayer, our mental, spiritual, and physical strength is renewed.**

But those who wait on the Lord shall renew their strength; they shall mount up with wings like eagles, they shall run and not be weary, they shall walk and not faint (Isaiah 40:31).

I. **According to the Scriptures, there is power in agreement. Whenever two or more people agree together in prayer on a particular matter, the results of their agreement will bring great rewards.**

Again I say to you that if two of you agree on earth concerning anything that they ask, it will be done for them by My Father in heaven. For where two or three are gathered together in My name, I am there in the midst of them (Matthew 18:19-20).

J. **When we pray with a believing heart, we are assured of God's answers.**

Therefore I say to you, whatever things you ask when you pray, believe that you receive them, and you will have them (Mark 11:24).

K. **When our prayers are in agreement with God's Word, we are assured our petitions are heard and answered.**

Now this is the confidence that we have in Him, that if we ask anything according to His will, He hears us. And if we know that He hears us, whatever we ask, we know that we have the petitions that we have asked of Him (I John 5:14-15).

III. Learning to Pray.

A. **The disciples asked Jesus to teach them how to pray.**

    1. They wanted to learn to pray in the same manner and power in which He prayed.

    2. They recognized that when Jesus prayed things happened and people's lives were changed.

B. **We can learn to pray by following the prayer of Jesus.**

In this manner, therefore, pray: Our Father in heaven, hallowed be Your name. Your kingdom come. Your will be done on earth as it is in heaven. Give us this day our daily bread. And forgive us our debts, as we forgive our debtors. And do not lead us into temptation, but deliver us from the evil one. For Yours is the kingdom and the power and the glory forever (Matthew 6:9-13).

    1. "Our Father in heaven."

        a. Beginning with "Our Father," Jesus placed an emphasis on our relationship with God. He established our confidence in prayer through the Father-child relationship.

101

Now this is the confidence that we have in Him, that if we ask anything according to His will, He hears us. And if we know that He hears us, whatever we ask, we know that we have the petitions that we have asked of Him (I John 5:14-15).

    b.   **This truth is beautifully portrayed in the story of the prodigal son as found in Luke 15. The tender compassion and grace of the father in the parable reflects how God, our Father, feels about us and how He responds to us when we repent of our failures.**

2.   "Hallowed be Your name."

    a.   **The word "hallowed," is translated as "holy." Jesus invites us to experience the life-changing power of the Holy Spirit as we enter into worship through our declaration: "Holy is Your name."**

    b.   **The concept of God's holiness speaks of His completeness. He lacks absolutely nothing in His person or in His ability to keep His Word.**

    c.   **As we present ourselves in worship to the Father, the Holy Spirit brings to completion those areas that have been rendered incomplete as a result of sin.**

3.   "Your kingdom come. Your will be done on earth as it is in heaven."

    a.   **We are to invite the purposes of God, as seen in His kingdom and expressed will, into every circumstance and arena of our lives.**

    b.   **We are inviting God's presence and power to work in reversing hell's agenda when we claim the kingdom and will of God.**

4. "Give us this day our daily bread."

   a. Jesus was not asking us to beg for God's promised provision in our lives; He was reminding us to declare our dependency on the Lord for our daily provision.

   b. When we declare our dependency on God for our provision, we are reminded of His unchanging commitment to provide for us.

   And my God shall supply all your need according to His riches in glory by Christ Jesus (Philippians 4:19).

5. "And forgive us our debts, as we forgive our debtors."

   a. Some Bible translations use the word "debts," while others use the word "trespasses." Both words are accurate and needful in order to understand both sides of our human failures.

      (1) Sins of commission: Wrongs we have committed in crossing the line set for us by God's Word, rendering us trespassers.

      (2) Sins of omission: Right things we have failed to do, rendering us to be debtors.

   b. Asking forgiveness releases us from the guilt of our trespasses; as well as, from the pain of neglect, which results in indebtedness.

6. "And do not lead us into temptation, but deliver us from the evil one."

   a. This portion of the prayer reminds us how vulnerable we are to daily temptations.

b. When we make this request we establish our steps for the day and commit ourselves to expect the Lord's deliverance.

c. Praying for God's deliverance will not remove us from temptation, but it will remind us that God has promised to make a way of escape.

No temptation has overtaken you except such as is common to man; but God is faithful, who will not allow you to be tempted beyond what you are able, but with the temptation will also make the way of escape, that you may be able to bear it (I Corinthians 10:13).

7. "For Yours is the kingdom and the power and the glory forever. Amen."

a. Our acknowledgement that the kingdom belongs to God reveals our willingness to submit to God's rulership in our lives.

b. We demonstrate our willingness to rest in His Lordship by placing the timing of all things into His abundantly capable hands.

Therefore humble yourselves under the mighty hand of God, that He may exalt you in due time, casting all your care upon Him, for He cares for you (I Peter 5:6-7).

Now thanks be to God who always leads us in triumph in Christ, and through us diffuses the fragrance of His knowledge in every place (II Corinthians 2:14).

IV. Types of Prayer.

A. Perseverance in prayer.

1. Perseverance in prayer speaks of our being steadfast and consistent in our investment of time in prayer.

2.   Perseverance in prayer recognizes that there is never a situation to which we need to surrender to the agenda of hell.

3.   The Gospel of Luke, chapters 11 and 18, teach us that we have a willing friend and a just judge in God; we can approach Him with the confidence that He will hear and respond to our request.

B. Supplication in prayer.

1.   Supplication in prayer is the passionate exercise of our God-given authority to bind hell's agenda. As we bind any action that is contrary to God's intended order, it will be arrested in its activity.

2.   Our supplication in prayer has the power to bind and release what has already been willed and provided for in heaven.

And I will give you the keys of the kingdom of heaven, and whatever you bind on earth will be bound in heaven, and whatever you loose on earth will be loosed in heaven (Matthew 16:19).

3.   The concept of "binding" in prayer is rooted in the idea of holding someone, or something, to a legal contract. It is our responsibility to recognize those areas that are contrary to God's plan and desire for humanity.

4.   We exercise authority as God's representatives; wherein, we bind circumstances to the will of God which was expressed in His Son, Jesus, on the cross.

5.   Calvary's contract states that whoever comes to Christ has the legal right to be saved, forgiven, healed, and delivered.

C. Intercession in prayer.

    1.   The call to intercession is to respond to the desire to pray and petition God on behalf of another.

    2.   As we are confronted by an adverse course of events in our own life and in the lives of those around us, we are prompted by the Holy Spirit to pray in faith and invite God's entry into the circumstance.

    3.   Intercessors recognize that they are God's representatives. They are vested with heaven's authority to speak the promises of God into every circumstance that is under the devil's attack.

    4.   Intercessors are driven to pray by a passionate awareness that unless someone prays, hell will successfully violate the covenant boundaries of heaven.

D. Thanksgiving in prayer.

    1.   The Bible does not instruct us to give thanks "for everything," because everything is not worthy of our thanksgiving.

    2.   However, the Bible does instruct us that "in everything," we are to give thanks to God. Regardless of how difficult our circumstance may be, we can give God thanks that He is there with us and that He will prove Himself faithful to us.

Rejoice always, pray without ceasing, in everything give thanks; for this is the will of God in Christ Jesus for you (I Thessalonians 5:16-18).

Therefore know that the Lord your God, He is God, the faithful God who keeps covenant and mercy for a thousand generations with those who love Him and keep His commandments (Deuteronomy 7:9).

E. Fasting in prayer.

1. **When we commit ourselves to fast, we unlock God's wisdom and direction for our lives. Jesus established fasting as a part of the Christian discipline.**

Then the disciples of John came to Him, saying, "Why do we and the Pharisees fast often, but Your disciples do not fast?" And Jesus said to them, "Can the friends of the bridegroom mourn as long as the bridegroom is with them? But the days will come when the bridegroom will be taken away from them, and then they will fast" (Matthew 9:14-15).

2. **There are any number of circumstances in life that should prompt us to fast and seek the Lord's guidance and wisdom.**

    a. **We should fast when we find ourselves in a time of transition; especially when that transition is a direct result of the enemy's work against us. King David fasted at the news of Saul's and Jonathan's death. He fully understood that the responsibility of the leadership of the nation would now fall on his shoulders.**

    And they mourned and wept and fasted until evening for Saul and for Jonathan his son, for the people of the Lord and for the house of Israel, because they had fallen by the sword (II Samuel 1:12).

    b. **We are to fast when it is evident that our survival is at stake. Through our fasting, we will discover God's plan for defeating the strategy of the enemy against us.**

    Go, gather all the Jews who are present in Shushan, and fast for me; neither eat nor drink for three days, night or day. My maids and I will fast likewise. And so I will go to the king, which is against the law; and if I perish, I perish (Esther 4:16)!

c. We are to fast for the future and for God's
    protection and provision when entering into a
    new season of life. The decisions that are
    made today will have a direct impact on the
    generations to come after us.

*Then I proclaimed a fast there at the river of Ahava, that
we might humble ourselves before our God, to seek from
Him the right way for us and our little ones and all our
possessions. For I was ashamed to request of the king an
escort of soldiers and horsemen to help us against the
enemy on the road, because we had spoken to the king,
saying, "The hand of our God is upon all those for good
who seek Him, but His power and His wrath are against
all those who forsake Him." So we fasted and entreated
our God for this, and He answered our prayer*
(Ezra 8:21-23).

d. We are to fast when waging spiritual warfare.
    Jesus taught us that fasting and prayer hold a
    dynamic power that is capable of breaking the
    power of evil and can stop hell's capacity to
    withstand the entry of God's kingdom.

*So He said to them, "This kind can come out by nothing
but prayer and fasting"* (Mark 9:29).

3. There are some practical guidelines we need to
    follow when we enter a time of fasting.

a. When you fast, seek the Holy Spirit's counsel
    as to how long you should fast. Consider your
    schedule when you enter a fast and keep in
    mind that a partial fast is acceptable to the
    Lord. Jesus fasted for forty days but it wasn't
    in the middle of His work week. Set time aside
    for an extended period of fasting.

*I ate no pleasant food, no meat or wine came into my
mouth, nor did I anoint myself at all, till three whole
weeks were fulfilled* (Daniel 10:3).

b.   When you fast, don't be foolish if you have medical reasons that restrict your fasting. Ask the Holy Spirit to show you ways you can enter into the spirit of a fast without jeopardizing your health.

c.   When you fast, remember that your body needs water, so make sure you stay hydrated.

d.   When you fast, schedule times to break for prayer and to feed on God's Word.

V. Developing the Desire to Pray.

A.   Jesus set the example of what our prayer life should be like. Throughout His ministry, He communed with His Father; each season of prayer resulted in the renewing of His strength and power for ministry.

Now in the morning, having risen a long while before daylight, He went out and departed to a solitary place; and there He prayed (Mark 1:35).

And when He had sent the multitudes away, He went up on the mountain by Himself to pray. And when evening had come, He was alone there (Matthew 14:23).

And coming out, He went to the Mount of Olives, as He was accustomed, and His disciples also followed Him. When He came to the place, He said to them, "Pray that you may not enter into temptation." And He was withdrawn from them about a stone's throw, and He knelt down and prayed (Luke 22:39-41).

Then Jesus said, "Father, forgive them, for they do not know what they do." And they divided His garments and cast lots (Luke 23:34).

Therefore He is also able to save to the uttermost those who come to God through Him, since He ever lives to make intercession for them (Hebrews 7:25).

B. Jesus taught that the purpose of the Temple, which was His Father's house, was to be a place of prayer. Today, individually, we are the temple or house of God; therefore, we are to be people of prayer.

1. **Just as Jesus cleansed the Temple of the money changers, so we must cleanse our hearts from sin.**

Then Jesus went into the temple of God and drove out all those who bought and sold in the temple, and overturned the tables of the money changers and the seats of those who sold doves (Matthew 21:12).

2. **Just as Jesus declared that the Temple should be a house of prayer, so must we develop a daily habit of prayer.**

And He said to them, "It is written, 'My house shall be called a house of prayer,' but you have made it a 'den of thieves' " (Matthew 21:13).

3. **Just as the power of God was manifested in the Temple after it was established as a house of prayer, so the power of God will be manifested in our lives as a result of our time in prayer.**

Then the blind and the lame came to Him in the temple, and He healed them (Matthew 21:14).

4. **Just as praise filled the Temple as a result of the manifestation of God's power; even so, praise will fill our hearts as we see the power of God released through prayer.**

But when the chief priests and scribes saw the wonderful things that He did, and the children crying out in the temple and saying, "Hosanna to the Son of David!" they were indignant and said to Him, "Do You hear what these are saying?" And Jesus said to them, "Yes. Have you never read, 'Out of the mouth of babes and nursing infants You have perfected praise'?" (Matthew 21:15-16).

C. The desire to pray is born within a heart that is hungry for God, and is evidenced by a driving desire to spend time in His presence.

   1. Having a desire to pray is not enough to develop the habit of prayer; it takes daily discipline.

   2. Our desire and daily discipline to spend time in the Lord's presence in prayer will be the delight of our hearts.

   You will show me the path of life; in Your presence is fullness of joy; at Your right hand are pleasures forevermore (Psalm 16:11).

Chapter Seven

Waging Spiritual Warfare

I. Understanding Your Enemy.

A. There are two powers attempting to work in our lives:

1. **One power seeking to work in our lives is God.**

   a. **God desires to bless our lives and fill us with the riches of His gift of life.**

   b. **God cares about redeeming us; thereby, bringing to completion those areas of life which have been broken or lost by sin.**

2. **The other power seeking to work in our lives is Satan and his demonic forces of darkness.**

   a. **Satan desires to rob us of the promises of God and ultimately, he desires to destroy us.**

   b. **Satan seeks to break our fellowship with God. He wants us to blame God for our problems; thereby, eroding our confidence in His Word.**

   The thief does not come except to steal, and to kill, and to destroy. I have come that they may have life, and that they may have it more abundantly (John 10:10).

B. Our enemy is Satan and his demonic forces of darkness—not people.

1. **Satan and his demons are fallen angels which are disembodied spirits. They rebelled against God and were cast out of heaven to the earth.**

   And war broke out in heaven: Michael and his angels fought with the dragon; and the dragon and his angels fought, but they did not prevail, nor was a place found for them in heaven any longer. So the great dragon was cast out, that serpent of old, called the Devil and Satan, who deceives the whole world; he was cast to the earth, and his angels were cast out with him (Revelation 12:7-9).

2. **Satan and his demons are not flesh and blood; however, they seek to influence those around us and control the circumstances of our lives. The devil's intimidation always gives birth to fear.**

Be sober, be vigilant; because your adversary the devil walks about like a roaring lion, seeking whom he may devour (I Peter 5:8).

C. **Our warfare against these forces of darkness must be waged from a spiritual perspective, not a physical one.**

Finally, my brethren, be strong in the Lord and in the power of His might. Put on the whole armor of God, that you may be able to stand against the wiles of the devil. For we do not wrestle against flesh and blood, but against principalities, against powers, against the rulers of the darkness of this age, against spiritual hosts of wickedness in the heavenly places (Ephesians 6:10-12).

For though we walk in the flesh, we do not war according to the flesh. For the weapons of our warfare are not carnal but mighty in God for pulling down strongholds (II Corinthians 10:3-4).

D. **Satan's attacks and strategies are an effort to keep us under the effects of the curse of the law.**

1. **The curse of the law was manifested in three ways: poverty; sickness; and death.**

2. **Jesus paid the ultimate price through His death on the cross to redeem us from the curse of the law.**

Christ has redeemed us from the curse of the law, having become a curse for us (for it is written, "Cursed is everyone who hangs on a tree") (Galatians 3:13).

3. **Jesus reversed the curse and positioned us to receive the covenant blessings of Abraham.**

That the blessing of Abraham might come upon the Gentiles in Christ Jesus, that we might receive the promise of the Spirit through faith (Galatians 3:14).

116

E. **Satan seeks to employ various strategies in order to defeat us. He seeks to wear down our resolve as we believe God and wait on Him by faith.**

   1. **Satan's strategy against us is to seek to delay God's answers to our prayers.**

      a. **He will do everything in his power to abort our miracles and block our answers to prayer.**

      b. **He knows that if he can delay our answers to prayer, he can weaken our faith and drain our strength to fight against his agenda.**

      Then he said to me, "Do not fear, Daniel, for from the first day that you set your heart to understand, and to humble yourself before your God, your words were heard; and I have come because of your words. But the prince of the kingdom of Persia withstood me twenty-one days; and behold, Michael, one of the chief princes, came to help me, for I had been left alone there with the kings of Persia" (Daniel 10:12-13).

   2. **Satan's strategy against us is to use deceit and tell us his lies.**

      a. **He lies about himself; about circumstances; and about our past, present, and future.**

      b. **He twists the truth and will make every effort to persuade us with his relentless lies.**

      c. **Satan is the consummate liar. Why would we believe anything he says about anything? Everything he says is rooted in a lie.**

      You are of your father the devil, and the desires of your father you want to do. He was a murderer from the beginning, and does not stand in the truth, because there is no truth in him. When he speaks a lie, he speaks from his own resources, for he is a liar and the father of it (John 8:44).

3. **Satan's strategy against us is to distract us from fulfilling our God-appointed purpose in life.**

    a. **He seeks to break our focus of faith; whereby, we look at our circumstances instead of God's promises and what God has called us to be.**

    And not being weak in faith, he did not consider his own body, already dead (since he was about a hundred years old), and the deadness of Sarah's womb. He did not waver at the promise of God through unbelief, but was strengthened in faith, giving glory to God, and being fully convinced that what He had promised He was also able to perform (Romans 4:19-21).

    b. **He distracts us by tempting us to engage in unhealthy activities; make unwise choices; and listen to unwarranted criticism.**

    Do not give place to the devil (Ephesians 4:27).

    But each one is tempted when he is drawn away by his own desires and enticed. Then, when desire has conceived, it gives birth to sin; and sin, when it is full-grown, brings forth death. Do not be deceived, my beloved brethren (James 1:14-16).

    c. **He places people in our lives who try to distract us from our purpose; they prove to be an unhealthy alliance.**

    Do not be deceived: Evil company corrupts good habits (I Corinthians 15:33).

    The righteous should choose his friends carefully, for the way of the wicked leads them astray (Proverbs 12:26).

4. **Satan's strategy is to touch and spoil the most important areas of our lives leaving us with the bitter taste of disappointment.**

    a. **When disappointment sets in, we lose hope of circumstances ever changing and we become spiritually sick in our hearts.**

b. **We are disappointed when things don't go according to plan; whether in marriage, children, relationships with friends, finances, health, or in our plans for the future.**

Hope deferred makes the heart sick, but when the desire comes, it is a tree of life (Proverbs 13:12).

Now hope does not disappoint, because the love of God has been poured out in our hearts by the Holy Spirit who was given to us (Romans 5:5).

c. **When we allow disappointment to settle into our hearts, we grow tired and stop doing the things that will turn circumstances around.**

And let us not grow weary while doing good, for in due season we shall reap if we do not lose heart (Galatians 6:9).

5. **Finally, one of Satan's strategies against us is to discourage us by pointing out the overwhelming odds against us.**

a. **He seeks to convince us that we don't have what it takes to win a particular battle.**

Then Caleb quieted the people before Moses, and said, "Let us go up at once and take possession, for we are well able to overcome it" (Numbers 13:30).

Look, the Lord your God has set the land before you; go up and possess it, as the Lord God of your fathers has spoken to you; do not fear or be discouraged (Deuteronomy 1:21).

b. **His goal is for us to surrender to his agenda and quit believing God for a miracle answer.**

Then the people of the land tried to discourage the people of Judah. They troubled them in building, and hired counselors against them to frustrate their purpose all the days of Cyrus king of Persia, even until the reign of Darius king of Persia (Ezra 4:4-5).

II. Standing in Christ's Victory.

A. **Jesus completely defeated Satan through His death on the cross and through His resurrection from the dead.**

1. **Jesus invites us to stand in His victory over the agenda of hell that is set against us.**

2. **As we learn to stand in Christ's victory Satan will be powerless to hold us captive and work his destructive plans against us.**

Having wiped out the handwriting of requirements that was against us, which was contrary to us. And He has taken it out of the way, having nailed it to the cross. Having disarmed principalities and powers, He made a public spectacle of them, triumphing over them in it (Colossians 2:14-15).

B. **The Scripture tells us that Jesus has destroyed the devil's power and work against us.**

1. **The word "destroyed," means "to render powerless, and to have no affect."**

2. **We still must deal with Satan's attacks; however, because of Jesus, his attacks will not be successful in defeating us.**

Inasmuch then as the children have partaken of flesh and blood, He Himself likewise shared in the same, that through death He might destroy him who had the power of death, that is, the devil (Hebrews 2:14).

He who sins is of the devil, for the devil has sinned from the beginning. For this purpose the Son of God was manifested, that He might destroy the works of the devil (I John 3:8).

C. **Jesus has not only defeated Satan, but He has now given us the right to exercise His authority over Satan and all of his demonic forces.**

Behold, I give you the authority to trample on serpents and scorpions, and over all the power of the enemy, and nothing shall by any means hurt you. Nevertheless do not rejoice in this, that the spirits are subject to you, but rather rejoice because your names are written in heaven (Luke 10:19-20).

And these signs will follow those who believe: In My name they will cast out demons; they will speak with new tongues; they will take up serpents; and if they drink anything deadly, it will by no means hurt them; they will lay hands on the sick, and they will recover (Mark 16:17-18).

D. In order for us to be able to stand in Christ's victory, we must guard our thoughts, words, and activities so as not to give Satan an entry point into our lives.

   1. Our willful disobedience to God's Word will result in sin and will give the devil access to our lives. Disobedience in God's eyes is rebellion; and God considers rebellion to be as the sin of witchcraft.

   2. We must avoid involvement with anything tied to the occult as it will give the devil access to our lives. Some of the many things to avoid include:

      a. New Age literature, crystals, games, movies, television shows, or music in which there is a satanic theme or involvement;

      b. And fortune tellers, psychics, horoscopes, and astrological signs.

   4. The afore-mentioned is not mere entertainment, even though portrayed in comedies and cartoons. It is a strategic attempt to desensitize people and present the dark-side as fun and harmless.

   5. There is absolutely nothing harmless, or remotely funny, about anything associated with the devil and his dark kingdom.

Nor give place to the devil (Ephesians 4:27).

E. **Satan is not omnipotent; he gains his knowledge of us by our words and our actions.**

1. **Our words and actions will activate and release one of two kingdoms to work for us or against us.**

2. **Satan fills our minds with negative thoughts in an attempt to get us to confess them; at which point, he uses our confession against us.**

The Lord is known by the judgment He executes; the wicked is snared in the work of his own hands (Psalm 9:16).

For as he thinks in his heart, so is he (Proverbs 23:7).

Brood of vipers! How can you, being evil, speak good things? For out of the abundance of the heart the mouth speaks. A good man out of the good treasure of his heart brings forth good things, and an evil man out of the evil treasure brings forth evil things. But I say to you that for every idle word men may speak, they will give account of it in the day of judgment. For by your words you will be justified, and by your words you will be condemned (Matthew 12:34-37).

You are snared by the words of your mouth; you are taken by the words of your mouth (Proverbs 6:2).

F. **Our thoughts must be centered on God and the promises of His Word. Without a proper focus, we will not be able to counter the enemy's attacks on our minds.**

1. **Meditating on the promises of God's Word will keep our mind focused on positive thoughts.**

Finally, brethren, whatever things are true, whatever things are noble, whatever things are just, whatever things are pure, whatever things are lovely, whatever things are of good report, if there is any virtue and if there is anything praiseworthy— meditate on these things (Philippians 4:8).

2. **Our words need to agree with the promises of the Scripture, then our words will be as praise.**

Therefore by Him let us continually offer the sacrifice of praise to God, that is, the fruit of our lips, giving thanks to His name (Hebrews 13:15).

G. Satan no longer has rights to anyone who has placed their trust in Jesus for He has delivered us from Satan's kingdom and his power over us.

He has delivered us from the power of darkness and conveyed us into the kingdom of the Son of His love (Colossians 1:13).

H. Jesus living within us makes us more than conquerors; wherein our victory is guaranteed over Satan and his agenda against us.

You are of God, little children, and have overcome them, because He who is in you is greater than he who is in the world (I John 4:4).

Yet in all these things we are more than conquerors through Him who loved us (Romans 8:37).

Now thanks be to God who always leads us in triumph in Christ, and through us diffuses the fragrance of His knowledge in every place (II Corinthians 2:14).

I. If we will submit ourselves to God, and resist the devil and his attack against us, Satan will flee from us.

Therefore submit to God. Resist the devil and he will flee from you (James 4:7).

J. The devil's weapons will not be successful against us. We are promised, that as we stand in the victory of Christ, that what was meant for our harm will turn for our good.

"No weapon formed against you shall prosper, and every tongue which rises against you in judgment you shall condemn. This is the heritage of the servants of the Lord, and their righteousness is from Me," says the Lord (Isaiah 54:17).

But as for you, you meant evil against me; but God meant it for good, in order to bring it about as it is this day, to save many people alive (Genesis 50:20).

123

III. The Armor of God.

A. **God has provided us a suit of armor to wear that will withstand any attack of the devil against us.**

    1. **We have learned the discipline of taking time to dress in natural clothes each day.**

    2. **We must also learn to discipline ourselves to dress in the armor of God each day.**

Put on the whole armor of God, that you may be able to stand against the wiles of the devil. For we do not wrestle against flesh and blood, but against principalities, against powers, against the rulers of the darkness of this age, against spiritual hosts of wickedness in the heavenly places. Therefore take up the whole armor of God, that you may be able to withstand in the evil day, and having done all, to stand. Stand therefore, having girded your waist with truth, having put on the breastplate of righteousness, and having shod your feet with the preparation of the gospel of peace; above all, taking the shield of faith with which you will be able to quench all the fiery darts of the wicked one. And take the helmet of salvation, and the sword of the Spirit, which is the word of God; praying always with all prayer and supplication in the Spirit, being watchful to this end with all perseverance and supplication for all the saints (Ephesians 6:11-18).

B. **Each piece of the armor of God is representative of Jesus, Himself.**

    1. **Jesus desires, and offers, to be our defense in every attack of Satan and his forces of darkness.**

    2. **The Scripture refers to the armor of God as being the armor of light. Light is a property that always overrules the darkness.**

The night is far spent, the day is at hand. Therefore let us cast off the works of darkness, and let us put on the armor of light (Romans 13:12).

3. **We must put on Jesus in the form of the armor of God; then we will have the ability to overpower the enemy's attack against us.**

But put on the Lord Jesus Christ, and make no provision for the flesh, to fulfill its lusts (Romans 13:14).

C. **We must declare our faith as we put on each piece of His armor.**

1. **We put on the Girdle of Truth by our faith declaration ... "Jesus, You are my Truth."**

Jesus said to him, "I am the way, the truth, and the life. No one comes to the Father except through Me" (John 14:6).

2. **We put on the Breastplate of Righteousness by our faith declaration ... "Jesus, You are my Righteousness."**

For He made Him who knew no sin to be sin for us, that we might become the righteousness of God in Him (II Corinthians 5:21).

3. **We put on the Shoes of Peace by our faith declaration ... "Jesus, You are my Peace."**

He has redeemed my soul in peace from the battle that was against me, for there were many against me (Psalm 55:18).

He will guard the feet of His saints, but the wicked shall be silent in darkness. For by strength no man shall prevail. The adversaries of the Lord shall be broken in pieces; from heaven He will thunder against them. The Lord will judge the ends of the earth. He will give strength to His king, and exalt the horn of His anointed (I Samuel 2:9-10).

4. **We put on the Shield of Faith by our faith declaration ... "Jesus, You are my Faith."**

I have been crucified with Christ; it is no longer I who live, but Christ lives in me; and the life which I now live in the flesh I live by faith in the Son of God, who loved me and gave Himself for me (Galatians 2:20).

5. **We put on the Helmet of Salvation by our faith declaration ... "Jesus, You are my Salvation."**

And having been perfected, He became the author of eternal salvation to all who obey Him (Hebrews 5:9).

6. **We take hold of the Sword of the Spirit, which is the Word of God by our faith declaration ... "Jesus, You are my Living Word."**

And the Word became flesh and dwelt among us, and we beheld His glory, the glory as of the only begotten of the Father, full of grace and truth (John 1:14).

7. **We fill our mouths with Prayer which is empowered by the Holy Spirit by our faith declaration ... "Jesus, You are my Intercessor."**

But He, because He continues forever, has an unchangeable priesthood. Therefore He is also able to save to the uttermost those who come to God through Him, since He always lives to make intercession for them (Hebrews 7:24-25).

D. **Finally, we must put on the armor of God that He has provided for us in His Word if we expect to withstand the attacks of hell's agenda that consistently comes against us. We will never be strong enough to withstand these attacks within our own might or strength.**

Finally, my brethren, be strong in the Lord and in the power of His might. Put on the whole armor of God, that you may be able to stand against the wiles of the devil. For we do not wrestle against flesh and blood, but against principalities, against powers, against the rulers of the darkness of this age, against spiritual hosts of wickedness in the heavenly places. Therefore take up the whole armor of God, that you may be able to withstand in the evil day, and having done all, to stand (Ephesians 6:10-13).

IV. The Weapons of War.

A. **It is critical to spiritual warfare that we realize that Satan is not just an enemy of Christianity but he is our personal enemy and has purposed to destroy our lives.**

Therefore rejoice, O heavens, and you who dwell in them! Woe to the inhabitants of the earth and the sea! For the devil has come down to you, having great wrath, because he knows that he has a short time (Revelation 12:12).

B. **The weapons of our warfare are powerful to pull down strongholds and to defeat the devil's purposes.**

For though we walk in the flesh, we do not war according to the flesh. For the weapons of our warfare are not carnal but mighty in God for pulling down strongholds, casting down arguments and every high thing that exalts itself against the knowledge of God, bringing every thought into captivity to the obedience of Christ (II Corinthians 10:3-5).

C. **There are ten powerful weapons of war given to us.**

1. The Word of God.

And Jesus answered and said to him, "Get behind Me, Satan! For it is written, 'You shall worship the Lord your God, and Him only you shall serve'" (Luke 4:8).

For the word of God is living and powerful, and sharper than any two-edged sword, piercing even to the division of soul and spirit, and of joints and marrow, and is a discerner of the thoughts and intents of the heart (Hebrews 4:12).

2. The name of Jesus.

And these signs will follow those who believe: In My name they will cast out demons; they will speak with new tongues; they will take up serpents; and if they drink anything deadly, it will by no means hurt them; they will lay hands on the sick, and they will recover (Mark 16:17-18).

And whatever you ask in My name, that I will do, that the Father may be glorified in the Son. If you ask anything in My name, I will do it (John 14:13-14).

3.   The blood of Jesus.

And they overcame him by the blood of the Lamb and by the word of their testimony, and they did not love their lives to the death (Revelation 12:11).

4.   Prayer and fasting.

However, this kind does not go out except by prayer and fasting (Matthew 17:21).

5.   The unity of praying believers as they claim God's promises and the devil's power to be broken.

Again I say to you that if two of you agree on earth concerning anything that they ask, it will be done for them by My Father in heaven (Matthew 18:19).

Five of you shall chase a hundred, and a hundred of you shall put ten thousand to flight; your enemies shall fall by the sword before you (Leviticus 26:8).

6.   The keys to the kingdom allow us to bind the enemy's activity to the contract of Calvary and release the power of God into every adversity.

And I will give you the keys of the kingdom of heaven, and whatever you bind on earth will be bound in heaven, and whatever you loose on earth will be loosed in heaven (Matthew 16:19).

7.   The joy of the Lord.

Then he said to them, "Go your way, eat the fat, drink the sweet, and send portions to those for whom nothing is prepared; for this day is holy to our Lord. Do not sorrow, for the joy of the Lord is your strength" (Nehemiah 8:10).

And now my head shall be lifted up above my enemies all around me; therefore I will offer sacrifices of joy in His tabernacle; I will sing, yes, I will sing praises to the Lord (Psalm 27:6).

8. Obedience to God's declared rights to the tithe.

"Bring all the tithes into the storehouse, that there may be food in My house, and try Me now in this," says the Lord of hosts, "if I will not open for you the windows of heaven and pour out for you such blessing that there will not be room enough to receive it. And I will rebuke the devourer for your sakes, so that he will not destroy the fruit of your ground, nor shall the vine fail to bear fruit for you in the field," says the Lord of hosts (Malachi 3:10).

9. The celebration of our praise to God.

"The voice of joy and the voice of gladness, the voice of the bridegroom and the voice of the bride, the voice of those who will say: 'Praise the Lord of hosts, for the Lord is good, for His mercy endures forever'— and of those who will bring the sacrifice of praise into the house of the Lord. For I will cause the captives of the land to return as at the first," says the Lord (Jeremiah 33:11).

And when he had consulted with the people, he appointed those who should sing to the Lord, and who should praise the beauty of holiness, as they went out before the army and were saying: "Praise the Lord, for His mercy endures forever." Now when they began to sing and to praise, the Lord set ambushes against the people of Ammon, Moab, and Mount Seir, who had come against Judah; and they were defeated (II Chronicles 20:21-22).

10. The exercise of our faith.

So Jesus answered and said to them, "Have faith in God. For assuredly, I say to you, whoever says to this mountain, 'Be removed and be cast into the sea,' and does not doubt in his heart, but believes that those things he says will be done, he will have whatever he says. Therefore I say to you, whatever things you ask when you pray, believe that you receive them, and you will have them" (Mark 11:22-24).

Jesus said to them, "Because of your unbelief; for assuredly, I say to you, if you have faith as a mustard seed, you will say to this mountain, 'Move from here to there,' and it will move; and nothing will be impossible for you" (Matthew 17:20).

Chapter Eight

How to Study the Bible

I. The Names and Titles of the Bible.

A. **We refer to the Word of God as the Bible.**

    1. **Our English word "Bible," is derived from the Greek word *biblios*, which means "book."**

    2. **The word "Bible," is not used in the Scripture. However, there are various books in the Bible referred to as "Bibles," where the Greek word *biblios*, is used.**

As it is written in the book of the words of Isaiah the prophet, saying: "The voice of one crying in the wilderness: 'Prepare the way of the Lord; Make His paths straight'" (Luke 3:4).

B. **The Bible is also referred to as the Word of God.**

    1. **The Scriptures are simply the words of God to man.**

    2. **The Scriptures refer to "the Word of God," whether stated, or alluded to, over two-thousand times.**

For this reason we also thank God without ceasing, because when you received the word of God which you heard from us, you welcomed it not as the word of men, but as it is in truth, the word of God, which also effectively works in you who believe (I Thessalonians 2:13).

    3. **Jesus is the living Word of God, while the Bible is the written Word of God.**

        a. **The living Word and the written Word are one, and the same.**

        b. **The written Word reveals the living Word to our hearts.**

In the beginning was the Word, and the Word was with God, and the Word was God. He was in the beginning with God (John 1:1-2).

And the Word became flesh and dwelt among us, and we beheld His glory, the glory as of the only begotten of the Father, full of grace and truth (John 1:14).

Then I said, "Behold, I have come—In the volume of the book it is written of Me—To do Your will, O God" (Hebrews 10:7).

C. The Bible is also referred to as the Scriptures.

1. The word "Scriptures" means "writings" and is used fifty-four times throughout the Bible.

2. The Holy Scriptures are set apart from all other uninspired writings of men.

And that from childhood you have known the Holy Scriptures, which are able to make you wise for salvation through faith which is in Christ Jesus (II Timothy 3:15).

D. The Bible is also referred to as the oracles of God.

1. The word "oracles" literally means "speaking place."

2. The Bible is God's oracle; His speaking place to the hearts of men.

Much in every way! Chiefly because to them were committed the oracles of God (Romans 3:2).

3. God will speak to our hearts from His Word and He will give us daily direction for our lives. He will never force us to listen to His directions so we must predetermine to obey His instructions.

Therefore, as the Holy Spirit says: "Today, if you will hear His voice, do not harden your hearts as in the rebellion, in the day of trial in the wilderness" (Hebrews 3:7-8).

II. The Structure of the Bible.

A. The Bible is the divinely "inspired" Word of God. The word "inspiration" means "God-breathed."

All Scripture is given by inspiration of God, and is profitable for doctrine, for reproof, for correction, for instruction in righteousness (II Timothy 3:16).

B. There are three modes or methods that God used in inspiring the Scriptures:

1. Revelation;

    a. Revelation is the communication of truth and it cannot be discovered by natural reasoning.

    b. Revelation is literally, God revealing Himself and His purposes to man.

2. Inspiration;

    a. Inspiration is the process by which God captures the attention of our heart, and of our mind.

    b. Inspiration is the means by which revelation is recorded and communicated.

3. And illumination;

    a. Illumination is the process by which the Holy Spirit enlightens our understanding to the truths of God.

    b. Illumination is the means by which the Holy Spirit helps us understand how the Word of God applies to the circumstances of our lives.

C. The Holy Spirit is the author of the Scriptures. He chose to use forty men, to write sixty-six books, in three languages, over a sixteen-hundred year period.

D. The Bible is divided into two "testaments." The word "testament" means "covenant."

   1. The Old Testament is called the "Covenant of Law."

   2. The New Testament is called the "Covenant of Grace."

   And for this reason He is the Mediator of the new covenant, by means of death, for the redemption of the transgressions under the first covenant, that those who are called may receive the promise of the eternal inheritance (Hebrews 9:15).

E. The Old Testament contains thirty-nine books and is divided into the following sections:

   1. Books of Law (Genesis through Deuteronomy);

   2. Books of History (Joshua through Esther);

   3. Books of Poetry (Job through Song of Solomon);

   4. Books of Prophecy (Isaiah through Malachi).

F. The New Testament contains twenty-seven books and is divided into the following sections:

   1. The Gospels (Matthew through John);

   2. Early Church History (Acts);

   3. Letters to the Churches (Romans through Jude);

   4. Prophecy (The Revelation).

G. The Bible is divided into two testaments; for God's revelation to man is progressive.

   1. The teachings and events recorded in the Old Testament prepared the way for the truths contained in the New Testament.

   2. The Old Testament reveals New Testament truths in shadow form and through types; especially as it applies to salvation and to the church.

   Whom will he teach knowledge? And whom will he make to understand the message? Those just weaned from milk? Those just drawn from the breasts? For precept must be upon precept, precept upon precept, line upon line, line upon line, here a little, there a little (Isaiah 28:9-10).

   Now all these things happened to them as examples, and they were written for our admonition, upon whom the ends of the ages have come (I Corinthians 10:11).

   For whatever things were written before were written for our learning, that we through the patience and comfort of the Scriptures might have hope (Romans 15:4).

   For the law, having a shadow of the good things to come, and not the very image of the things, can never with these same sacrifices, which they offer continually year by year, make those who approach perfect (Hebrews 10:1).

H. It is critical to the operation of our faith that we believe the Bible to be the absolute truth of God. We must believe that it is authoritative and inherent.

   Knowing this first, that no prophecy of Scripture is of any private interpretation, for prophecy never came by the will of man, but holy men of God spoke as they were moved by the Holy Spirit (II Peter 1:20-21).

   Sanctify them by Your truth. Your word is truth (John 17:17).

   The entirety of Your word is truth, and every one of Your righteous judgments endures forever (Psalm 119:160).

1. **The Bible is infallible, accurate, and dependable in all that it teaches.**

Therefore all Your precepts concerning all things I consider to be right; I hate every false way (Psalm 119:128).

2. **The teachings of the Word of God are completely trustworthy for daily living.**

The law of the Lord is perfect, converting the soul; the testimony of the Lord is sure, making wise the simple; the statutes of the Lord are right, rejoicing the heart; the commandment of the Lord is pure, enlightening the eyes; the fear of the Lord is clean, enduring forever; the judgments of the Lord are true and righteous altogether. More to be desired are they than gold, yea, than much fine gold; sweeter also than honey and the honeycomb. Moreover by them Your servant is warned, and in keeping them there is great reward (Psalm 19:7-11).

I. **The Bible is complete and is forever settled in its content and in its relevant truth.**

Forever, O Lord, Your word is settled in heaven (Psalm 119:89).

Do not think that I came to destroy the Law or the Prophets. I did not come to destroy but to fulfill. For assuredly, I say to you, till heaven and earth pass away, one jot or one tittle will by no means pass from the law till all is fulfilled. Whoever therefore breaks one of the least of these commandments, and teaches men so, shall be called least in the kingdom of heaven; but whoever does and teaches them, he shall be called great in the kingdom of heaven (Matthew 5:17-19).

1. **The Bible is completely sufficient to answer anything we need to know about eternal salvation.**

2. **The Bible is completely sufficient to give the practical wisdom to deal with the issues of life.**

Every word of God is pure; He is a shield to those who put their trust in Him. Do not add to His words, lest He rebuke you, and you be found a liar (Proverbs 30:5-6).

138

J.   The Bible is a living document and it is relevant to every area of life today.

In the beginning was the Word, and the Word was with God, and the Word was God. He was in the beginning with God. All things were made through Him, and without Him nothing was made that was made. In Him was life, and the life was the light of men (John 1:1-4).

For the word of God is living and powerful, and sharper than any two-edged sword, piercing even to the division of soul and spirit, and of joints and marrow, and is a discerner of the thoughts and intents of the heart (Hebrews 4:12).

Let the high praises of God be in their mouth, and a two-edged sword in their hand, to execute vengeance on the nations, and punishments on the peoples; to bind their kings with chains, and their nobles with fetters of iron; to execute on them the written judgment—this honor have all His saints. Praise the Lord (Psalm 149:6-9)!

K.   We must live in absolute obedience to the teachings of His Word; whereby, we validate our claim that we love Jesus and call Him the Lord of our lives.

   1.   Our obedience is a tangible proof that we really do love Jesus.

   If you love Me, keep My commandments (John 14:15).

   2.   Our obedience is tangible proof that we have made Jesus the Lord of our lives.

   But why do you call Me "Lord, Lord," and do not do the things which I say (Luke 6:46)?

L.   Our opinions must line up with the Word of God. We must let go of anything that is not consistent with the teachings of the Word of God.

Casting down arguments and every high thing that exalts itself against the knowledge of God, bringing every thought into captivity to the obedience of Christ (II Corinthians 10:5).

III. The Symbols of the Bible.

A. The Word of God is like a fire and a hammer.

1. It is like a fire, in that it cleanses and purges all that is contrary to its holy standard.

2. It is like a hammer in that it strikes a blow that will destroy evil.

"Is not My word like a fire?" says the Lord, "and like a hammer that breaks the rock in pieces" (Jeremiah 23:29)?

B. The Word of God is like a mirror.

1. It shows us what we are now and what we can become in Christ.

2. It reveals the areas of weakness where we need to repent and allow the Holy Spirit to work in us.

For if anyone is a hearer of the word and not a doer, he is like a man observing his natural face in a mirror; for he observes himself, goes away, and immediately forgets what kind of man he was. But he who looks into the perfect law of liberty and continues in it, and is not a forgetful hearer but a doer of the work, this one will be blessed in what he does (James 1:23-25).

C. The Word of God is like milk.

1. Just as milk fills and nourishes a young child, so the Word fills and nourishes the young Christian that is seeking after God.

2. Just as milk provides calcium for the building of strong bones in a growing body, so the Word builds a strong foundation in the heart of a believer as they grow in their faith.

As newborn babes, desire the pure milk of the word, that you may grow thereby (I Peter 2:2).

140

D. The Word of God is like a lamp.

   1. It is an instrument of light which overrules the darkness.

   2. It illuminates our understanding to the truths and ways of God.

Your word is a lamp to my feet and a light to my path
(Psalm 119:105).

E. The Word of God is like a seed.

   1. It is like a seed that is life-producing, germinating, and has the potential of eternal life to all who will receive it.

Having been born again, not of corruptible seed but incorruptible, through the word of God which lives and abides forever (I Peter 1:23).

   2. It will always produce the harvest for which it has been sown, and will do so without fail.

So shall My word be that goes forth from My mouth; It shall not return to Me void, but it shall accomplish what I please, and it shall prosper in the thing for which I sent it (Isaiah 55:11).

F. The Word is like honey.

   1. It is sweet to the taste, when consumed.

How sweet are Your words to my taste, sweeter than honey to my mouth (Psalm 119:103).

   2. It will release the joy of the Lord in us. The Word will create a longing within us for fellowship with God and a desire to walk in His ways.

Your words were found, and I ate them, and Your word was to me the joy and rejoicing of my heart; for I am called by Your name, O Lord God of hosts (Jeremiah 15:16).

G. The Word of God is like a sword.

   1. It is sharp and dual-edged in its operation.

   2. It separates the flesh from the things of the Spirit.

   For the word of God is living and powerful, and sharper than any two-edged sword, piercing even to the division of soul and spirit, and of joints and marrow, and is a discerner of the thoughts and intents of the heart (Hebrews 4:12).

H. The Word of God is like an ox-goad and a nail.

   1. An ox-goad is an instrument which prods the oxen into fulfilling their duties.

   2. The Word of God is like a nail, in that when it is applied to our lives we are secured by its truth; which allows us to rest in safety.

   The words of the wise are like goads, and the words of scholars are like well-driven nails, given by one Shepherd (Ecclesiastes 12:11).

I. The Word of God is like bread.

   1. It is the staff of life; ever fresh and nourishing.

   2. It is meant for our daily consumption.

   But He answered and said, "It is written, 'Man shall not live by bread alone, but by every word that proceeds from the mouth of God'" (Matthew 4:4).

J. The Word of God is like water.

   1. It is life-giving and refreshing to a thirsty soul.

   2. It is a cleansing agent that washes the filth of our fleshly deeds from our spirits.

   That He might sanctify and cleanse her with the washing of water by the word (Ephesians 5:26).

K. **The Word of God is like an anchor.**

1. **It secures the believer in every storm of life.**

2. **It keeps us from drifting from our fellowship with God and in our doctrines and beliefs about God.**

Thus God, determining to show more abundantly to the heirs of promise the immutability of His counsel, confirmed it by an oath, that by two immutable things, in which it is impossible for God to lie, we might have strong consolation, who have fled for refuge to lay hold of the hope set before us. This hope we have as an anchor of the soul, both sure and steadfast, and which enters the Presence behind the veil (Hebrews 6:17-19).

L. **The Word of God is like a rod.**

1. **The Word is the divine measuring instrument God uses to measure all matters of faith and practice.**

2. **Everything we do is measured by God's standard.**

He has shown you, O man, what is good; and what does the Lord require of you but to do justly, to love mercy, and to walk humbly with your God? The Lord's voice cries to the city— Wisdom shall see Your name: Hear the Rod! Who has appointed it (Micah 6:8-9)?

Then I was given a reed like a measuring rod. And the angel stood, saying, "Rise and measure the temple of God, the altar, and those who worship there" (Revelation 11:1).

There shall come forth a Rod from the stem of Jesse, and a Branch shall grow out of his roots. The Spirit of the Lord shall rest upon Him, the Spirit of wisdom and understanding, the Spirit of counsel and might, the Spirit of knowledge and of the fear of the Lord. His delight is in the fear of the Lord, and He shall not judge by the sight of His eyes, nor decide by the hearing of His ears; But with righteousness He shall judge the poor, and decide with equity for the meek of the earth; He shall strike the earth with the rod of His mouth, and with the breath of His lips He shall slay the wicked. Righteousness shall be the belt of His loins, and faithfulness the belt of His waist (Isaiah 11:1-5).

IV. Committing to Study the Scriptures.

A. The treasures of God's wisdom are hidden in the Word. It is not only our privilege, but it is our responsibility, to search out these nuggets of truth.

It is the glory of God to conceal a matter, but the glory of kings is to search out a matter (Proverbs 25:2).

B. We must commit to study the Scriptures every day to find success in life.

This Book of the Law shall not depart from your mouth, but you shall meditate in it day and night, that you may observe to do according to all that is written in it. For then you will make your way prosperous, and then you will have good success (Joshua 1:8).

But his delight is in the law of the Lord, and in His law he meditates day and night (Psalm 1:2).

Oh, how I love Your law! It is my meditation all the day (Psalm 119:97).

C. Before we begin we should ask the Holy Spirit to open the truths found in the passages we are about to study.

Open my eyes, that I may see wondrous things from Your law (Psalm 119:18).

D. Studying the Scriptures is a command of God. If we are to grow and mature in Christ, our dedication and discipline will be demanded.

Be diligent to present yourself approved to God, a worker who does not need to be ashamed, rightly dividing the word of truth (II Timothy 2:15).

Therefore you shall lay up these words of mine in your heart and in your soul, and bind them as a sign on your hand, and they shall be as frontlets between your eyes. You shall teach them to your children, speaking of them when you sit in your house, when you walk by the way, when you lie down, and when you rise up (Deuteronomy 11:18-19).

*Let the word of Christ dwell in you richly in all wisdom,
teaching and admonishing one another in psalms and hymns
and spiritual songs, singing with grace in your hearts to the
Lord* (Colossians 3:16).

1. Developing a daily Bible study habit is difficult; it demands the determination of our will.

*Therefore be very courageous to keep and to do all that is
written in the Book of the Law of Moses, lest you turn aside
from it to the right hand or to the left* (Joshua 23:6).

*I have not departed from the commandment of His lips; I have
treasured the words of His mouth more than my necessary food*
(Job 23:12).

2. Our minds and bodies will try to convince us that we are too busy and tired. Paul knew the battle to be waged when dealing with spiritual matters.

*But I discipline my body and bring it into subjection, lest, when
I have preached to others, I myself should become disqualified*
(I Corinthians 9:27).

E. Satan opposes our time in the Word as He knows his access will be limited and his influence defeated.

1. The devil knows he is defeated when we start using the Word of God against him.

*Then I heard a loud voice saying in heaven, "Now salvation,
and strength, and the kingdom of our God, and the power of
His Christ have come, for the accuser of our brethren, who
accused them before our God day and night, has been cast
down. And they overcame him by the blood of the Lamb and
by the word of their testimony, and they did not love their lives
to the death"* (Revelation 12:10-11).

2. Jesus used the Word of God against the devil.

*Then Jesus said to him, "Away with you, Satan! For it is
written, 'You shall worship the Lord your God, and Him only
you shall serve.'" Then the devil left Him, and behold, angels
came and ministered to Him* (Matthew 4:10-11).

V. The Benefits of Studying the Bible.

A. Studying the Scriptures will release God's joy into our hearts and will supply us with strength.

These things I have spoken to you, that My joy may remain in you, and that your joy may be full (John 15:11).

Your words were found, and I ate them, and Your word was to me the joy and rejoicing of my heart; for I am called by Your name, O Lord God of hosts (Jeremiah 15:16).

You will show me the path of life; in Your presence is fullness of joy; at Your right hand are pleasures forevermore (Psalm 16:11).

The king shall have joy in Your strength, O Lord (Psalm 21:1).

B. Studying the Scriptures will help us understand God's ways and keep us from practicing sin.

How can a young man cleanse his way? By taking heed according to Your word. With my whole heart I have sought You; oh, let me not wander from Your commandments! Your word I have hidden in my heart, that I might not sin against You (Psalm 119:9-11).

C. Studying the Scriptures will keep the devil from deceiving us and working his destruction in our lives.

My people are destroyed for lack of knowledge. Because you have rejected knowledge, I also will reject you from being priest for Me; because you have forgotten the law of your God, I also will forget your children (Hosea 4:6).

Jesus answered and said to them, "You are mistaken, not knowing the Scriptures nor the power of God" (Matthew 22:29).

D. Studying the Scriptures will increase our vocabulary in prayer and will give us confidence as we pray.

If you abide in Me, and My words abide in you, you will ask what you desire, and it shall be done for you (John 15:7).

E. Studying the Scriptures will increase our spiritual strength and will release God's divine energy into our bodies.

It is the Spirit who gives life; the flesh profits nothing. The words that I speak to you are spirit, and they are life (John 6:63).

F. Studying the Scriptures will cleanse our hearts.

You are already clean because of the word which I have spoken to you (John 15:3).

G. Studying the Scriptures will produce the fruit of Christ's nature and character in us.

But his delight is in the law of the Lord, and in His law he meditates day and night. He shall be like a tree planted by the rivers of water, that brings forth its fruit in its season, whose leaf also shall not wither; and whatever he does shall prosper (Psalm 1:2-3).

H. Studying the Scriptures will release the peace of God to our hearts and minds.

Great peace have those who love Your law, and nothing causes them to stumble (Psalm 119:165).

I. Studying the Scriptures will open our hearts to receive the revelation of the Holy Spirit.

But as it is written: "Eye has not seen, nor ear heard, nor have entered into the heart of man the things which God has prepared for those who love Him." But God has revealed them to us through His Spirit. For the Spirit searches all things, yes, the deep things of God. For what man knows the things of a man except the spirit of the man which is in him? Even so no one knows the things of God except the Spirit of God. Now we have received, not the spirit of the world, but the Spirit who is from God, that we might know the things that have been freely given to us by God. These things we also speak, not in words which man's wisdom teaches but which the Holy Spirit teaches, comparing spiritual things with spiritual" (I Corinthians 2:9-13).

147

J. **Studying the Scriptures will impart God's wisdom to our hearts and will make us wiser than our enemies.**

You, through Your commandments, make me wiser than my enemies; for they are ever with me (Psalm 119:98).

K. **Studying the Scriptures will warn us about the traps the devil has set for our lives.**

The wicked have laid a snare for me, yet I have not strayed from Your precepts (Psalm 119:110).

Then Jesus said to those Jews who believed Him, "If you abide in My word, you are My disciples indeed. And you shall know the truth, and the truth shall make you free" (John 8:31-32).

L. **Studying the Scriptures will help us avoid confusion and will keep us from making embarrassing and foolish mistakes.**

You have commanded us to keep Your precepts diligently. Oh, that my ways were directed to keep Your statutes! Then I would not be ashamed, when I look into all Your commandments (Psalm 119:4-6).

M. **Studying the Scriptures will lay a solid spiritual foundation in our lives.**

Therefore whoever hears these sayings of Mine, and does them, I will liken him to a wise man who built his house on the rock: and the rain descended, the floods came, and the winds blew and beat on that house; and it did not fall, for it was founded on the rock. But everyone who hears these sayings of Mine, and does not do them, will be like a foolish man who built his house on the sand: and the rain descended, the floods came, and the winds blew and beat on that house; and it fell. And great was its fall (Matthew 7:24-27).

N. **Studying the Scriptures will equip us for our service to God.**

Be diligent to present yourself approved to God, a worker who does not need to be ashamed, rightly dividing the word of truth (II Timothy 2:15).

O. **Studying the Scriptures will build our faith.**

So then faith comes by hearing, and hearing by the word of God (Romans 10:17).

P. **In order to receive God's wisdom, we must make the Scriptures our number one pursuit in life.**

Wisdom is the principal thing; therefore get wisdom. And in all your getting, get understanding (Proverbs 4:7).

Chapter Nine

Living by Faith

I. The Origin of Our Faith.

A. There are many wonderful explanations that will help us understand the meaning of faith.

  1. Faith is the ability to believe in the promises of God as we trust Him to fulfill those promises.

  2. Faith enables you to treat the future as the present as you believe the promises of God's Word.

  3. Faith enables you to willingly embrace your answer from God before you see it manifested.

  4. Faith is built on the foundation of our convictions about God and the integrity of His Word.

  5. Faith is sustained on the wings of our expectations that God will fulfill what He has promised.

  Now faith is the substance of things hoped for, the evidence of things not seen (Hebrews 11:1).

B. Faith originates from God.

  In the beginning God created the heavens and the earth (Genesis 1:1).

  John answered and said, "A man can receive nothing unless it has been given to him from heaven" (John 3:27).

  Every good gift and every perfect gift is from above, and comes down from the Father of lights, with whom there is no variation or shadow of turning (James 1:17).

  For by grace you have been saved through faith and that not of yourselves; it is the gift of God (Ephesians 2:8).

C. When we use the faith that God has given us, we can be victorious over challenges that face us.

  I can do all things through Christ who strengthens me (Philippians 4:13).

D. Our faith rests upon the character of God and the moral integrity of His holiness; no further proof is required.

1. The fact that God declares His truth is enough, even if it contradicts all of the conclusions of our logic.

Certainly not! Indeed, let God be true but every man a liar. As it is written: "That You may be justified in Your words, and may overcome when You are judged" (Romans 3:4).

He who believes in the Son of God has the witness in himself; he who does not believe God has made Him a liar, because he has not believed the testimony that God has given of His Son (I John 5:10).

2. Unbelievers may have the mental capacity to give intellectual assent to the Scriptures, but they don't have the faith to believe the promises of the Scriptures.

And that we may be delivered from unreasonable and wicked men; for not all have faith (II Thessalonians 3:2).

E. Jesus is the author of our faith.

Looking unto Jesus, the author and finisher of our faith, who for the joy that was set before Him endured the cross, despising the shame, and has sat down at the right hand of the throne of God (Hebrews 12:2).

F. The same faith that was resident in Jesus has now become the gift of God to every believer.

For I say, through the grace given to me, to everyone who is among you, not to think of himself more highly than he ought to think, but to think soberly, as God has dealt to each one a measure of faith (Romans 12:3).

I have been crucified with Christ; it is no longer I who live, but Christ lives in me; and the life which I now live in the flesh I live by faith in the Son of God, who loved me and gave Himself for me (Galatians 2:20).

154

G. Faith internalizes the knowledge of God and of His son, Jesus Christ, as revealed in the Word of God. This internalization of truth results in the release of our faith to believe God.

And those who know Your name will put their trust in You; for You, Lord, have not forsaken those who seek You (Psalm 9:10).

H. Faith will always demand that we be absolutely convinced that God is faithful; therefore, He is worthy of our trust.

    1. Faith accepts the wisdom of the ways of God, even if His ways are not currently comprehendible to our natural mind.

    2. Faith resolves that God loves us and is on our side. Faith rests in the conviction that He will do what is ultimately best for us.

When I cry out to You, then my enemies will turn back; this I know, because God is for me. In God (I will praise His word), in the Lord (I will praise His word), in God I have put my trust; I will not be afraid. What can man do to me (Psalm 56:9-11)?

I. Faith is to the Christian, what water is to fish, and air is to birds. Faith is the medium in which we, as Christians, live and operate. We will never be victorious or successful if we try to operate outside faith.

For I am not ashamed of the gospel of Christ, for it is the power of God to salvation for everyone who believes, for the Jew first and also for the Greek. For in it the righteousness of God is revealed from faith to faith; as it is written, "The just shall live by faith" (Romans 1:16-17).

For we walk by faith, not by sight (II Corinthians 5:7).

II. The Operation of Our Faith.

A. The operation of our faith is critical; whatever we do apart from faith is considered to be sin in God's eyes.

But he who doubts is condemned if he eats, because he does not eat from faith; for whatever is not from faith is sin (Romans 14:23).

1. Obedience is tangible proof that our faith is active.

Then the word of God spread, and the number of the disciples multiplied greatly in Jerusalem, and a great many of the priests were obedient to the faith (Acts 6:7).

Through Him we have received grace and apostleship for obedience to the faith among all nations for His name (Romans 1:5).

But now has been made manifest, and by the prophetic Scriptures has been made known to all nations, according to the commandment of the everlasting God, for obedience to the faith (Romans 16:26).

2. Disobedience ultimately hinders the operation of our faith.

And to whom did He swear that they would not enter His rest, but to those who did not obey? So we see that they could not enter in because of unbelief (Hebrews 3:18-19).

B. It is the nature of man to make decisions based on conclusions that have been drawn from data that is received from our five senses.

1. Our five senses utilize information that is gathered from an ever-changing and fallen world.

2. However, our faith utilizes information from conclusions drawn from God's unchanging Word, even if it goes against our five senses.

For we walk by faith, not by sight (II Corinthians 5:7).

156

C. **Faith requires us to see through the eyes of our spirits. We must make a corresponding action to the commands of God; not only in our confession but in our conduct.**

What does it profit, my brethren, if someone says he has faith but does not have works? Can faith save him? Thus also faith by itself, if it does not have works, is dead (James 2:14, 17).

So Jesus answered and said to them, "Have faith in God. For assuredly, I say to you, whoever says to this mountain, 'Be removed and be cast into the sea,' and does not doubt in his heart, but believes that those things he says will be done, he will have whatever he says. Therefore I say to you, whatever things you ask when you pray, believe that you receive them, and you will have them" (Mark 11:22-24).

1. **We must posture ourselves to rely on the promises of God's Word in any circumstance that faces us. Our decisions cannot be based on what we see, feel, hear, or think.**

2. **The Word of God should be the only source that moves us to a responsive action or influences our confession.**

He did not waver at the promise of God through unbelief, but was strengthened in faith, giving glory to God, and being fully convinced that what He had promised He was also able to perform. And therefore "it was accounted to him for righteousness" (Romans 4:20-22).

D. **God reveals His righteousness to us through the vehicle of faith. He expects us to live in His righteousness by our faith.**

For I am not ashamed of the gospel of Christ, for it is the power of God to salvation for everyone who believes, for the Jew first and also for the Greek. For in it the righteousness of God is revealed from faith to faith; as it is written, "The just shall live by faith" (Romans 1:16-17).

E. Faith is simply—believing God. Faith is living our lives trusting God in every facet of life. Without an active faith it is impossible to please God.

But without faith it is impossible to please Him, for he who comes to God must believe that He is, and that He is a rewarder of those who diligently seek Him (Hebrews 11:6).

1. It is through the agency of faith that we are saved.

For by grace you have been saved through faith, and that not of yourselves; it is the gift of God, not of works, lest anyone should boast (Ephesians 2:8-9).

2. It is through our faith that we are born into the family of God and become the children of God.

For you are all sons of God through faith in Christ Jesus (Galatians 3:26).

3. It is through our faith that we are justified in the eyes of God.

Therefore, having been justified by faith, we have peace with God through our Lord Jesus Christ (Romans 5:1).

4. It is through our faith that we have access to the grace of God.

Through whom also we have access by faith into this grace in which we stand, and rejoice in hope of the glory of God (Romans 5:2).

5. It is through our faith that we receive the promise of the Holy Spirit.

That the blessing of Abraham might come upon the Gentiles in Christ Jesus, that we might receive the promise of the Spirit through faith (Galatians 3:14).

6. It is through our faith that we are overcomers.

For whatever is born of God overcomes the world. And this is the victory that has overcome the world—our faith (I John 5:4).

7. It is through our faith that all things become possible to us.

Jesus said to him, "If you can believe, all things are possible to him who believes" (Mark 9:23).

8. It is through our faith that we are sustained in the midst of every trial.

That the genuineness of your faith, being much more precious than gold that perishes, though it is tested by fire, may be found to praise, honor, and glory at the revelation of Jesus Christ (I Peter 1:7).

9. It is through our faith that we are shielded from the attacks of the devil.

Above all, taking the shield of faith with which you will be able to quench all the fiery darts of the wicked one (Ephesians 6:16).

10. It is through the prayer of faith that healing will be brought to the sick. We find in James 5 the command to pray for the sick. The words found in reference to our prayer are, "avails much," which means "to prevail with great power."

Is anyone among you sick? Let him call for the elders of the church, and let them pray over him, anointing him with oil in the name of the Lord. And the prayer of faith will save the sick, and the Lord will raise him up. And if he has committed sins, he will be forgiven. Confess your trespasses to one another, and pray for one another, that you may be healed. The effective, fervent prayer of a righteous man avails much (James 5:14-16).

11. It is through our faith that we bring glory to the Father.

He did not waver at the promise of God through unbelief, but was strengthened in faith, giving glory to God (Romans 4:20).

III. The Confession of Our Faith.

A.   Our confession of faith must be rooted in the promises of God's Word and not in the carnal desires of our fleshly nature.

You ask and do not receive, because you ask amiss, that you may spend it on your pleasures (James 4:3).

B.   We are to confess our faith in the promises of God's Word; we must then stand in faith with the expectation that God will honor His Word.

So Jesus answered and said to them, "Have faith in God. For assuredly, I say to you, whoever says to this mountain, 'Be removed and be cast into the sea,' and does not doubt in his heart, but believes that those things he says will be done, he will have whatever he says. Therefore I say to you, whatever things you ask when you pray, believe that you receive them, and you will have them" (Mark 11:22-24).

So Jesus said to them, "Because of your unbelief; for assuredly, I say to you, if you have faith as a mustard seed, you will say to this mountain, 'Move from here to there,' and it will move; and nothing will be impossible for you" (Matthew 17:20).

Now this is the confidence that we have in Him, that if we ask anything according to His will, He hears us. And if we know that He hears us, whatever we ask, we know that we have the petitions that we have asked of Him (I John 5:14-15).

C.   Jesus taught that the devil's agenda for our lives is vastly different from God's agenda for us. We need to bring our confession into agreement with what God is saying about us, and not what the devil is saying.

The thief does not come except to steal, and to kill, and to destroy. I have come that they may have life, and that they may have it more abundantly (John 10:10).

For I know the thoughts that I think toward you, says the Lord, thoughts of peace and not of evil, to give you a future and a hope (Jeremiah 29:11).

D. **What we confess, and how we act, will have a profound impact on our lives. Our response will give permission for God to bless us, or the devil to work against us. We must remember that the devil is not a mind reader and he is limited in his knowledge of us.**

Do not give place to the devil (Ephesians 4:27).

The Lord is known by the judgment He executes; the wicked is snared in the work of his own hands (Psalm 9:16).

Death and life are in the power of the tongue, and those who love it will eat its fruit (Proverbs 18:21).

You are snared by the words of your mouth; you are taken by the words of your mouth (Proverbs 6:2).

E. **We are a product of our confession; and our confession is a product of what we really believe about our circumstances. Our confession will always bring us to a crossroad that will demand a decision.**

1. **We can choose to confess by faith the promises of God's Word, and stand in that faith.**

2. **Or, we can choose to confess all the negatives of our circumstances and stand in fear.**

F. **We must align our confession with the Word of God and guard against speaking words rooted in unbelief. When we do not waver in our confession of faith, God will prove Himself faithful to us and to His Word.**

Brood of vipers! How can you, being evil, speak good things? For out of the abundance of the heart the mouth speaks. A good man out of the good treasure of his heart brings forth good things, and an evil man out of the evil treasure brings forth evil things. But I say to you that for every idle word men may speak, they will give account of it in the day of judgment. For by your words you will be justified, and by your words you will be condemned (Matthew 12:34-37).

Let us hold fast the confession of our hope without wavering, for He who promised is faithful (Hebrews 10:23).

G. We must never allow the testimony of another's experience to validate, or invalidate, the truth of God's Word and the relevance of His promises for us today.

For what if some did not believe? Will their unbelief make the faithfulness of God without effect? Certainly not! Indeed, let God be true but every man a liar. As it is written: "That You may be justified in Your words, and may overcome when You are judged" (Romans 3:3-4).

H. Our God is a mighty God who knows absolutely no impossibilities and He is worthy of our trust.

Ah, Lord God! Behold, You have made the heavens and the earth by Your great power and outstretched arm. There is nothing too hard for You (Jeremiah 32:17).

Behold, I am the Lord, the God of all flesh. Is there anything too hard for Me (Jeremiah 32:27)?

But Jesus looked at them and said, "With men it is impossible, but not with God; for with God all things are possible" (Mark 10:27).

IV. The Building of Our Faith.

A. Every believer has been given a measure of faith and it is more than adequate for all of life's circumstances.

1. The same faith that Jesus used to open blind eyes; make the lame to walk; heal the sick; calm the storm; and raise the dead; is resident within us.

2. We do not need to pray and ask God to give us more faith, because the faith we have been given is more than adequate for any need.

Jesus said to them, "Because of your unbelief; for assuredly, I say to you, if you have faith as a mustard seed, you will say to this mountain, 'Move from here to there,' and it will move; and nothing will be impossible for you" (Matthew 17:20).

B. **Instead of praying for more faith, we should be praying that our faith would be increased and strengthened.**

Not boasting of things beyond measure, that is, in other men's labors, but having hope, that as your faith is increased, we shall be greatly enlarged by you in our sphere (II Corinthians 10:15).

So then faith comes by hearing, and hearing by the word of God (Romans 10:17).

C. **Faith is like a muscle; using a muscle strengthens the muscle. To gain size and strength in the muscle, you have to exercise to the muscles maximum capacity.**

1. **Our faith is strengthened and increased in the same manner when we are tested.**

2. **Our faith is tried through adversity; and the trying of our faith produces patience.**

My brethren, count it all joy when you fall into various trials, knowing that the testing of your faith produces patience. But let patience have its perfect work, that you may be perfect and complete, lacking nothing (James 1:2-4).

D. **God's blessings are recorded in His Word and they are revealed by His Spirit. Once discovered, we must believe that God will manifest them in our lives.**

That your faith should not be in the wisdom of men but in the power of God (I Corinthians 2:5).

But as it is written: "Eye has not seen, nor ear heard, nor have entered into the heart of man the things which God has prepared for those who love Him." But God has revealed them to us through His Spirit. For the Spirit searches all things, yes, the deep things of God. For what man knows the things of a man except the spirit of the man which is in him? Even so no one knows the things of God except the Spirit of God. Now we have received, not the spirit of the world, but the Spirit who is from God, that we might know the things that have been freely given to us by God (I Corinthians 2:9-12).

E. God's Word is the revelation to us of God's promises and His will for our lives. Our faith must be rooted and grounded in the truths declared in the promises of Scripture.

    1. Our faith will never rise above our knowledge and acceptance of God's Word.

    2. Faith is the fruit of our coming to know God and His ways. When we know God and His desires for us, we will choose to act upon His Word.

For in it the righteousness of God is revealed from faith to faith; as it is written, "The just shall live by faith" (Romans 1:17).

Teach me, O Lord, the way of Your statutes, and I shall keep it to the end. Give me understanding, and I shall keep Your law; indeed, I shall observe it with my whole heart (Psalm 119:33-34).

I will never forget Your precepts, for by them You have given me life (Psalm 119:93).

The entrance of Your words gives light; It gives understanding to the simple (Psalm 119:130).

F. In order for our faith to operate successfully, we must be absolutely persuaded that God is who He claims to be in His Word.

    1. We must be absolutely convinced that God is willing to do what He has promised.

    2. We must also be absolutely convinced that God is not only willing, but that He is able to do all that He has promised.

But without faith it is impossible to please Him, for he who comes to God must believe that He is, and that He is a rewarder of those who diligently seek Him (Hebrews 11:6).

V. The Principles of Faith.

A. **There are four key principles that are found in Hebrews 11:13 which will help us understand how to operate in faith.**

*These all died in faith, not having received the promises, but having **seen them** afar off **were assured** of them, **embraced them** and **confessed** that they were strangers and pilgrims on the earth* (Hebrews 11:13). *(emphasis mine)*

1. **First Principle: SEE THE PROMISE.**

   a. **We must see the promises of God's Word for our particular area of need.**

   b. **We must set our focus on the promises of God's Word. We must never allow ourselves the opportunity to focus on our problem or circumstance.**

   My son, give attention to my words; incline your ear to my sayings. Do not let them depart from your eyes; keep them in the midst of your heart (Proverbs 4:20-21).

2. **Second Principle: BELIEVE THE PROMISE.**

   a. **We must choose to believe that the promises of God are absolutely true and that they belong to us.**

   The entirety of Your word is truth, and every one of Your righteous judgments endures forever (Psalm 119:160).

   b. **We must choose to believe that God will be faithful to His promises. We must also believe that He will be faithful to manifest those promises in our lives.**

   Your testimonies, which You have commanded, are righteous and very faithful (Psalm 119:138).

3. **Third Principle: EMBRACE THE PROMISE.**

    a. **For us to embrace the promises of God, we must believe that the promises actually belong to us. We must stand in faith until it is manifested.**

    b. **Faith demands absolute obedience. We must be willing to meet the conditions of the promise if we expect to receive the promise.**

    c. **Faith is simply acting out what you believe.**

    Thus also faith by itself, if it does not have works, is dead (James 2:17).

4. **Fourth Principle: CONFESS THE PROMISE.**

    a. **We must confess the promises of God's Word by faith and believe that what we are confessing will come to pass.**

    So Jesus answered and said to them, "Have faith in God. For assuredly, I say to you, whoever says to this mountain 'Be removed and be cast into the sea,' and does not doubt in his heart, but believes that those things he says will be done, he will have whatever he says. Therefore I say to you, whatever things you ask when you pray, believe that you receive them, and you will have them" (Mark 11:22-24).

    b. **We must guard our confession to make sure it is in accordance with the Word of God.**

    You will also declare a thing, and it will be established for you; so light will shine on your ways (Job 22:28).

    Then the Lord said to me, "You have seen well, for I am ready to perform My word" (Jeremiah 1:12).

Chapter Ten

The Structure of God's Church

I. The Church: The Body of Christ.

A. The word "church" is derived from the Greek word, *ecclesia* which means "the called out ones."

B. There are two dynamics through which the church of Jesus Christ is recognized and acknowledged:

   1. First, there is the invisible church. This invisible church is made up of the invisible union of all believers from every generation.

   But you have come to Mount Zion and to the city of the living God, the heavenly Jerusalem, to an innumerable company of angels, to the general assembly and church of the firstborn who are registered in heaven, to God the Judge of all, to the spirits of just men made perfect (Hebrews 12:22-23).

   2. Second, there is the visible church. This visible church is comprised of the visible union of two or more believers who are bonded to Christ, and to each other, in the name of Christ.

   For where two or three are gathered together in My name, I am there in the midst of them (Matthew 18:20).

C. Jesus is both the head, and owner, of His church: He is the master architect and builder of His church.

   And I also say to you that you are Peter, and on this rock I will build My church, and the gates of Hades shall not prevail against it. And I will give you the keys of the kingdom of heaven, and whatever you bind on earth will be bound in heaven, and whatever you loose on earth will be loosed in heaven (Matthew 16:18-19).

   1. Jesus intends for His church to be powerful. He expects us to prevail and overthrow hell's agenda.

   And He put all things under His feet, and gave Him to be head over all things to the church, which is His body, the fullness of Him who fills all in all (Ephesians 1:22-23).

2. **Jesus is building His church through the person and power of the Holy Spirit.**

So he answered and said to me: "This is the word of the Lord to Zerubbabel: 'Not by might nor by power, but by My Spirit,' says the Lord of hosts" (Zechariah 4:6).

D. **The church is referred to by four different names in the Scripture. Each name reveals a particular truth about the church.**

1. **A Temple: The church is the individual and collective habitation of God by His Spirit on the earth.**

Now, therefore, you are no longer strangers and foreigners, but fellow citizens with the saints and members of the household of God, having been built on the foundation of the apostles and prophets, Jesus Christ Himself being the chief cornerstone, in whom the whole building, being fitted together, grows into a holy temple in the Lord, in whom you also are being built together for a dwelling place of God in the Spirit (Ephesians 2:19-22).

And what agreement has the temple of God with idols? For you are the temple of the living God. As God has said: "I will dwell in them and walk among them. I will be their God, and they shall be My people" (II Corinthians 6:16).

2. **A Family: The church is the spiritual family of God. The love, care, and protection, as seen in the relationships of a natural family, are also found in the spiritual family.**

For it was fitting for Him, for whom are all things and by whom are all things, in bringing many sons to glory, to make the captain of their salvation perfect through sufferings (Hebrews 2:10).

The Spirit Himself bears witness with our spirit that we are children of God, and if children, then heirs—heirs of God and joint heirs with Christ, if indeed we suffer with Him, that we may also be glorified together (Romans 8:16-17).

3. **A Bride:**   **The church is Christ's bride. We are**
                     to be as loving, committed, and loyal
                     to Christ, as a bride to her beloved.

*He who has the bride is the bridegroom; but the friend of the
bridegroom, who stands and hears him, rejoices greatly
because of the bridegroom's voice. Therefore this joy of mine is
fulfilled* (John 3:29).

*Then one of the seven angels who had the seven bowls filled
with the seven last plagues came to me and talked with me,
saying, "Come, I will show you the bride, the Lamb's wife"*
(Revelation 21:9).

*Let us be glad and rejoice and give Him glory, for the
marriage of the Lamb has come, and His wife has made herself
ready* (Revelation 19:7).

4. **A Body:**   **The church is the body of Christ and**
                     we are to carry on His ministry in
                     unity. We are members of His body;
                     therefore, members of each other.

Now you are the body of Christ, and members individually
(I Corinthians 12:27).

*For as the body is one and has many members, but all the
members of that one body, being many, are one body, so also is
Christ. For by one Spirit we were all baptized into one body—
whether Jews or Greeks, whether slaves or free—and have all
been made to drink into one Spirit. For in fact the body is not
one member but many* (I Corinthians 12:12-14).

E. Christ, Himself, indwells the church.

*To them God willed to make known what are the riches of the
glory of this mystery among the Gentiles: which is Christ in
you, the hope of glory* (Colossians 1:27).

F. Jesus identifies with His church: He is inseparable
from His church. To love and serve Him is to love and
serve His church.

*He who receives you receives Me, and he who receives Me
receives Him who sent Me* (Matthew 10:40).

II. The Purpose of the Church.

A. There are two definitive statements made by Jesus that identify the focus of ministry for His church.

    1. The first definitive statement is found in the Great Commandment given to His disciples. Jesus identifies two assignments given to His church:

        a. First, we are to love God with every fiber of our being, and with our lives.

        b. Second, we are to love people with the same measure of love we afford ourselves.

        Jesus said to him, "You shall love the Lord your God with all your heart, with all your soul, and with all your mind. This is the first and great commandment. And the second is like it: 'You shall love your neighbor as yourself.' On these two commandments hang all the Law and the Prophets" (Matthew 22:37-40).

    2. The second definitive statement is found in the Great Commission as Jesus identifies three assignments He has given to His church:

        a. First, we are to make disciples out of converts;

        b. Second, we are to baptize them and enfold them into the fellowship of the local body;

        c. Third, we are to teach these new disciples the Word and the ways of the Lord.

        Go therefore and make disciples of all the nations, baptizing them in the name of the Father and of the Son and of the Holy Spirit, teaching them to observe all things that I have commanded you; and lo, I am with you always, even to the end of the age. Amen (Matthew 28:19-20).

B. There are five dominate purposes that should be evident in the church.

    1. First Purpose: Worship.

        a. The first purpose, and the highest priority of the church, is to love God and express that love to Him in times of celebration and intimacy.

        b. Worship is far more than just an activity of the corporate service on Sunday; it is to be the lifestyle of every follower of Christ.

Oh come, let us worship and bow down; let us kneel before the Lord our Maker (Psalm 95:6).

Then Jesus said to him, "Away with you, Satan! For it is written, 'You shall worship the Lord your God, and Him only you shall serve'" (Matthew 4:10).

    2. Second Purpose: Relationship.

        a. The second purpose of the church is to baptize new converts and enfold them into the fellowship of the church.

        b. As believers, we are called to "belong" not just to "believe."

        c. Every believer needs a relationship with other believers that will hold them accountable and encourage them in their Christian walk.

Now, therefore, you are no longer strangers and foreigners, but fellow citizens with the saints and members of the household of God, having been built on the foundation of the apostles and prophets, Jesus Christ Himself being the chief cornerstone, in whom the whole building, being fitted together, grows into a holy temple in the Lord, in whom you also are being built together for a dwelling place of God in the Spirit (Ephesians 2:19-22).

3. **Third Purpose: Discipleship.**

   a. **The third purpose of the church is to teach believers the principles and precepts of the Word of God. This teaching, when received, will enable believers to mature in spiritual matters and thereby be conformed into the image of Christ.**

   b. **Every believer needs to grow in their knowledge of the Word of God. However, knowledge is not enough; we must allow His Word to transform us so we can live our lives according to God's standards and principles.**

   c. **Our lives must be lived in accordance with the Word of God. The Holy Spirit will then have the freedom to make us effective in every area of our life as He purposes to produce the nature and character of Christ in us.**

   Him we preach, warning every man and teaching every man in all wisdom, that we may present every man perfect in Christ Jesus (Colossians 1:28).

   Till we all come to the unity of the faith and of the knowledge of the Son of God, to a perfect man, to the measure of the stature of the fullness of Christ; that we should no longer be children, tossed to and fro and carried about with every wind of doctrine, by the trickery of men, in the cunning craftiness of deceitful plotting (Ephesians 4:13-14).

4. **Fourth Purpose: Ministry.**

   a. **The fourth purpose of the church is to serve God by serving others. God has given abilities and gifts to each member of His family; these are to be used to minister to others around us who are in need.**

b. It is the responsibility of every believer to discover, develop, and invest their ministry gifts into people's lives; thereby, becoming a source of encouragement and compassion.

But, speaking the truth in love, may grow up in all things into Him who is the head—Christ— from whom the whole body, joined and knit together by what every joint supplies, according to the effective working by which every part does its share, causes growth of the body for the edifying of itself in love (Ephesians 4:15-16).

5. **Fifth Purpose: Mission.**

   a. The fifth purpose of the church is to reach out beyond its four walls and win souls to Jesus Christ.

   b. We must first reach out to our immediate circle of influence by sharing how Jesus saved us and what a difference He has made in our lives.

   c. We are responsible to find practical ways to express Christ's love to those who are hurting. We must reach out to those outside our immediate circle of influence.

   d. We are required to reach out to the nations and tell them of the life-changing love of Christ. We must tell them of the peace, hope, and joy that only He can give.

But you shall receive power when the Holy Spirit has come upon you; and you shall be witnesses to Me in Jerusalem, and in all Judea and Samaria, and to the end of the earth (Acts 1:8).

So Jesus said to them again, "Peace to you! As the Father has sent Me, I also send you" (John 20:21).

III. The Ministries of the Church.

A. **Jesus gave five specific gift-ministries to His church; the prophet, apostle, evangelist, pastor, and teacher.**

But to each one of us grace was given according to the measure of Christ's gift. Therefore He says: "When He ascended on high, He led captivity captive, and gave gifts to men." (Now this, "He ascended"—what does it mean but that He also first descended into the lower parts of the earth? He who descended is also the One who ascended far above all the heavens, that He might fill all things.) And He Himself gave some to be apostles, some prophets, some evangelists, and some pastors and teachers (Ephesians 4:8-11).

B. **Each gift-ministry performs a specific purpose in the church.**

For the equipping of the saints for the work of ministry, for the edifying of the body of Christ, till we all come to the unity of the faith and of the knowledge of the Son of God, to a perfect man, to the measure of the stature of the fullness of Christ; that we should no longer be children, tossed to and fro and carried about with every wind of doctrine, by the trickery of men, in the cunning craftiness of deceitful plotting, but, speaking the truth in love, may grow up in all things into Him who is the head— Christ—from whom the whole body, joined and knit together by what every joint supplies, according to the effective working by which every part does its share, causes growth of the body for the edifying of itself in love (Ephesians 4:12-16).

1. **These gift-ministries train believers for the work of ministry as they help them discover, develop, and invest their gifts.**

2. **They reveal Jesus to His church through their gifts; and they establish the church in the doctrines of Christ. They also are responsible to edify (build up, encourage, and strengthen), and promote unity of the church.**

C. When the five gift-ministries work together, they confirm and compliment the other's ministry.

    1. The Apostle: The word "apostle" means "one who is sent."

        a. The primary ministry of the apostle is to establish new churches.

        b. They are involved in training leadership and grounding the church in Christ's doctrines.

Am I not an apostle? Am I not free? Have I not seen Jesus Christ our Lord? Are you not my work in the Lord? If I am not an apostle to others, yet doubtless I am to you. For you are the seal of my apostleship in the Lord (I Corinthians 9:1-2).

Now, therefore, you are no longer strangers and foreigners, but fellow citizens with the saints and members of the household of God, having been built on the foundation of the apostles and prophets, Jesus Christ Himself being the chief cornerstone (Ephesians 2:19-20).

    2. The Prophet: The ministry of the "prophet" is to exhort, edify, and comfort:

        a. First, they "fore-tell" what God is about to do; and how He is about to work in the earth.

        b. Second, they "forth-tell" the Word of God.

But he who prophesies speaks edification and exhortation and comfort to men (I Corinthians 14:3).

    3. The Evangelist: The word "evangelist" means "a proclaimer of good news."

        a. The evangelist preaches the good news of God's love and of His offer of salvation.

b. The evangelist is personally involved in soul-winning on a one-to-one basis.

Then Philip went down to the city of Samaria and preached Christ to them. And the multitudes with one accord heeded the things spoken by Philip, hearing and seeing the miracles which he did. For unclean spirits, crying with a loud voice, came out of many who were possessed; and many who were paralyzed and lame were healed. And there was great joy in that city (Acts 8:5-8).

But when they believed Philip as he preached the things concerning the kingdom of God and the name of Jesus Christ, both men and women were baptized (Acts 8:12).

4. The Pastor: **The word "pastor" means "shepherd."**

a. The pastor is charged with the oversight of the ministries within the local church.

b. The pastor is responsible to feed, lead, guide, love, govern, care for, and defend the local church.

Shepherd the flock of God which is among you, serving as overseers, not by compulsion but willingly, not for dishonest gain but eagerly; nor as being lords over those entrusted to you, but being examples to the flock (I Peter 5:2-3).

5. The Teacher: **The primary responsibility of the teacher is to ground the church in God's Word and in His ways.**

These things command and teach (I Timothy 4:11).

And a servant of the Lord must not quarrel but be gentle to all, able to teach, patient, in humility correcting those who are in opposition, if God perhaps will grant them repentance, so that they may know the truth, and that they may come to their senses and escape the snare of the devil, having been taken captive by him to do his wil (II Timothy 2:24-26).

IV. The Offices of the Church.

A. **The governmental structure of the church is a theocracy: God is the ultimate ruler of His church.**

1. The church is not governed by a democracy where the majority votes and rules.

2. The decisions are made by God; they are communicated to the five gift-ministries; and then they are confirmed by the body of elders.

B. **God established the offices of elder and deacon in the local church to assist the five gift-ministries in the work of the ministry.**

1. The word "elder" means "senior or elderly."

   a. In natural terms, it means one who is older and potentially wiser by virtue of years lived. However, in spiritual terms, it means "the opposite of a novice." An elder is measured by spiritual maturity, not by chronological years.

   b. An elder is raised up by God and ministers under the Pastor's authority; they must meet the Scriptural qualifications to serve.

   For this reason I left you in Crete, that you should set in order the things that are lacking, and appoint elders in every city as I commanded you— if a man is blameless, the husband of one wife, having faithful children not accused of dissipation or insubordination. For a bishop must be blameless, as a steward of God, not self-willed, not quick-tempered, not given to wine, not violent, not greedy for money, but hospitable, a lover of what is good, sober-minded, just, holy, self-controlled, holding fast the faithful word as he has been taught, that he may be able, by sound doctrine, both to exhort and convict those who contradict (Titus 1:5-9).

c.   **The elder's work is primarily in the areas of counseling, teaching, visitation, and assisting in spiritual oversight. There may be times that an elder has a pastor's calling and anointing.**

The elders who are among you I exhort, I who am a fellow elder and a witness of the sufferings of Christ, and also a partaker of the glory that will be revealed: Shepherd the flock of God which is among you, serving as overseers, not by compulsion but willingly, not for dishonest gain but eagerly; nor as being lords over those entrusted to you, but being examples to the flock (I Peter 5:1-3).

Let the elders who rule well be counted worthy of double honor, especially those who labor in the word and doctrine (I Timothy 5:17).

2.   **The word "deacon" means "servant."**

a.   **Deacons are generally elected by the church from those meeting Scriptural qualifications.**

b.   **Deacons are not part of the governing body. Deacons assist the pastors and the elders in the physical administrations of ministry.**

Therefore, brethren, seek out from among you seven men of good reputation, full of the Holy Spirit and wisdom, whom we may appoint over this business; but we will give ourselves continually to prayer and to the ministry of the word (Acts 6:3-4).

Likewise deacons must be reverent, not double-tongued, not given to much wine, not greedy for money, holding the mystery of the faith with a pure conscience. But let these also first be tested; then let them serve as deacons, being found blameless. Likewise their wives must be reverent, not slanderers, temperate, faithful in all things. Let deacons be the husbands of one wife, ruling their children and their own houses well. For those who have served well as deacons obtain for themselves a good standing and great boldness in the faith which is in Christ Jesus (I Timothy 3:8-13).

180

V. The Responsibilities of the Church.

A. The church is the expression of Christ in the earth; it is therefore imperative that we are connected to a local congregation.

    1. Jesus died for His church. If Jesus felt strongly enough to die for the church, we should feel strongly enough to be identified with the church.

And He is the head of the body, the church, who is the beginning, the firstborn from the dead, that in all things He may have the preeminence (Colossians 1:18).

    2. The New Testament pattern teaches that believers were participating members who identified with the local church.

So continuing daily with one accord in the temple, and breaking bread from house to house, they ate their food with gladness and simplicity of heart, praising God and having favor with all the people. And the Lord added to the church daily those who were being saved (Acts 2:46-47).

B. Every believer is blessed and gifted with abilities that are to be shared for the benefit of the church.

From whom the whole body, joined and knit together by what every joint supplies, according to the effective working by which every part does its share, causes growth of the body for the edifying of itself in love (Ephesians 4:16).

C. The Scripture mandates that we pray for one another, encourage one another, and bear one another's burdens. This will require first-hand knowledge of what is happening in the lives of others.

Bear one another's burdens, and so fulfill the law of Christ (Galatians 6:2).

Confess your trespasses to one another, and pray for one another, that you may be healed. The effective, fervent prayer of a righteous man avails much (James 5:16).

D. The Scripture teaches that we are to live submitted lives:

1. We are to submit ourselves to the Lord;

2. We are to submit to one another in Christ's love;

3. We are to submit to our spiritual leaders.

Submitting to one another in the fear of God (Ephesians 5:21).

Obey those who rule over you, and be submissive, for they watch out for your souls, as those who must give account. Let them do so with joy and not with grief, for that would be unprofitable for you (Hebrews 13:17).

E. The Scriptures teach that believers are to faithfully support the local church with their tithes and offerings.

"Bring all the tithes into the storehouse, that there may be food in My house, and try Me now in this," says the Lord of hosts, "If I will not open for you the windows of heaven and pour out for you such blessing that there will not be room enough to receive it" (Malachi 3:10).

Now concerning the collection for the saints, as I have given orders to the churches of Galatia, so you must do also: On the first day of the week let each one of you lay something aside, storing up as he may prosper, that there be no collections when I come (I Corinthians 16:1-2).

F. The Lord plants us in the local church of His choosing. It is important that we remain where the Lord has planted us so that the purposes of God can be realized, not only in our lives, but also in the church.

But now God has set the members, each one of them, in the body just as He pleased (I Corinthians 12:18).

1. The Scriptures teach us to be faithful in our attendance of the church services and ministries.

2. **It will be impossible to minister to each other if we do not commit to a local church. We must become acquainted with each other if we are to fulfill the mandates of the Word.**

And let us consider one another in order to stir up love and good works, not forsaking the assembling of ourselves together, as is the manner of some, but exhorting one another, and so much the more as you see the Day approaching (Hebrews 10:24-25).

Chapter Eleven

Embracing the Ordinances of the Church

I. Water Baptism.

A. There are three Greek words which describe the English word, "baptism."

    1. The first word *cheo* **means "to pour."**

    2. The second word *rantizo* **means "to sprinkle."**

    3. The third word *baptize* **means "to immerse."**

        a. The expanded definition of *baptizo* **is "to dip or plunge; to immerse; to put into or under water, to entirely immerse or submerge."**

        b. The word, *baptizo,* **is used in reference to water baptism throughout the Scripture. We can therefore conclude that the mode of water baptism is in the form of immersion.**

        So he commanded the chariot to stand still. And both Philip and the eunuch went down into the water, and he baptized him (Acts 8:38).

B. Jesus commanded that every believer be baptized.

He who believes and is baptized will be saved; but he who does not believe will be condemned (Mark 16:16).

Go therefore and make disciples of all the nations, baptizing them in the name of the Father and of the Son and of the Holy Spirit, teaching them to observe all things that I have commanded you; and lo, I am with you always, even to the end of the age (Matthew 28:19-20).

C. Jesus set the example for us to follow when He submitted Himself to John the Baptist for baptism.

When all the people were baptized, it came to pass that Jesus also was baptized; and while He prayed, the heaven was opened (Luke 3:21).

D. Water baptism is an act of obedience; whereby, our love for the Lord's instructions is demonstrated.

By this we know that we love the children of God, when we love God and keep His commandments. For this is the love of God, that we keep His commandments. And His commandments are not burdensome (I John 5:2-3).

If you love Me, keep My commandments (John 14:15).

E. The Apostles taught that believers were to be baptized.

Then Peter said to them, "Repent, and let every one of you be baptized in the name of Jesus Christ for the remission of sins; and you shall receive the gift of the Holy Spirit" (Acts 2:38).

F. Water baptism is symbolic of the spiritual transaction that has taken place in the believer's heart.

1. Baptism pictures the death of Christ.

a. For the believer, baptism becomes the picture of the death of our old nature.

Or do you not know that as many of us as were baptized into Christ Jesus were baptized into His death? Therefore we were buried with Him through baptism into death, that just as Christ was raised from the dead by the glory of the Father, even so we also should walk in newness of life (Romans 6:3-4).

b. Our new nature is dead to the practice of sin.

Knowing this, that our old man was crucified with Him, that the body of sin might be done away with, that we should no longer be slaves of sin. For he who has died has been freed from sin. Now if we died with Christ, we believe that we shall also live with Him, knowing that Christ, having been raised from the dead, dies no more. Death no longer has dominion over Him. For the death that He died, He died to sin once for all; but the life that He lives, He lives to God. Likewise you also, reckon yourselves to be dead indeed to sin, but alive to God in Christ Jesus our Lord (Romans 6:6-11).

2. **Baptism pictures Christ's burial.**

   a. **Baptism is a picture of the burial of our old nature.**

   b. **The water symbolizes the grave in which our old nature is put away, or buried.**

   Buried with Him in baptism, in which you also were raised with Him through faith in the working of God, who raised Him from the dead (Colossians 2:12).

3. **Baptism pictures Christ's resurrection.**

   a. **Baptism is a picture of Christ's resurrection from the dead; to the believer it symbolizes the resurrection of our new nature from death.**

   b. **Our old nature, being reckoned dead and buried, is now raised to a new life. Our new nature will seek the pleasure of God.**

   Therefore we were buried with Him through baptism into death, that just as Christ was raised from the dead by the glory of the Father, even so we also should walk in newness of life (Romans 6:4-5).

4. **Baptism identifies believers as followers of Christ and identifies them as members of His church.**

   I have been crucified with Christ; it is no longer I who live, but Christ lives in me; and the life which I now live in the flesh I live by faith in the Son of God, who loved me and gave Himself for me (Galatians 2:20).

   For as many of you as were baptized into Christ have put on Christ (Galatians 3:27).

5. **Baptism is the sign of the New Covenant just as circumcision was the sign of the Old Covenant. Baptism pictures the circumcision of our hearts and the cutting away of our carnal nature.**

189

There is also an antitype which now saves us—baptism (not the removal of the filth of the flesh, but the answer of a good conscience toward God), through the resurrection of Jesus Christ (I Peter 3:21).

And you are complete in Him, who is the head of all principality and power. In Him you were also circumcised with the circumcision made without hands, by putting off the body of the sins of the flesh, by the circumcision of Christ, buried with Him in baptism, in which you also were raised with Him through faith in the working of God, who raised Him from the dead (Colossians 2:10-12).

6. **The requirement of Scripture for the rite of water baptism is one must be a believer in Jesus Christ.**

   a. **We must confess and repent of our sins.**

   b. **We must place our faith in Jesus and confess Him to be our Savior and Lord.**

   That if you confess with your mouth the Lord Jesus and believe in your heart that God has raised Him from the dead, you will be saved. For with the heart one believes unto righteousness, and with the mouth confession is made unto salvation (Romans 10:9-10).

7. **Baptism is a believer's exercise.**

   a. **Infant baptism is not valid due to the infant's inability to comply with the requirements: the exercise of faith; repentance; and confession.**

   b. **The Scripture does teach the dedication of infants to the Lord and to His service; it is a meaningful experience for the infant's family.**

   "For this child I prayed, and the Lord has granted me my petition which I asked of Him. Therefore I also have lent him to the Lord; as long as he lives he shall be lent to the Lord." So they worshiped the Lord there (I Samuel 1:27-28).

II. The Holy Communion.

A. **Celebrating the Holy Communion is a celebration of the New Covenant. The bread and the wine are the elements of communion.**

 1. **As we partake of these elements we are reminded of the price that Jesus paid. We are convicted of unrepentant sin and areas not surrendered to His Lordship and the leadership of the Holy Spirit.**

 2. **As we partake of the elements of communion we are inspired to release our praise and worship for the overwhelming demonstration of His love.**

 3. **As we partake of the elements of communion we are reminded of God's covenant promises to us and our faith is released to embrace them.**

B. **Communion is known by various names in Scripture:**

 1. **The Lord's Supper;**

 Therefore when you come together in one place, it is not to eat the Lord's Supper (I Corinthians 11:20).

 2. **The Lord's Table;**

 You cannot drink the cup of the Lord and the cup of demons; you cannot partake of the Lord's Table and of the table of demons (I Corinthians 10:21).

 3. **The Communion;**

 The cup of blessing which we bless, is it not the communion of the blood of Christ? The bread which we break, is it not the communion of the body of Christ (I Corinthians 10:16)?

 4. **The Breaking of Bread.**

 And they continued steadfastly in the apostles' doctrine and fellowship, in the breaking of bread, and in prayer (Acts 2:42).

C. Jesus instituted the celebration of the New Covenant at the Feast of Passover.

So His disciples went out, and came into the city, and found it just as He had said to them; and they prepared the Passover. And as they were eating, Jesus took bread, blessed and broke it, and gave it to them and said, "Take, eat; this is My body." Then He took the cup, and when He had given thanks He gave it to them, and they all drank from it. And He said to them, "This is My blood of the new covenant, which is shed for many" (Mark 14:16, 22-24).

D. Paul instructed the Corinthian Church to celebrate the New Covenant as they observed Holy Communion.

For I received from the Lord that which I also delivered to you: that the Lord Jesus on the same night in which He was betrayed took bread; and when He had given thanks, He broke it and said, "Take, eat; this is My body which is broken for you; do this in remembrance of Me." In the same manner He also took the cup after supper, saying, "This cup is the new covenant in My blood. This do, as often as you drink it, in remembrance of Me" (I Corinthians 11:23-25).

E. There are several symbols of the Holy Communion:

1. The Table;

a. The Table is a place to demonstrate humility and servanthood.

But the priests, the Levites, the sons of Zadok, who kept charge of My sanctuary when the children of Israel went astray from Me, they shall come near Me to minister to Me; and they shall stand before Me to offer to Me the fat and the blood, says the Lord God. They shall enter My sanctuary, and they shall come near My table to minister to Me, and they shall keep My charge (Ezekiel 44:15-16).

b. The Table is a place to enjoy fellowship.

Behold, I stand at the door and knock. If anyone hears My voice and opens the door, I will come in to him and dine with him, and he with Me (Revelation 3:20).

2. **The Bread;**

   a. **The Bread represents the body of Christ which was broken for us.**

   And as they were eating, Jesus took bread, blessed and broke it, and gave it to the disciples and said, "Take, eat; this is My body" (Matthew 26:26).

   b. **The Bread represents our communion with Christ.**

   The cup of blessing which we bless, is it not the communion of the blood of Christ? The bread which we break, is it not the communion of the body of Christ (I Corinthians 10:16)?

3. **The Wine;**

   a. **The Wine represents the blood of the Lord which established the New Covenant. It causes us to remember the blood that was shed for the remission of our sins.**

   Then He took the cup, and gave thanks, and gave it to them, saying, "Drink from it, all of you. For this is My blood of the new covenant, which is shed for many for the remission of sins" (Matthew 26:27-28).

   b. **The Wine reminds us that Jesus removed the barrier of sin; therefore, mankind can have relationship and fellowship with God.**

   In the same manner He also took the cup after supper, saying, "This cup is the new covenant in My blood. This do, as often as you drink it, in remembrance of Me" (I Corinthians 11:25).

F. **There are several characteristics that should mark our celebration of the Holy Communion.**

   1. **We should follow the example of Jesus and have a deep desire to celebrate the Table of the Lord.**

193

When the hour had come, He sat down, and the twelve apostles with Him. Then He said to them, "With fervent desire I have desired to eat this Passover with you before I suffer" (Luke 22:14-15).

2. We should come to the Table of the Lord with thankful hearts for His blessings and His faithfulness to keep His promises to us.

Then He took the cup, and gave thanks, and said, "Take this and divide it among yourselves" (Luke 22:17).

But without faith it is impossible to please Him, for he who comes to God must believe that He is, and that He is a rewarder of those who diligently seek Him (Hebrews 11:6).

3. We should come to the Table of the Lord in unity.

For we, though many, are one bread and one body; for we all partake of that one bread (I Corinthians 10:17).

Therefore, my brethren, when you come together to eat, wait for one another (I Corinthians 11:33).

4. We should come to the Table of the Lord with joy.

So continuing daily with one accord in the temple, and breaking bread from house to house, they ate their food with gladness and simplicity of heart, praising God and having favor with all the people. And the Lord added to the church daily those who were being saved (Acts 2:46-47).

5. We should come to the Table of the Lord with the expectation of receiving God's life-giving power.

Whoever eats My flesh and drinks My blood has eternal life, and I will raise him up at the last day. For My flesh is food indeed, and My blood is drink indeed. He who eats My flesh and drinks My blood abides in Me, and I in him. As the living Father sent Me, and I live because of the Father, so he who feeds on Me will live because of Me. This is the bread which came down from heaven—not as your fathers ate the manna, and are dead. He who eats this bread will live forever (John 6:54-58).

G. The Scripture instructs us to celebrate the Table of the Lord in remembrance of Him.

   1. Celebrating the Lord's Table in remembrance of Him does not mean that we are to only focus on the cross and commiserate over Christ's sufferings for our sins; wherein, we become appropriately somber and sad.

   2. We are to remember Christ's victory over the power of sin and His triumph over death; hell; and the grave.

   3. We are to remember that Christ's triumph belongs to us.

For I received from the Lord that which I also delivered to you: that the Lord Jesus on the same night in which He was betrayed took bread; and when He had given thanks, He broke it and said, "Take, eat; this is My body which is broken for you; do this in remembrance of Me." In the same manner He also took the cup after supper, saying, "This cup is the new covenant in My blood. This do, as often as you drink it, in remembrance of Me" (I Corinthians 11:23-25).

H. Celebrating the Table of the Lord is a celebration of Christ's victory.

And they overcame him by the blood of the Lamb and by the word of their testimony, and they did not love their lives to the death (Revelation 12:11).

   1. We can celebrate because, through the blood of Jesus, we have been given dominion over the rulers and powers of darkness, and over the agenda of hell against us.

   2. We are to celebrate Christ's great announcement from the cross ... "It is finished."

a. Because of the finished work of the cross, our salvation has been made complete and our sins are forever forgiven.

b. Because of the finished work of the cross, we stand before God justified and are robed in Christ's righteousness.

3. The Greek word *eucharisteo* from which we get our English word "Eucharist" means "I thank."

   a. We celebrate with thanksgiving by remembering that Christ's sacrifice on the cross purchased our salvation and total forgiveness of sin.

   b. We celebrate with thanksgiving by remembering Christ's victory over hell's powers. In this victory, Christ purchased our healing and our deliverance from the enslaving power of sin.

I. Celebrating the Table of the Lord is a declaration of our complete redemption and a proclamation of the truths surrounding His death and resurrection.

For as often as you eat this bread and drink this cup, you proclaim the Lord's death till He comes (I Corinthians 11:26).

1. Through Christ's death and resurrection we are redeemed from the hand of the devil and from his ability to control and enslave our lives.

He has delivered us from the power of darkness and conveyed us into the kingdom of the Son of His love, in whom we have redemption through His blood, the forgiveness of sins (Colossians 1:13-14).

2. Celebrating the Table of the Lord heightens our anticipation of Christ's promised return.

But I say to you, "I will not drink of this fruit of the vine from now on until that day when I drink it new with you in My Father's kingdom" (Matthew 26:29).

3. **When we celebrate the Table of the Lord, we declare our faith in our ultimate redemption from this world when Christ returns.**

Then they will see the Son of Man coming in a cloud with power and great glory. Now when these things begin to happen, look up and lift up your heads, because your redemption draws near (Luke 21:27-28).

J. **Celebrating the Table of the Lord is a declaration of our complete dependence on the Lord for all things pertaining to life.**

1. **Celebrating the Table of the Lord is a declaration of our dependency on the Lord for our spiritual nourishment and strength.**

Then Jesus said to them, "Most assuredly, I say to you, unless you eat the flesh of the Son of Man and drink His blood, you have no life in you. Whoever eats My flesh and drinks My blood has eternal life, and I will raise him up at the last day. For My flesh is food indeed, and My blood is drink indeed. He who eats My flesh and drinks My blood abides in Me, and I in him. As the living Father sent Me, and I live because of the Father, so he who feeds on Me will live because of Me. This is the bread which came down from heaven—not as your fathers ate the manna, and are dead. He who eats this bread will live forever" (John 6:53-58).

2. **Jesus explained to His disciples that "eating His flesh and drinking His blood" would become their source of spiritual strength and life (this statement is not literal; rather, it is a figurative application of entering into covenant relationship with Him).**

It is the Spirit who gives life; the flesh profits nothing. The words that I speak to you are spirit, and they are life (John 6:63).

3. Just as natural food nourishes our bodies giving us physical strength; celebrating His Table gives us spiritual nourishment and strength.

K. Celebrating the Table of the Lord is a time for self-examination.

But let a man examine himself, and so let him eat of the bread and drink of the cup (I Corinthians 11:28).

1. The word "examine" comes from a Greek word which means "a running test."

2. We are to examine our hearts in two areas:

   a. First, we must examine our hearts in regards to our relationship with God. We are to confess our sins so that we can approach His Table with a heart that is clean before Him.

   If we confess our sins, He is faithful and just to forgive us our sins and to cleanse us from all unrighteousness (I John 1:9).

   b. Second, we must examine our hearts in regards to our relationship with others. We cannot approach His Table with a heart that is full of unforgiveness. We are to love and forgive others as Christ has loved and forgiven us.

   A new commandment I give to you, that you love one another; as I have loved you, that you also love one another. By this all will know that you are My disciples, if you have love for one another (John 13:34-35).

   And be kind to one another, tenderhearted, forgiving one another, just as God in Christ forgave you (Ephesians 4:32).

L. Celebrating the Table of the Lord is a reminder of God's provision for healing.

1.   The Apostle Paul warned against approaching the Table of the Lord in an "unworthy manner."

For he who eats and drinks in an unworthy manner eats and drinks judgment to himself, not discerning the Lord's body (I Corinthians 11:29).

2.   Truthfully, we are always "unworthy" of any blessing that the Lord gives us.

3.   There is absolutely nothing we can do in our human effort to make us "worthy" to receive anything from God.

4.   The Greek word for "worthy" is *axios* which deals with the concept of "weight," not "perfection."

   a.   In ancient times the value of a coin was determined by its weight.

   b.   A coin would lose some of its weight through use and therefore, some of its value.

5.   The Apostle Paul encourages us to come to the Table of the Lord with an understanding of the Lord's body so that we can find forgiveness; healing; and spiritual strength.

   a.   When we receive the bread, which symbolically represents His body, we must release our faith to believe God for His promised provision for every need we have in the physical realm of life.

   b.   When we receive the wine, which symbolically represents His blood, we must release our faith to believe God for His promised provision for every need we have in the spiritual realm of life.

III. The Laying on of Hands.

A. The only authority we have as believers is the authority that Jesus has given to us.

    1. When we lay our hands on someone and pray in the name of Jesus there is a spiritual impartation from God to that person.

    2. Our hands symbolically become the hands of the Lord to the individual we are praying for.

B. The Old Testament sets forth the example for us to follow when we lay hands on another in faith; we must expect a divine impartation.

    1. God instructed Moses to lay his hands on Joshua and charge him with the leadership of the children of Israel.

And the Lord said to Moses: "Take Joshua the son of Nun with you, a man in whom is the Spirit, and lay your hand on him; set him before Eleazar the priest and before all the congregation, and inaugurate him in their sight. And you shall give some of your authority to him, that all the congregation of the children of Israel may be obedient. He shall stand before Eleazar the priest, who shall inquire before the Lord for him by the judgment of the Urim. At his word they shall go out, and at his word they shall come in, he and all the children of Israel with him—all the congregation." So Moses did as the Lord commanded him. He took Joshua and set him before Eleazar the priest and before all the congregation. And he laid his hands on him and inaugurated him, just as the Lord commanded by the hand of Moses (Numbers 27:18-23).

    2. Joshua would never be the same after this event.

Now Joshua the son of Nun was full of the spirit of wisdom, for Moses had laid his hands on him; so the children of Israel heeded him, and did as the Lord had commanded Moses (Deuteronomy 34:9).

C. The Scripture instructs us concerning the various reasons for the laying on of hands.

1. We lay on hands to impart the Baptism of Jesus in the Holy Spirit.

Then they laid hands on them, and they received the Holy Spirit. And when Simon saw that through the laying on of the apostles' hands the Holy Spirit was given, he offered them money, saying, "Give me this power also, that anyone on whom I lay hands may receive the Holy Spirit" (Acts 8:17-19).

2. We lay on hands to impart spiritual gifts.

For I long to see you, that I may impart to you some spiritual gift, so that you may be established (Romans 1:11).

That good thing which was committed to you, keep by the Holy Spirit who dwells in us (II Timothy 1:14).

Do not neglect the gift that is in you, which was given to you by prophecy with the laying on of the hands of the eldership (I Timothy 4:14).

3. We lay on hands to ordain ministers.

And they chose Stephen, a man full of faith and the Holy Spirit, and Philip, Prochorus, Nicanor, Timon, Parmenas, and Nicolas, a proselyte from Antioch, whom they set before the apostles; and when they had prayed, they laid hands on them (Acts 6:5-6).

4. We lay on hands to send out ministers.

As they ministered to the Lord and fasted, the Holy Spirit said, "Now separate to Me Barnabas and Saul for the work to which I have called them." Then, having fasted and prayed and laid hands on them, they sent them away (Acts 13:2-3).

5. We lay on hands for healing.

They will lay hands on the sick, and they will recover (Mark 16:18).

6. We lay on hands to bless children.

Then they brought little children to Him, that He might touch them; but the disciples rebuked those who brought them. But when Jesus saw it, He was greatly displeased and said to them, "Let the little children come to Me, and do not forbid them; for of such is the kingdom of God. Assuredly, I say to you, whoever does not receive the kingdom of God as a little child will by no means enter it." And He took them up in His arms, put His hands on them, and blessed them (Mark 10:13-16).

D. There are two fundamental rules found in Scripture that govern the ministry of laying on of hands:

1. First, we are not to show partiality or prejudice when ministering through the laying on of hands; we are not to favor one person over another.

I charge you before God and the Lord Jesus Christ and the elect angels that you observe these things without prejudice, doing nothing with partiality (I Timothy 5:21).

2. And second we are to use discernment when we lay hands on another. We must seek the leadership of the Holy Spirit and listen to His voice.

Do not lay hands on anyone hastily, nor share in other people's sins; keep yourself pure (I Timothy 5:22).

Your ears shall hear a word behind you, saying, "This is the way, walk in it," whenever you turn to the right hand or whenever you turn to the left" (Isaiah 30:21).

Chapter Twelve

Understanding God's Financial Plan

I. Stewardship.

A. Stewardship recognizes that God is the owner of all created things.

The earth is the Lord's, and all its fullness, the world and those who dwell therein (Psalm 24:1).

B. Stewardship recognizes that everything we have has come from the hand of God.

Now therefore, our God, we thank You and praise Your glorious name. But who am I, and who are my people, that we should be able to offer so willingly as this? For all things come from You, and of Your own we have given You (I Chronicles 29:13-14).

1. Stewardship recognizes that the ownership of one's person; one's power; and one's possessions; belong to God.

Yours, O Lord, is the greatness, the power and the glory, the victory and the majesty; for all that is in heaven and in earth is Yours; Yours is the kingdom, O Lord, and You are exalted as head over all. Both riches and honor come from You, and You reign over all. In Your hand is power and might; in Your hand it is to make great and to give strength to all (I Chronicles 29:11-12).

2. Stewardship acknowledges that we are both responsible, and accountable, for all that we have been given.

After a long time the lord of those servants came and settled accounts with them (Matthew 25:19).

So he called him and said to him, "What is this I hear about you? Give an account of your stewardship, for you can no longer be steward" (Luke 16:2).

C. The Scriptures mandate that we be good stewards of the abundant resources which we have received.

1. **Stewardship requires that we have a right attitude regarding our resources. When our attitude is right, our actions will bring about the systematic and proportionate giving of our talents; time; and possessions.**

2. **As stewards of our resources we are entrusted with the responsibility to release them into the service of God for the advancement of His kingdom on earth.**

D. **There are defining characteristics of a good steward.**

1. **A good steward is faithful.**

Let a man so consider us, as servants of Christ and stewards of the mysteries of God. Moreover it is required in stewards that one be found faithful (I Corinthians 4:1-2).

2. **A good steward honors the tithe.**

"Bring all the tithes into the storehouse, that there may be food in My house, and prove Me now in this," says the Lord of hosts, "If I will not open for you the windows of heaven and pour out for you such blessing that there will not be room enough to receive it" (Malachi 3:10).

4. **A good steward is giving.**

Give, and it will be given to you: good measure, pressed down, shaken together, and running over will be put into your bosom. For with the same measure that you use, it will be measured back to you (Luke 6:38).

5. **A good steward is hospitable.**

Distributing to the needs of the saints, given to hospitality (Romans 12:13).

E. **God will punish the unfaithful steward.**

Then the steward said within himself, "What shall I do? For my master is taking the stewardship away from me. I cannot dig; I am ashamed to beg" (Luke 16:3).

He who is faithful in what is least is faithful also in much; and he who is unjust in what is least is unjust also in much. Therefore if you have not been faithful in the unrighteous mammon, who will commit to your trust the true riches? And if you have not been faithful in what is another man's, who will give you what is your own (Luke 16:10-12)?

F. God will reward the faithful steward.

Blessed is that servant whom his master, when he comes, will find so doing (Matthew 24:46).

His lord said to him, "Well done, good and faithful servant; you were faithful over a few things, I will make you ruler over many things. Enter into the joy of your lord" (Matthew 25:21).

II. The Tithe.

A. The starting point for learning to live in the economy of God is learning to honor the tithe.

1. The tithe is considered to be ten-percent of your total earnings.

And this stone which I have set as a pillar shall be God's house, and of all that You give me I will surely give a tenth to You (Genesis 28:22).

2. The tithe belongs to the Lord; He considers it to be holy and sacred.

And all the tithe of the land, whether of the seed of the land or of the fruit of the tree, is the Lord's. It is holy to the Lord (Leviticus 27:30).

B. The concept of honoring the tithe is perhaps best understood in terms of recognizing God's rights to the portion of our income that He claims as His own. We must be obedient to release His portion back to Him.

1. When we honor the tithe, we recognize that ten-percent of our income belongs to God. We are honoring the difference between what belongs to God, and what He has given to us for our discretional use.

2. God spoke through the Prophet Malachi to call His people to repent, and to return to Him. In doing so, He dealt with the issue of not recognizing His rights to their provision. God pointed out to them that this problem was generations deep.

"Yet from the days of your fathers you have gone away from My ordinances and have not kept them. Return to Me, and I will return to you," says the Lord of hosts. "But you said, 'In what way shall we return?' Will a man rob God? Yet you have robbed Me! But you say, 'In what way have we robbed You?' In tithes and offerings" (Malachi 3:7-8).

C. God gave Adam and Eve stewardship in the Garden of Eden over the entirety of His creation. God placed only one stipulation on them; they were to honor His rights to the tree of the knowledge of good and evil and not eat of its fruit.

Then God blessed them, and God said to them, "Be fruitful and multiply; fill the earth and subdue it; have dominion over the fish of the sea, over the birds of the air, and over every living thing that moves on the earth" (Genesis 1:28).

And the Lord God commanded the man, saying, "Of every tree of the garden you may freely eat; but of the tree of the knowledge of good and evil you shall not eat, for in the day that you eat of it you shall surely die" (Genesis 2:16-17).

1. The issue at hand was not about whether to eat or not to eat; it was much deeper.

2. The issue at hand was over recognizing God's rights to what He claimed as His own.

D. **When we honor the tithe, our obedience positions us to receive God's promised blessings.**

"Bring all the tithes into the storehouse, that there may be food in My house, and prove Me now in this," says the Lord of hosts, "If I will not open for you the windows of heaven and pour out for you such blessing that there will not be room enough to receive it. And I will rebuke the devourer for your sakes, so that he will not destroy the fruit of your ground, nor shall the vine fail to bear fruit for you in the field," says the Lord of hosts (Malachi 3:10-11).

1. **God promises to respond to our obedience, of returning His portion of our resources to Him, by opening the windows of heaven over our lives and pouring His blessings upon us.**

2. **When we become a Christian, we experience the redeeming grace of Christ which redeems us in every area of life. This outpouring of God's blessings is evidenced in a variety of expressions:**

   a. **Our homes will overflow with joy and happiness;**

   b. **Our business dealings will be crowned with God's favor, resulting in prosperity;**

   c. **Our hearts and minds will rest on the provision of God's peace and confidence;**

   d. **Our bodies will enjoy divine health and contentment;**

   e. **Our God-given dreams and desires will become a manifest reality;**

   f. **And our resources will be preserved and our endeavors will be fruitful. The Lord will hold the agenda of hell (to abort and diminish our lives) at bay.**

E. When we make the choice not to honor the tithe, we can safely predict that we are opening ourselves to negative consequences.

1. God stated that when we fail to recognize His rights to His predetermined portion of our provision, we are robbing Him.

Will a man rob God? Yet you have robbed Me! But you say, "in what way have we robbed You?" In tithes and offering (Malachi 3:8).

a. There is a difference between stealing from someone and robbing someone.

(1) When we steal from someone, we do so under the cloak of secrecy.

(2) When we rob someone, we do so in an open confrontation, face to face.

b. When we withhold our tithe, we are robbing God, face to face, with an open act of disobedience.

2. When we withhold our tithe, we rob God of His opportunity to bless us. Now we are dealing with more than just stolen resources; we are also dealing with stolen opportunities.

3. God warns us that when our tithe is withheld, we open ourselves to the consequences of the curse.

You are cursed with a curse, for you have robbed Me, even this whole nation (Malachi 3:9).

a. When we disobey a directive of Scripture we invert, or reverse, the promises of Scripture. Literally, blessings become curses to us.

b. God does not place a curse on us, for that is not consistent with His nature. However, when we disobey we willfully step out from under the canopy of His protective grace and are subjected to the consequences of the curse.

4. When we honor the Lord's tithe, we are placing our trust in Him to continually provide for our needs.

   a. When we withhold our tithe, we are making a dangerous statement to the Lord, "I can manage my money better than You."

   b. We give in to our vulnerability to place our confidence in our own management skills rather than placing our faith in the money management principles of God.

F. We are to give our tithe to the storehouse, which is the local church to which we belong.

"Bring all the tithes into the storehouse, that there may be food in My house, and prove Me now in this," says the Lord of hosts, "If I will not open for you the windows of heaven and pour out for you such blessing that there will not be room enough to receive it" (Malachi 3:10).

1. The treasury was located within the Temple: It became the clearing house for the distribution of the treasury's resources.

2. A common misconception among Christians is that they have the freedom to choose where they will invest their tithe within the greater work of God.

3. The tithe is to be given to the local church so the resources will be available for the work of the local ministry which cares for the individual.

G. **It is a misconception that tithing was only a requirement in the Old Testament practice of the Mosaic Law.**

    1. **The Law of Moses mandated the practice of tithing.**

And all the tithe of the land, whether of the seed of the land or of the fruit of the tree, is the Lord's. It is holy to the Lord. If a man wants at all to redeem any of his tithes, he shall add one-fifth to it. And concerning the tithe of the herd or the flock, of whatever passes under the rod, the tenth one shall be holy to the Lord (Leviticus 27:30-32).

    2. **Jesus, however, affirmed that tithing is a timeless instruction. This was confirmed when He championed the Pharisee's practice of tithing, while rebuking their attitudes towards justice, mercy, and faith.**

Woe to you, scribes and Pharisees, hypocrites! For you pay tithe of mint and anise and cummin, and have neglected the weightier matters of the law: justice and mercy and faith. These you ought to have done, without leaving the others undone (Matthew 23:23).

        a. **Jesus explained that tithing was a moral imperative in His use of the word "ought" in the above passage of Scripture.**

        b. **By stating that "these you ought to have done," Jesus pointed out that there is a higher, divine precept that should not be violated.**

    3. **A logical question one might ask when analyzing this principle would be, "Why would Jesus commend an Old Testament practice that was not going to become a part of the New Testament economy?"**

H. The New Testament teaches that we should follow the patterns of faith exhibited in the life of Abraham; Abraham is called "The Father of Faith."

1. Abraham paid a tithe to Melchizedek (who was an Old Testament picture of Jesus), before the Law of Moses was ever established.

Then Melchizedek king of Salem brought out bread and wine; he was the priest of God Most High. And he blessed him and said: "Blessed be Abram of God Most High, Possessor of heaven and earth; And blessed be God Most High, Who has delivered your enemies into your hand." And he gave him a tithe of all (Genesis 14:18-20).

2. Abraham gave his tithe as an act of worship; thereby, he acknowledged that God was the source of his blessings.

But Abram said to the king of Sodom, "I have lifted my hand to the Lord, God Most High, the Possessor of heaven and earth" (Genesis 14:22).

3. Melchizedek received Abraham's tithe and pronounced a blessing on him.

And he blessed him and said: "Blessed be Abram of God Most High, Possessor of heaven and earth; And blessed be God Most High, who has delivered your enemies into your hand" (Genesis 14:19-20).

I. A question often asked is whether we are to tithe on the net, or the gross, of our income. The Scriptural answer to this question is found in the phrase, "the firstfruits of all your increase." We are to offer God His tithe first, before any other financial obligation is considered.

Honor the Lord with your possessions, and with the firstfruits of all your increase; So your barns will be filled with plenty, and your vats will overflow with new wine (Proverbs 3:9-10).

III. The Offering.

A. **Offerings are not assigned specific amounts in the Bible; the matter is determined by the heart.**

1. **Offerings were given as a source of pleasure to God in the Old Testament.**

Now the Lord spoke to Moses, saying, "Command the children of Israel, and say to them, 'My offering, My food for My offerings made by fire as a sweet aroma to Me, you shall be careful to offer to Me at their appointed time'" (Numbers 28:1-2).

2. **The practice of giving offerings is carried over into the New Testament. The Apostle Paul acknowledged the love offerings of the Philippian church as being pleasing to the Lord.**

Indeed I have all and abound. I am full, having received from Epaphroditus the things which were sent from you, a sweet-smelling aroma, an acceptable sacrifice, well pleasing to God (Philippians 4:18).

B. **Offerings are a part of our worship experience. When we give offerings, we acknowledge the worthiness of the Lord to be worshiped.**

Give to the Lord the glory due His name; bring an offering, and come into His courts. Oh, worship the Lord in the beauty of holiness! Tremble before Him, all the earth (Psalm 96:8-9).

1. **Offerings are the fruit of a sincere heart that is seeking to worship, and serve the Lord. First, we give ourselves to God in worship; secondly, we give of our offerings for the work of ministry.**

Imploring us with much urgency that we would receive the gift and the fellowship of the ministering to the saints. And this they did not as we had hoped, but they first gave themselves to the Lord, and then to us by the will of God (II Corinthians 8:4-5).

2. **We are to release our offerings to the Lord with a cheerful heart.**

So let each one give as he purposes in his heart, not grudgingly or of necessity; for God loves a cheerful giver
(II Corinthians 9:7).

C. **The Scriptures speak of three different offerings:**

1. **Gratitude Offerings;**

   a. **This offering is given out of the firstfruits of the harvest.**

   b. **This was an annual offering given to express gratitude to God for His faithfulness to provide for His people.**

   The first of the firstfruits of your land you shall bring into the house of the Lord your God (Exodus 23:19).

2. **Ministry Offerings;**

   a. **This offering was given to help with the work of the ministry.**

   b. **This offering was to establish, maintain, and expand the ministry.**

   Then everyone came whose heart was stirred, and everyone whose spirit was willing, and they brought the Lord's offering for the work of the tabernacle of meeting, for all its service, and for the holy garments
   (Exodus 35:21).

3. **The Humanitarian Offerings;**

   a. **This offering was given to assist in helping to meet the needs of the poor in the community.**

   b. **Our attitudes in giving to the poor reflect our respect for the Lord.**

215

He who oppresses the poor reproaches his Maker, but he who honors Him has mercy on the needy (Proverbs 14:31).

    c.   God promises to take care of those who take care of the poor. He also promises to pay back what he has given.

He who gives to the poor will not lack, but he who hides his eyes will have many curses (Proverbs 28:27).

He who has pity on the poor lends to the Lord, and He will pay back what he has given (Proverbs 19:17).

D.   There are attitudes that should govern our giving.

    1.   We are to give willingly.

For if there is first a willing mind, it is accepted according to what one has, and not according to what he does not have (II Corinthians 8:12).

    2.   We are to give cheerfully.

So let each one give as he purposes in his heart, not grudgingly or of necessity; for God loves a cheerful giver (II Corinthians 9:7).

    3.   We are to give liberally.

But this I say: He who sows sparingly will also reap sparingly, and he who sows bountifully will also reap bountifully (II Corinthians 9:6).

    4.   We are to give according to the measure of God's blessings in our lives.

Every man shall give as he is able, according to the blessing of the Lord your God which He has given you (Deuteronomy 16:17).

    5.   We are to give with regularity.

On the first day of the week let each one of you lay something aside, storing up as he may prosper, that there be no collections when I come (I Corinthians 16:2).

6.   We are to give with simplicity. The actual word for "liberality," is the word simplicity.

He who exhorts, in exhortation; he who gives, with liberality; he who leads, with diligence; he who shows mercy, with cheerfulness (Romans 12:8).

7.   We are to give freely.

Heal the sick, cleanse the lepers, raise the dead, cast out demons. Freely you have received, freely give (Matthew 10:8).

IV. The Law of the Seed.

A.   The "law of the seed" involves the principles of sowing and reaping as established in the Word of God.

1.   First Principle: Within every seed there is an invisible assignment that will determine its harvest.

Then God said, "Let the earth bring forth grass, the herb that yields seed, and the fruit tree that yields fruit according to its kind, whose seed is in itself, on the earth"; and it was so. And the earth brought forth grass, the herb that yields seed according to its kind, and the tree that yields fruit, whose seed is in itself according to its kind. And God saw that it was good (Genesis 1:11-12).

Do not be deceived, God is not mocked; for whatever a man sows, that he will also reap (Galatians 6:7).

2.   Second Principle: Every seed that is planted will produce its assigned harvest in time.

While the earth remains, seedtime and harvest, and cold and heat, and winter and summer, and day and night shall not cease (Genesis 8:22).

3.   **Third Principle:**   **The size of the harvest is determined by the amount of seed that is planted.**

But this I say: He who sows sparingly will also reap sparingly, and he who sows bountifully will also reap bountifully (II Corinthians 9:6).

Give, and it will be given to you: good measure, pressed down, shaken together, and running over will be put into your bosom. For with the same measure that you use, it will be measured back to you (Luke 6:38).

4.   **Fourth Principle:**   **Seed that is planted will produce the specific harvest for which it was planted.**

So let each one give as he purposes in his heart, not grudgingly or of necessity; for God loves a cheerful giver (II Corinthians 9:7).

B.   **The stewardship of our resources will be impacted by not only our obedience, but by our disobedience.**

1.   **Obedience to the instructions of God's Word will bring prosperity into our lives.**

This Book of the Law shall not depart from your mouth, but you shall meditate in it day and night, that you may observe to do according to all that is written in it. For then you will make your way prosperous, and then you will have good success (Joshua 1:8).

Honor the Lord with your possessions, and with the firstfruits of all your increase; so your barns will be filled with plenty, and your vats will overflow with new wine (Proverbs 3:9-10).

2.   **Disobedience to the instructions of God's Word will bring a curse into our lives.**

It shall come to pass, if you do not obey the voice of the Lord your God, to observe carefully all His commandments and His statutes which I command you today, that all these curses will come upon you and overtake you (Deuteronomy 28:15).

V. Prosperity and the Heart of God.

A. Prosperity should not be defined as the accumulation of money or things. Prosperity means you have enough resources to accomplish your purpose and assignment given to you by God.

And God is able to make all grace abound toward you, that you, always having all sufficiency in all things, have an abundance for every good work. As it is written: "He has dispersed abroad, He has given to the poor; His righteousness endures forever." Now may He who supplies seed to the sower, and bread for food, supply and multiply the seed you have sown and increase the fruits of your righteousness, while you are enriched in everything for all liberality, which causes thanksgiving through us to God (II Corinthians 9:8-11).

B. Jesus promised a hundred-fold return when we give sacrificially.

Then Peter began to say to Him, "See, we have left all and followed You." So Jesus answered and said, "Assuredly, I say to you, there is no one who has left house or brothers or sisters or father or mother or wife or children or lands, for My sake and the gospel's, who shall not receive a hundredfold now in this time—houses and brothers and sisters and mothers and children and lands, with persecutions—and in the age to come, eternal life" (Mark 10:28-30).

C. Jesus taught that we should expect a harvest on every seed that we sow.

Ask, and it will be given to you; seek, and you will find; knock, and it will be opened to you. For everyone who asks receives, and he who seeks finds, and to him who knocks it will be opened (Matthew 7:7-8).

Give, and it will be given to you: good measure, pressed down, shaken together, and running over will be put into your bosom. For with the same measure that you use, it will be measured back to you (Luke 6:38).

D. We can securely rest in the fact that the heart of God is pleased when we prosper.

Let them shout for joy and be glad, who favor my righteous cause; and let them say continually, "Let the Lord be magnified, Who has pleasure in the prosperity of His servant" (Psalm 35:27).

Beloved, I pray that you may prosper in all things and be in health, just as your soul prospers (III John 2).

E. There are several reasons that God wants His people to prosper and have more than enough.

1. God wants us to have more than enough finances to pay our taxes and meet all of our obligations.

Render therefore to Caesar the things that are Caesar's, and to God the things that are God's (Matthew 22:21).

2. God wants us to have more than enough finances to return the tithe back to His house, the church.

And all the tithe of the land, whether of the seed of the land or of the fruit of the tree, is the Lord's. It is holy to the Lord (Leviticus 27:30).

"Bring all the tithes into the storehouse, that there may be food in My house, and prove Me now in this," says the Lord of hosts, "If I will not open for you the windows of heaven and pour out for you such blessing that there will not be room enough to receive it" (Malachi 3:10).

3. God wants us to have more than enough finances to provide for the ministries that have touched us.

Let the elders who rule well be counted worthy of double honor, especially those who labor in the word and doctrine. For the Scripture says, "You shall not muzzle an ox while it treads out the grain," and, "The laborer is worthy of his wages" (I Timothy 5:17-18).

4. God wants us to have more than enough finances to help meet the needs of the poor.

He who has pity on the poor lends to the Lord, and He will pay back what he has given (Proverbs 19:17).

5. God wants us to have more than enough finances to help spread the gospel around the world.

And how shall they preach unless they are sent? As it is written: "How beautiful are the feet of those who preach the gospel of peace, who bring glad tidings of good things" (Romans 10:15)!

Chapter Thirteen

Discovering Your Life's Purpose

I. The Transferable Ministry of Jesus.

A. The ministry of Jesus encompassed four predominant areas:

    1. The first emphasis in the ministry of Jesus was to demonstrate God's love for all of mankind;

        a. Jesus taught people of God's unfailing love for them.

        b. Jesus confirmed God's love through the miracles He performed on their behalf.

        c. Jesus changed the quality of the lives of people through His miracle ministry; and in doing so, He changed their hearts as well.

"The Spirit of the Lord is upon Me, because He has anointed Me to preach the gospel to the poor; He has sent Me to heal the brokenhearted, to preach deliverance to the captives and recovery of sight to the blind, to set at liberty those who are oppressed; to preach the acceptable year of the Lord." Then He closed the book, and gave it back to the attendant and sat down. And the eyes of all who were in the synagogue were fixed on Him. And He began to say to them, "Today this Scripture is fulfilled in your hearing" (Luke 4:18-21).

    2. The second emphasis in the ministry of Jesus was to reveal the Father to all of mankind;

        a. Man lost his understanding of the loving nature of God, and His desire for fellowship with man, as a result of his sin in the Garden of Eden.

        b. Man's confidence in a loving relationship with God was soon replaced with a fear of God.

c. **Jesus modeled the loving and compassionate nature of God in an attempt to restore man's knowledge of God and to remove man's fear of God.**

All things have been delivered to Me by My Father, and no one knows the Son except the Father. Nor does anyone know the Father except the Son, and he to whom the Son wills to reveal Him (Matthew 11:27).

"If you had known Me, you would have known My Father also; and from now on you know Him and have seen Him." Philip said to Him, "Lord, show us the Father, and it is sufficient for us." Jesus said to him, "Have I been with you so long, and yet you have not known Me, Philip? He who has seen Me has seen the Father; so how can you say, 'Show us the Father'" (John 14:7-9)?

3. **The third emphasis in the ministry of Jesus was to do the will of His Father;**

a. **Jesus only spoke and acted on the instructions of His Father.**

b. **Jesus clearly revealed the will of God to men through His words and by His actions.**

For I have come down from heaven, not to do My own will, but the will of Him who sent Me (John 6:38).

Then Jesus answered and said to them, "Most assuredly, I say to you, the Son can do nothing of Himself, but what He sees the Father do; for whatever He does, the Son also does in like manner. For the Father loves the Son, and shows Him all things that He Himself does; and He will show Him greater works than these, that you may marvel. For as the Father raises the dead and gives life to them, even so the Son gives life to whom He will. For the Father judges no one, but has committed all judgment to the Son, that all should honor the Son just as they honor the Father. He who does not honor the Son does not honor the Father who sent Him" (John 5:19-23).

4. The fourth emphasis in the ministry of Jesus was to redeem all that was lost to the redemptive plan of God.

   a. As a result of sin the plan of God was spoiled in the Garden of Eden.

   b. As a result of sin man lost his intimate relationship with a God who had created him for fellowship.

   c. As a result of sin man died spiritually and from that point on, he also began to die physically.

   d. As a result of sin man lost his ability to effectively rule over the circumstances of his life. He also lost the ability to rule over the natural environment that he was entrusted with.

   e. As a result of sin man lost his dignity, his confidence, and his sense of self-worth. Man now lived under the burden of guilt, shame, and condemnation.

   f. Jesus came to recover all that had been lost in the Garden of Eden because of man's sin. He came to restore man to the original plan of God.

   For the Son of Man has come to seek and to save that which was lost (Luke 19:10).

B. Jesus intends for His ministry to continue today through the church. Therefore, He has transferred charge of His ministry to every faithful believer who has chosen to follow Him.

1. **Jesus has sent us out to minister life in His name, just as His Father in heaven sent Him to minister life to us.**

So Jesus said to them again, "Peace to you! As the Father has sent Me, I also send you" (John 20:21).

2. **Jesus gave the Great Commission to His followers; wherein, He charged to them to take His message of love to the nations.**

   a. **First, we are to make new converts of the people with whom we share the news of God's love.**

   b. **Secondly, we are to teach these new converts about the love of God and how to obey the disciplines of His doctrines.**

And Jesus came and spoke to them, saying, "All authority has been given to Me in heaven and on earth. Go therefore and make disciples of all the nations, baptizing them in the name of the Father and of the Son and of the Holy Spirit, teaching them to observe all things that I have commanded you; and lo, I am with you always, even to the end of the age (Matthew 28:18-20).

3. **When we make a choice to follow Jesus and make Him Lord of our lives, He promises that He will use us as His messengers to win souls to His kingdom.**

And He said to them, "Follow Me, and I will make you fishers of men" (Matthew 4:19).

4. **God looks on any Christian who wins souls as being wise.**

The fruit of the righteous is a tree of life, and he who wins souls is wise (Proverbs 11:30).

5. **Jesus taught, that in order for us to be effective witnesses for Him, we need the power and help of the Holy Spirit.**

But you shall receive power when the Holy Spirit has come upon you; and you shall be witnesses to Me in Jerusalem, and in all Judea and Samaria, and to the end of the earth (Acts 1:8).

Then He said to them, "Thus it is written, and thus it was necessary for the Christ to suffer and to rise from the dead the third day, and that repentance and remission of sins should be preached in His name to all nations, beginning at Jerusalem. And you are witnesses of these things. Behold, I send the Promise of My Father upon you; but tarry in the city of Jerusalem until you are endued with power from on high" (Luke 24:46-49).

6. **Jesus promises to confirm our witness with miraculous signs and wonders as we share our faith with others.**

And these signs will follow those who believe: in My name they will cast out demons; they will speak with new tongues; they will take up serpents; and if they drink anything deadly, it will by no means hurt them; they will lay hands on the sick, and they will recover (Mark 16:17-18).

7. **Jesus has given to everyone, who has confessed Him as Lord, the ministry of reconciliation. We are to help restore people to a right relationship with God.**

Now all things are of God, who has reconciled us to Himself through Jesus Christ, and has given us the ministry of reconciliation, that is, that God was in Christ reconciling the world to Himself, not imputing their trespasses to them, and has committed to us the word of reconciliation. Therefore, we are ambassadors for Christ, as though God were pleading through us: we implore you on Christ's behalf, be reconciled to God (II Corinthians 5:18-20).

II. Convictions That Motivate Soul-Winning.

A. We must be absolutely convinced about certain things in order to effectively share our faith with those around us. Without these convictions, it is doubtful that we will share our faith with anyone, much less, be effective.

   1. We must believe that every man is lost apart from a personal faith in Jesus Christ. Jesus is the only hope of escaping a literal place called "hell," and gaining a literal eternal home called "heaven."

   For all have sinned and fall short of the glory of God (Romans 3:23).

   For the wages of sin is death, but the gift of God is eternal life in Christ Jesus our Lord (Romans 6:23).

   He who believes in the Son has everlasting life; and he who does not believe the Son shall not see life, but the wrath of God abides on him (John 3:36).

   And do not fear those who kill the body but cannot kill the soul. But rather fear Him who is able to destroy both soul and body in hell (Matthew 10:28).

   In My Father's house are many mansions; if it were not so, I would have told you. I go to prepare a place for you (John 14:2).

   Jesus said to him, "I am the way, the truth, and the life. No one comes to the Father except through Me" (John 14:6).

   2. We must believe that no one can be totally fulfilled in life, or live in heaven for eternity, apart from having a personal relationship with Jesus Christ.

   For what is a man profited if he gains the whole world, and loses his own soul? Or what will a man give in exchange for his soul (Matthew 16:26)?

   These things I have spoken to you, that My joy may remain in you, and that your joy may be full (John 15:11).

230

3. **We must believe that the invitation to receive salvation is available to everyone who asks and is willing to accept the Lord's terms for relationship.**

For the Scripture says, "Whoever believes on Him will not be put to shame." For there is no distinction between Jew and Greek, for the same Lord over all is rich to all who call upon Him. For "whoever calls on the name of the Lord shall be saved" (Romans 10:11-13).

Therefore whoever confesses Me before men, him I will also confess before My Father who is in heaven. But whoever denies Me before men, him I will also deny before My Father who is in heaven (Matthew 10:32-33).

And the Spirit and the bride say, "Come!" And let him who hears say, "Come!" And let him who thirsts come. And whoever desires, let him take the water of life freely (Revelation 22:17).

B. **There are two common misconceptions about witnessing to others that keep many Christians from sharing their faith.**

1. **The first misconception is that before we share our faith with another, we need to wait for a special instruction or a special leading from the Lord.**

    a. **We don't need to wait for a special instruction; we have already been given a special instruction from the Word of God. We are expected to share the knowledge of our faith with others who do not know about Him.**

    Go therefore and make disciples of all the nations, baptizing them in the name of the Father and of the Son and of the Holy Spirit, teaching them to observe all things that I have commanded you; and lo, I am with you always, even to the end of the age. Amen (Matthew 28:19-20).

b. We don't need to wait for a special burden to touch our hearts before we share our faith. All we need to do is look around us and we will see many who are burdened with the cares of life and they need to know about the liberating love of Jesus.

The Lord God has given Me the tongue of the learned, that I should know how to speak a word in season to him who is weary. He awakens Me morning by morning, He awakens My ear to hear as the learned (Isaiah 50:4).

2. The second misconception is that we need to be sure that it is the Lord who is leading us to share our faith with someone, and not the devil trying to influence us.

   a. We need to realize that the devil will never inspire us, or instruct us to share our faith with anyone. It is far too dangerous to his agenda ... they might believe what they hear and get saved.

   b. We need to remember that as we begin each day by surrendering our hearts to the Lord, and ask for His leadership and direction, that He promises to direct our steps.

   c. We need to realize that when the Lord is the one who is directing our steps, He will lead us to people, and lead people to us, so He can reach out to them with His unfailing love.

The steps of a good man are ordered by the Lord, and He delights in his way (Psalm 37:23).

C. When we make the commitment to share our faith, the Lord will not only lead us to people, but He will also help us in three important areas:

232

1. **First, God will give us the unique ability to speak on His behalf. He will enable us to speak with authority as though we had been specifically trained;**

The Lord God has given Me the tongue of the learned, that I should know how to speak a word in season to him who is weary. He awakens Me morning by morning, He awakens My ear to hear as the learned (Isaiah 50:4).

2. **Secondly, God will tell us the words He wants us to speak in each circumstance. Literally, the Holy Spirit will give us the words He wants spoken through us;**

And I have put My words in your mouth; I have covered you with the shadow of My hand (Isaiah 51:16).

But when they deliver you up, do not worry about how or what you should speak. For it will be given to you in that hour what you should speak; for it is not you who speak, but the Spirit of your Father who speaks in you (Matthew 10:19-20).

3. **Thirdly, God will make sure that the season or, in other words, the timing, is right for us to share our faith with the one we have chosen to speak with concerning Christ and His redemptive love for them.**

The Lord God has given Me the tongue of the learned, that I should know how to speak a word in season to him who is weary. He awakens Me morning by morning, He awakens My ear to hear as the learned (Isaiah 50:4).

My times are in Your hand (Psalm 31:15).

A man has joy by the answer of his mouth, and a word spoken in due season, how good it is (Proverbs 15:23)!

To everything there is a season, a time for every purpose under heaven. (Ecclesiastes 3:1).

A time to keep silence, and a time to speak (Ecclesiastes 3:7).

III. The Scope of Our Witness for Christ.

A. Just before Jesus ascended back into heaven, He told His disciples that their witness on His behalf was to reach into three areas or regions of life.

But you shall receive power when the Holy Spirit has come upon you; and you shall be witnesses to Me in Jerusalem, and in all Judea and Samaria, and to the end of the earth (Acts 1:8).

1. The first area where we are to share our witness for Christ is to our "Jerusalem."

   a. Our "Jerusalem" is comprised of people who are the closest to us, including those who habitually cross our paths; our family, friends, neighbors, and co-workers.

   b. We are to simply tell what Jesus has done for us and that He will do the same for them.

   Now the man from whom the demons had departed begged Him that he might be with Him. But Jesus sent him away, saying, "Return to your own house, and tell what great things God has done for you." And he went his way and proclaimed throughout the whole city what great things Jesus had done for him (Luke 8:38-39).

   c. We need to be prepared to share our faith in Christ as the opportunity presents itself to us.

   But sanctify the Lord God in your hearts, and always be ready to give a defense to everyone who asks you a reason for the hope that is in you, with meekness and fear (I Peter 3:15).

   d. We will share our faith once we internalize that it is not God's desire for anyone, who falls in the category of our "Jerusalem," to miss heaven and spend eternity in hell.

234

The Lord is not slack concerning His promise, as some count slackness, but is longsuffering toward us, not willing that any should perish but that all should come to repentance (II Peter 3:9).

2. **The second area where we are to share our witness for Christ is to the nearby "Judea and Samaria."**

    a. **Our "Judea and Samaria" is comprised of those who are close to us, but who are culturally, socially, or economically different.**

    b. **When we realize that all people share the same spiritual needs as we have, it will motivate us to reach beyond our comfort zone and share Christ's love with them.**

    To the weak I became as weak, that I might win the weak. I have become all things to all men, that I might by all means save some (I Corinthians 9:22).

    c. **We are called to bear each others burdens, including those within our "Judea and Samaria." However, we cannot bear another's burden if our hand is never extended.**

    Bear one another's burdens, and so fulfill the law of Christ (Galatians 6:2).

    d. **The law of Christ's love is to be the compelling force that causes us to reach out and love others near to us.**

    "Honor your father and your mother," and "You shall love your neighbor as yourself" (Matthew 19:19).

    e. **The evidence that we love Jesus will be seen in how we reach out and share Christ's love.**

    Pure and undefiled religion before God and the Father is this: to visit orphans and widows in their trouble, and to keep oneself unspotted from the world (James 1:27).

f. **Jesus told us that He will one day measure the quality of our confessed love for Him by what we have done for others who are in need.**

For I was hungry and you gave Me food; I was thirsty and you gave Me drink; I was a stranger and you took Me in; I was naked and you clothed Me; I was sick and you visited Me; I was in prison and you came to Me
(Matthew 25:35-36).

g. **Jesus promised to abundantly bless anyone who willingly serves Him and He will reward their sacrifice.**

So Jesus answered and said, "Assuredly, I say to you, there is no one who has left house or brothers or sisters or father or mother or wife or children or lands, for My sake and the gospel's, who shall not receive a hundredfold now in this time—houses and brothers and sisters and mothers and children and lands, with persecutions—and in the age to come, eternal life (Mark 10:29-30).

3. **The third area where we are to share our witness for Christ is to the "ends of the earth."**

a. **The "ends of the earth" means ... the people of the whole world.**

b. **Jesus commissioned His faithful followers to take His story of love; grace; and salvation; to the whole world. Just as Jesus commissioned them, we are to take the news to the nations.**

For God so loved the world that He gave His only begotten Son, that whoever believes in Him should not perish but have everlasting life. For God did not send His Son into the world to condemn the world, but that the world through Him might be saved (John 3:16-17).

And He said to them, "Go into all the world and preach the gospel to every creature" (Mark 16:15).

IV. The Soul-Winners Tools.

A. **Our first and most effective tool for winning souls to Christ is our personal testimony.**

   1. **People can argue the finer points of theology and doctrine with us, but no one can argue about the tremendous difference that Jesus has made in our lives. We can assure them that He desires to do the same for them.**

   2. **We must be sincere in sharing our faith. We must remember that the goal in soul-winning is to make a difference in people's lives.**

   Now it happened in Iconium that they went together to the synagogue of the Jews, and so spoke that a great multitude both of the Jews and of the Greeks believed. But the unbelieving Jews stirred up the Gentiles and poisoned their minds against the brethren. Therefore they stayed there a long time, speaking boldly in the Lord, who was bearing witness to the word of His grace, granting signs and wonders to be done by their hands (Acts 14:1-3).

B. **We need to learn how to use the Scriptures to lead someone to a saving knowledge of Jesus. One collection of Scriptures that is often used is comprised of six basic steps and is called the "Roman Road to Salvation."**

   1. Step One: **Even with our best efforts to achieve righteousness (to be in right standing with God), we will never be good enough to measure up to God's standard of righteousness.**

   As it is written: "There is none righteous, no, not one; There is none who understands; There is none who seeks after God. They have all gone out of the way; They have together become unprofitable; There is none who does good, no, not one" (Romans 3:10-12).

2. **Step Two: We have all been born with a sin nature that is in direct opposition to God and separates us from Him.**

For all have sinned and fall short of the glory of God (Romans 3:23).

Therefore, just as through one man sin entered the world, and death through sin, and thus death spread to all men, because all sinned (Romans 5:12).

3. **Step Three: The penalty for sin is to spiritually die and be eternally separated from God in a place called Hell. However, God offers the gift of eternal life to all who will place their faith in Jesus.**

For the wages of sin is death, but the gift of God is eternal life in Christ Jesus our Lord (Romans 6:23).

4. **Step Four: God loves us so much that He sent His only Son, Jesus, to die on the cross to pay our sin penalty in full.**

But God demonstrates His own love toward us, in that while we were still sinners, Christ died for us (Romans 5:8).

5. **Step Five: We are saved by faith. Faith is the declaration of what we believe. If we believe in our heart, and confess with our mouth, that Jesus Christ is the only Son of God; He died on the cross for our sins; He was buried; He was raised from the dead; and He is alive in heaven today ... we will be saved.**

But what does it say? "The word is near you, in your mouth and in your heart" (that is, the word of faith which we preach): that if you confess with your mouth the Lord Jesus and believe in your heart that God has raised Him from the dead, you will be saved. For with the heart one believes unto righteousness and with the mouth confession is made unto salvation (Romans 10:8-10).

6. **Step Six:** **Anyone who chooses to believe in Jesus Christ, and by faith ask Him to forgive them of their sins and give them His free gift of eternal life ... will be saved.**

For "whoever calls on the name of the Lord shall be saved" (Romans 10:13).

C. Here is a simple prayer that can be used to help lead someone to Christ:

"Lord Jesus, I believe that You are the Son of God, and that You died on the cross to pay my sin penalty. I believe that You were buried and that God raised You from the dead on the third day. I acknowledge that I am a sinner and that I cannot save myself. I humbly ask You to forgive me of my sins and save me. I now invite You to live forever in my heart and to rule over my life from the throne of my heart. I gratefully receive Your gift of eternal life; and in return, I pledge to love and serve You for the rest of my life. Amen."

Chapter Fourteen

How to Be Led By the Spirit of God

I. The Holy Spirit Desires to Lead Us.

A. **The first truth that must be established in order to be led by the Holy Spirit is that God attempts to speak to us each day.**

Therefore, as the Holy Spirit says: "Today, if you will hear His voice, do not harden your hearts as in the rebellion, in the day of trial in the wilderness" (Hebrews 3:7-8).

B. **God desires to guide and instruct us regarding every step we take and every decision we make in life.**

Receive, please, instruction from His mouth, and lay up His words in your heart (Job 22:22).

I will instruct you and teach you in the way you should go; I will guide you with My eye (Psalm 32:8).

Your ears shall hear a word behind you, saying, "This is the way, walk in it," whenever you turn to the right hand or whenever you turn to the left (Isaiah 30:21).

C. **The Lord's voice is distinguishable from all other voices that we may hear. However, we must train ourselves to discern His voice.**

Most assuredly, I say to you, he who does not enter the sheepfold by the door, but climbs up some other way, the same is a thief and a robber. But he who enters by the door is the shepherd of the sheep. To him the doorkeeper opens, and the sheep hear his voice; and he calls his own sheep by name and leads them out. And when he brings out his own sheep, he goes before them; and the sheep follow him, for they know his voice. Yet they will by no means follow a stranger, but will flee from him, for they do not know the voice of strangers (John 10:1-5).

D. **God speaks to us today through the revelation of His Son, Jesus. When He speaks, our understanding is enlightened through the work of the Holy Spirit who resides within us.**

God, who at various times and in various ways spoke in time past to the fathers by the prophets, has in these last days spoken to us by His Son, whom He has appointed heir of all things, through whom also He made the worlds (Hebrews 1:1-2).

But as it is written: "Eye has not seen, nor ear heard, nor have entered into the heart of man the things which God has prepared for those who love Him." But God has revealed them to us through His Spirit. For the Spirit searches all things, yes, the deep things of God. For what man knows the things of a man except the spirit of the man which is in him? Even so no one knows the things of God except the Spirit of God. Now we have received, not the spirit of the world, but the Spirit who is from God, that we might know the things that have been freely given to us by God (I Corinthians 2:9-12).

E.   **If we are to be successfully led by the Holy Spirit, we must trust Him in every decision we make and in every step we take.**

1.   **The Holy Spirit is the source of all knowledge. He promises to impart His wisdom for our daily decisions.**

Trust in the Lord with all your heart, and lean not on your own understanding; in all your ways acknowledge Him, and He shall direct your paths (Proverbs 3:5-6).

You will show me the path of life; in Your presence is fullness of joy; at Your right hand are pleasures forevermore (Psalm 16:11).

The steps of a good man are ordered by the Lord, and He delights in his way (Psalm 37:23).

For as many as are led by the Spirit of God, these are sons of God (Romans 8:14).

2.   **The Holy Spirit promises to liberally give answers to our requests. However, we are required to ask in faith, without doubting, if we are to receive answers from Him.**

244

If any of you lacks wisdom, let him ask of God, who gives to all liberally and without reproach, and it will be given to him. But let him ask in faith, with no doubting, for he who doubts is like a wave of the sea driven and tossed by the wind. For let not that man suppose that he will receive anything from the Lord; he is a double-minded man, unstable in all his ways (James 1:5-8).

F. We can easily make wrong decisions if we are not firmly convinced that the only source of leadership we can trust is the Spirit of God. We must understand that God will guide us through our spirit; not through our five senses, our emotions, or our intellect.

The spirit of a man is the lamp of the Lord, searching all the inner depths of his heart (Proverbs 20:27).

The Spirit Himself bears witness with our spirit that we are children of God (Romans 8:16).

G. Man is a tri-unity: he is a spirit; that lives in a body; and has a mind.

Now may the God of peace Himself sanctify you completely; and may your whole spirit, soul, and body be preserved blameless at the coming of our Lord Jesus Christ (I Thessalonians 5:23).

1. When we make the decision to come to Christ and confess Him as our Savior and Lord, we are born again. This new birth occurs in our spirit, not in our body.

Jesus answered and said to him, "Most assuredly, I say to you, unless one is born again, he cannot see the kingdom of God." Nicodemus said to Him, "How can a man be born when he is old? Can he enter a second time into his mother's womb and be born?" Jesus answered, "Most assuredly, I say to you, unless one is born of water and the Spirit, he cannot enter the kingdom of God. That which is born of the flesh is flesh, and that which is born of the Spirit is spirit" (John 3:3-6).

2. The words "heart" and "spirit" are often interchangeable in the Scripture; in other words, the heart of a man is the same as the spirit of a man.

3. The only trustworthy source from which to receive guidance is from the Lord.

   a. We can trust His guidance as we allow Him to daily renew our spirit by His power.

   b. We cannot trust our mind alone. Our mind weakens over time and our bodies grow older with each passing day.

Therefore we do not lose heart. Even though our outward man is perishing, yet the inward man is being renewed day by day (II Corinthians 4:16).

H. Our soul, spirit, and body are separate entities which are distinguishable from each other. The Word tells us we are responsible to bring each of them into subjection to the Word of God.

For the word of God is living and powerful, and sharper than any two-edged sword, piercing even to the division of soul and spirit, and of joints and marrow, and is a discerner of the thoughts and intents of the heart (Hebrews 4:12).

1. The body is the source by which we contact the physical realm of our life.

2. The soul is the source by which we contact the intellectual realm of our life. The soul is comprised of the intellect, the will, and the emotions.

3. The spirit is the source by which we contact the spiritual realm of our life.

II. Leadership in the Old Testament.

A. **In the Old Testament we find that there were two ways that the Holy Spirit led people to seek Him for direction and to do His will.**

1. **The first way was through the act of fleecing God. Fleecing was a specific request used to receive an answer to a question or to receive direction. The act of fleecing God is clearly seen in the Old Testament story of Gideon.**

    So Gideon said to God, "If You will save Israel by my hand as You have said— look, I shall put a fleece of wool on the threshing floor; if there is dew on the fleece only, and it is dry on all the ground, then I shall know that You will save Israel by my hand, as You have said." And it was so. When he rose early the next morning and squeezed the fleece together, he wrung the dew out of the fleece, a bowl full of water. Then Gideon said to God, "Do not be angry with me, but let me speak just once more: Let me test, I pray, just once more with the fleece; let it now be dry only on the fleece, but on all the ground let there be dew." And God did so that night. It was dry on the fleece only, but there was dew on all the ground (Judges 6:36-40).*

    a. **Fleecing God, or asking for direction through a sign, carries a great risk. The Word reveals to us that the devil can duplicate the sign requested; thereby, we can receive a false sense of direction.**

    b. **The duplication of signs is clearly seen in the story of Moses and his confrontation with Pharaoh. Moses performed various signs and wonders to convince Pharaoh to let the Israelites go. However, Pharaoh's magicians duplicated each of the signs which further hardened the heart of Pharaoh.**

Then the Lord spoke to Moses and Aaron, saying, "When Pharaoh speaks to you, saying, 'Show a miracle for yourselves,' then you shall say to Aaron, 'Take your rod and cast it before Pharaoh, and let it become a serpent.'" So Moses and Aaron went in to Pharaoh, and they did so, just as the Lord commanded. And Aaron cast down his rod before Pharaoh and before his servants, and it became a serpent. But Pharaoh also called the wise men and the sorcerers; so the magicians of Egypt, they also did in like manner with their enchantments. For every man threw down his rod, and they became serpents. But Aaron's rod swallowed up their rods. And Pharaoh's heart grew hard, and he did not heed them, as the Lord had said (Exodus 7:8-13).

2. **The second way they received guidance from the Holy Spirit was through the voice of the prophets.**

    a. **God used the prophets as the primary means by which He would give direction to His people. He warned them of future judgment if they did not repent of their evil ways.**

    And they rose early in the morning and went out into the Wilderness of Tekoa; and as they went out, Jehoshaphat stood and said, "Hear me, O Judah and you inhabitants of Jerusalem: Believe in the Lord your God, and you shall be established; believe His prophets, and you shall prosper" (II Chronicles 20:20).

    And the Lord God of their fathers sent warnings to them by His messengers, rising up early and sending them, because He had compassion on His people and on His dwelling place. But they mocked the messengers of God, despised His words, and scoffed at His prophets, until the wrath of the Lord arose against His people, till there was no remedy (II Chronicles 36:15-16).

    b. **The voice of the Holy Spirit was not accessible to everyone like it is today; only the prophets of God and a few of the kings enjoyed this privilege.**

III. Leadership in the New Testament.

A. Today, because we live in the New Testament economy, we don't need to place a fleece before the Lord or seek out the words of a prophet in order to gain God's direction and leadership for our lives.

    1. In the New Testament economy we are to be led by the Holy Spirit.

For as many as are led by the Spirit of God, these are sons of God (Romans 8:14).

    2. Every believer has the Holy Spirit living within their hearts and He will reveal the will of God on a daily basis if we ask Him.

But God has revealed them to us through His Spirit. For the Spirit searches all things, yes, the deep things of God. For what man knows the things of a man except the spirit of the man which is in him? Even so no one knows the things of God except the Spirit of God. Now we have received, not the spirit of the world, but the Spirit who is from God, that we might know the things that have been freely given to us by God (I Corinthians 2:10-12).

B. The Holy Spirit will lead us through an "inward witness."

    1. When God's answer to our request is "no," or if we are headed in the wrong direction, God will give us a "check" in our spirits, much like a red light that governs traffic.

Now when much time had been spent, and sailing was now dangerous because the Fast was already over, Paul advised them, saying, "Men, I perceive that this voyage will end with disaster and much loss, not only of the cargo and ship, but also our lives" (Acts 27:9-10).

a.   When we ignore the "check" in our spirit, not only have we disobeyed God, but we have opened ourselves to Satan's agenda.

b.   We must believe that God knows what we do not know and that He always has our best interest at heart.

For I know the thoughts that I think toward you, says the Lord, thoughts of peace and not of evil, to give you a future and a hope (Jeremiah 29:11).

c.   There are times when an earthly parent must say "no" to their children out of love and a desire to protect them. So also, God must sometimes say "no" to us, His children, to express His love for us and protect us.

d.   We need to recognize that God's restrictions are not given to limit us, but they are given to liberate us for God's intended best.

For to be carnally minded is death, but to be spiritually minded is life and peace (Romans 8:6).

For if you live according to the flesh you will die; but if by the Spirit you put to death the deeds of the body, you will live (Romans 8:13).

2.   When God's answer is "yes," He will confirm His answer by giving peace to our spirit.

a.   Our intellect won't always understand God's ways or be willing to embrace His terms.

"For My thoughts are not your thoughts, nor are your ways My ways," says the Lord. "For as the heavens are higher than the earth, so are My ways higher than your ways, and My thoughts than your thoughts" (Isaiah 55:8-9).

b.   However, if we trust the Lord and yield to His leadership, the favor of God will rest on us.

Now therefore, listen to me, my children, for blessed are those who keep my ways. Hear instruction and be wise, and do not disdain it. Blessed is the man who listens to me, watching daily at my gates, waiting at the posts of my doors. For whoever finds me finds life, and obtains favor from the Lord (Proverbs 8:32-35).

C. **The Holy Spirit will lead us through an "inward voice."**

    1. **The "inward voice" is the voice of our spirits.**

        a. **Some refer to this voice as the "still, small voice of our hearts."**

        b. **Others refer to it as the voice of "conscience."**

I tell the truth in Christ, I am not lying, my conscience also bearing me witness in the Holy Spirit (Romans 9:1).

Then Paul, looking earnestly at the council, said, "Men and brethren, I have lived in all good conscience before God until this day" (Acts 23:1).

For You will light my lamp; the Lord my God will enlighten my darkness (Psalm 18:28).

    2. **We need to daily confess that the life of God that resides in our spirit dominates us; therefore, we purpose to walk in the light of His life.**

In Him was life, and the life was the light of men (John 1:4).

These things I have written to you who believe in the name of the Son of God, that you may know that you have eternal life, and that you may continue to believe in the name of the Son of God (I John 5:13).

    3. **God dwells within our spirit by the Holy Spirit and He communicates His direction for us through our spirit. It is very important to discern the difference between the voices that seek to guide our life.**

a.   The voice of our body is our "feelings."

b.   The voice of our soul is our "logic."

c.   The voice of our spirit is our "conscience."

However, when He, the Spirit of truth, has come, He will guide you into all truth; for He will not speak on His own authority, but whatever He hears He will speak; and He will tell you things to come. He will glorify Me, for He will take of what is Mine and declare it to you. All things that the Father has are Mine. Therefore I said that He will take of Mine and declare it to you (John 16:13-15).

And what agreement has the temple of God with idols? For you are the temple of the living God. As God has said: "I will dwell in them and walk among them. I will be their God, and they shall be My people" (II Corinthians 6:16).

Do you not know that you are the temple of God and that the Spirit of God dwells in you (I Corinthians 3:16)?

4.   It is imperative that we keep our heart (spirit) tender towards the directives of the Holy Spirit.

Keep your heart with all diligence, for out of it spring the issues of life (Proverbs 4:23).

a.   Sin will sear our conscience and harden our heart towards the things of God.

Now the Spirit expressly says that in latter times some will depart from the faith, giving heed to deceiving spirits and doctrines of demons, speaking lies in hypocrisy, having their own conscience seared with a hot iron (I Timothy 4:1-2).

But when his heart was lifted up, and his spirit was hardened in pride, he was deposed from his kingly throne, and they took his glory from him (Daniel 5:20).

b.   However, if our heart is pure and does not condemn us, then we can be assured that we are being led by the Spirit.

252

For if our heart condemns us, God is greater than our heart, and knows all things. Beloved, if our heart does not condemn us, we have confidence toward God. And whatever we ask we receive from Him, because we keep His commandments and do those things that are pleasing in His sight (I John 3:20-22).

D. The Holy Spirit will also lead us by directly speaking to us in His own voice.

Your ears shall hear a word behind you, saying, "This is the way, walk in it," whenever you turn to the right hand or whenever you turn to the left (Isaiah 30:21).

While Peter thought about the vision, the Spirit said to him, "Behold, three men are seeking you. Arise therefore, go down and go with them, doubting nothing; for I have sent them" (Acts 10:19-20).

1. All guidance that we receive must be judged by the Word of God. Remember, God will not circumvent His Word when giving you direction.

Do not quench the Spirit. Do not despise prophecies. Test all things; hold fast what is good (I Thessalonians 5:19-21).

Your word I have hidden in my heart, that I might not sin against You (Psalm 119:11).

Your word is a lamp to my feet and a light to my path (Psalm 119:105).

2. We are not to build our lives on anything but the Word: this includes any personal prophecies that we receive regardless of the person's sincerity.

Test all things; hold fast what is good (I Thessalonians 5:21).

a. A personal prophecy will only confirm what God has spoken to our hearts; if it doesn't, we are not to receive it as being from the Lord.

b. However, we must be careful to judge the prophecy, not the person who gives it to us.

IV. The Holy Spirit will Train Our Spirit.

A. We must develop our spirit; our soul; and our body; to be receptive to the leadership of the Holy Spirit.

    1. Our spirit will be developed when we fellowship with the Holy Spirit through prayer. This can be accomplished by allowing Him to assist us in prayer. We will become sensitive to His voice when we allow Him to pray through us.

Likewise the Spirit also helps in our weaknesses. For we do not know what we should pray for as we ought, but the Spirit Himself makes intercession for us with groanings which cannot be uttered. Now He who searches the hearts knows what the mind of the Spirit is, because He makes intercession for the saints according to the will of God (Romans 8:26-27).

    2. Our soul will be developed by the renewing of our mind. We will learn to think like God thinks when we spend time studying His Word.

And do not be conformed to this world, but be transformed by the renewing of your mind, that you may prove what is that good and acceptable and perfect will of God (Romans 12:2).

He restores my soul; He leads me in the paths of righteousness for His name's sake (Psalm 23:3).

Let this mind be in you which was also in Christ Jesus (Philippians 2:5).

    3. Our body will be spiritually developed by refusing to yield to our carnal desires and appetites. We must learn to bring our carnal nature under subjection to the Word of God.

I beseech you therefore, brethren, by the mercies of God, that you present your bodies a living sacrifice, holy, acceptable to God, which is your reasonable service. And do not be conformed to this world, but be transformed by the renewing of your mind, that you may prove what is that good and acceptable and perfect will of God (Romans 12:1-2).

254

But I discipline my body and bring it into subjection, lest, when I have preached to others, I myself should become disqualified (I Corinthians 9:27).

Likewise you also, reckon yourselves to be dead indeed to sin, but alive to God in Christ Jesus our Lord. Therefore do not let sin reign in your mortal body, that you should obey it in its lusts. And do not present your members as instruments of unrighteousness to sin, but present yourselves to God as being alive from the dead, and your members as instruments of righteousness to God. For sin shall not have dominion over you, for you are not under law but under grace (Romans 6:11-14).

B. There are four things that we can do to train our spirit to be led by the Holy Spirit:

1. The first thing we can do to train our spirit is to develop a daily Bible reading habit;

a. The Bible is the primary medium through which God speaks today.

What advantage then has the Jew, or what is the profit of circumcision? Much in every way! Chiefly because to them were committed the oracles of God (Romans 3:1-2).

(1) The word "oracle" means "the speaking place."

(2) The Bible is God's "speaking place"; in other words, that place from which God primarily speaks.

b. Developing a daily Bible reading habit is critical if we want the Holy Spirit to guide us.

This Book of the Law shall not depart from your mouth, but you shall meditate in it day and night, that you may observe to do according to all that is written in it. For then you will make your way prosperous, and then you will have good success (Joshua 1:8).

*Blessed is the man who walks not in the counsel of the
ungodly, nor stands in the path of sinners, nor sits in the
seat of the scornful; but his delight is in the law of the
Lord, and in His law he meditates day and night*
(Psalm 1:1-2).

2. The second thing we can do to train our spirit is to daily meditate on the Word of God;

Oh, how I love Your law! It is my meditation all the day
(Psalm 119:97).

a. The Hebrew word for "meditate" also means "to mutter." Literally, we are to "mutter" the Word of God to ourselves as we meditate.

*This Book of the Law shall not depart from your mouth,
but you shall meditate in it day and night, that you may
observe to do according to all that is written in it. For
then you will make your way prosperous, and then you
will have good success* (Joshua 1:8).

b. The Holy Spirit will use the Scriptures to prepare our heart and mind to hear God's voice and to understand His truths.

*Open my eyes, that I may see wondrous things from Your
law* (Psalm 119:18).

*Teach me, O Lord, the way of Your statutes, and I shall
keep it to the end. Give me understanding, and I shall keep
Your law; indeed, I shall observe it with my whole heart.
Make me walk in the path of Your commandments, for I
delight in it* (Psalm 119:33-35).

*The entrance of Your words gives light; it gives
understanding to the simple* (Psalm 119:130).

c. The Holy Spirit will use the Scriptures to help us discern any traps the devil has set for us.

*The wicked have laid a snare for me, yet I have not
strayed from Your precepts* (Psalm 119:110).

Concerning the works of men, by the word of Your lips, I have kept myself from the paths of the destroyer (Psalm 17:4).

3. **The third thing we can do to train our spirit is to practice the Word of God;**

   a. **We must become doers of the Word, and not just hearers only.**

   But be doers of the word, and not hearers only, deceiving yourselves. For if anyone is a hearer of the word and not a doer, he is like a man observing his natural face in a mirror; for he observes himself, goes away, and immediately forgets what kind of man he was. But he who looks into the perfect law of liberty and continues in it, and is not a forgetful hearer but a doer of the work, this one will be blessed in what he does (James 1:22-25).

   b. **The Holy Spirit will use the Scriptures to keep us from making mistakes in life. He will chart the path for the steps we are to take.**

   Jesus answered and said to them, "You are mistaken, not knowing the Scriptures nor the power of God" (Matthew 22:29).

   You have commanded us to keep Your precepts diligently. Oh, that my ways were directed to keep Your statutes! Then I would not be ashamed, when I look into all Your commandments (Psalm 119:4-6).

   c. **The Holy Spirit will use the Scriptures to help us build our lives on a solid foundation which cannot be destroyed by the storms of life.**

   Therefore whoever hears these sayings of Mine, and does them, I will liken him to a wise man who built his house on the rock: and the rain descended, the floods came, and the winds blew and beat on that house; and it did not fall, for it was founded on the rock (Matthew 7:24-25).

d. **The Holy Spirit will never lead us in a way that would circumvent the Scriptures. His guidance will be consistent with the Word.**

Your Word is a lamp to my feet and a light to my path (Psalm 119:105).

Therefore all Your precepts concerning all things I consider to be right; I hate every false way (Psalm 119:128).

The entirety of Your word is truth, and every one of Your righteous judgments endures forever (Psalm 119:160).

For the Lord gives wisdom; from His mouth come knowledge and understanding; He stores up sound wisdom for the upright; He is a shield to those who walk uprightly; He guards the paths of justice, and preserves the way of His saints. Then you will understand righteousness and justice, equity and every good path. When wisdom enters your heart, and knowledge is pleasant to your soul, discretion will keep you, to deliver you from the way of evil. (Proverbs 2:6-11).

We also have the prophetic word made sure, which you do well to heed as a light that shines in a dark place, until the day dawns and the morning star rises in your hearts; knowing this first, that no prophecy of Scripture is of any private interpretation, for prophecy never came by the will of man, but holy men of God spoke as they were moved by the Holy Spirit (II Peter 1:19-21).

4. **Finally, the fourth thing we can do to train our spirit is to give the Word of God first place in our life. His Word must be the first and final authority in every area of life.**

My son, give attention to my words; incline your ear to my sayings. Do not let them depart from your eyes; keep them in the midst of your heart; for they are life to those who find them, and health to all their flesh (Proverbs 4:20-22).

I have not departed from the commandment of His lips; I have treasured the words of His mouth more than my necessary food (Job 23:12).

258

Chapter Fifteen

Living in the Community of Faith

I. God's Community of Faith.

A. The concept of "community" finds its origins in God: He is the living example of community.

    1. Genesis presents God as a community; a multiplicity of Persons, yet indivisibly unified.

        a. Genesis 1:1 reveals God the Father: He is the Creator and the Father of Life.

In the beginning God created the heavens and the earth (Genesis 1:1).

        b. Genesis 1:2 reveals God the Holy Spirit: He is hovering over creation as He protects, and redeems His creation.

The earth was without form, and void; and darkness was on the face of the deep. And the Spirit of God was hovering over the face of the waters (Genesis 1:2).

        c. Genesis 1:3 reveals God the Son: He declares His Word to become His will.

Then God said, "Let there be light"; and there was light (Genesis 1:3).

    2. The church expressed as a community is not an option ... it is a compelling necessity. It is to be modeled after the community expressed in the Godhead; the Father, Son, and Holy Spirit.

B. God's desire was to create man in His own image; His image consists of plurality in oneness.

    1. God created Adam in His own image.

And the Lord God formed man of the dust of the ground, and breathed into his nostrils the breath of life; and man became a living being (Genesis 2:7).

Then God said, "Let Us make man in Our image, according to Our likeness; let them have dominion over the fish of the sea, over the birds of the air, and over the cattle, over all the earth and over every creeping thing that creeps on the earth." So God created man in His own image; in the image of God He created him; male and female He created them (Genesis 1:26-27).

2. God saw that Adam was living without the benefits of a community; therefore, God said that it is not good that man should be alone.

And the Lord God said, "It is not good that man should be alone; I will make him a helper comparable to him" (Genesis 2:18).

3. God created Eve out of Adam's substance and she became a helpmate and companion for Adam.

And the Lord God caused a deep sleep to fall on Adam, and he slept; and He took one of his ribs, and closed up the flesh in its place. Then the rib which the Lord God had taken from man He made into a woman, and He brought her to the man. And Adam said: "This is now bone of my bones and flesh of my flesh; She shall be called Woman, because she was taken out of Man" (Genesis 2:21-23).

4. The first community on the earth was comprised of God; Adam; and Eve.

5. The benefits and the dynamics of community were tragically lost as a result of Adam and Eve's sin.

And they heard the sound of the Lord God walking in the garden in the cool of the day, and Adam and his wife hid themselves from the presence of the Lord God among the trees of the garden. Then the Lord God called to Adam and said to him, "Where are you" (Genesis 3:8-9)?

a. Adam and Eve's love for God was replaced by their new-found fear of God.

So he said, "I heard Your voice in the garden, and I was
afraid because I was naked; and I hid myself"
(Genesis 3:10).

    b.   **Adam and Eve's trust in each other eroded**
        and their relationship became clouded with
        suspicion.

    c.   **Each of them pointed a finger at another in a**
        feeble attempt to escape their responsibility in
        the matter of their sin.

And He said, "Who told you that you were naked? Have
you eaten from the tree of which I commanded you that
you should not eat?" Then the man said, "The woman
whom You gave to be with me, she gave me of the tree,
and I ate." And the Lord God said to the woman, "What is
this you have done?" The woman said, "The serpent
deceived me, and I ate" (Genesis 3:11-13).

C. **Bible history records the failure of mankind to live in**
    God's intended community of faith.

    1. **God instructed Noah and his family to repopulate**
        the whole earth after the great flood.

        a.   **Not long after Noah's days, His descendants**
           decided not to scatter and repopulate the
           earth as God had instructed; instead, they
           gathered to build a city and tower at Babel.

And they said, "Come, let us build ourselves a city, and a
tower whose top is in the heavens; let us make a name for
ourselves, lest we be scattered abroad over the face of the
whole earth" (Genesis 11:4).

        b.   **However, God stepped into the picture and**
           confused their language so that they lost their
           ability to communicate with each other. This
           forced them to follow God's instruction to
           scatter throughout the earth.

But the Lord came down to see the city and the tower which the sons of men had built. And He said, "Indeed the people are one and they all have one language, and this is what they begin to do; now nothing that they propose to do will be withheld from them. Come, let Us go down and confuse their language, that they may not understand one another's speech." So the Lord scattered them abroad from there over the face of all the earth, and they ceased building the city. Therefore its name is called Babel, because there the Lord confused the language of all the earth; and from there the Lord scattered them abroad over the face of the earth (Genesis 11:5-9).

2.   **God sought to reestablish the concept of community through Abraham.**

   a.   **The name Abram means "the father of one clan." However, the name Abraham means "the father of many nations."**

   b.   **God desired to bring a new community of faith through the loins of Abraham.**

Now the Lord had said to Abram: "Get out of your country, from your kindred and from your father's house, to a land that I will show you. I will make you a great nation; I will bless you and make your name great; and you shall be a blessing. I will bless those who bless you, and I will curse him who curses you; and in you all the families of the earth shall be blessed" (Genesis 12:1-3).

   c.   **Abraham's family of faith was compromised through the generations because of rebellion. They refused to hear the warnings of God's prophets to turn from idolatry and return to Him.**

   d.   **Tragically, Abraham's family of faith was almost lost as God's judgments fell because of sin. They not only suffered a divided kingdom but were also taken captive into exile.**

264

D. Jesus came to fulfill God's desire to have a community of faith. The most compelling argument for the Gospel is the unity within His community.

    1. Jesus gave two commandments that reveal how life in the community of faith is to be lived.

        a. First, Jesus summed up the Old Testament economy by stating that we are to love God with all of our being.

        Jesus said to him, "You shall love the Lord your God with all your heart, with all your soul, and with all your mind. This is the first and great commandment" (Matthew 22:37-38).

        b. Second, Jesus said that loving God means that we are to love each other as we love ourselves.

        And the second is like it: "You shall love your neighbor as yourself." On these two commandments hang all the Law and the Prophets (Matthew 22:39-40).

    2. Celebrating the Passover with His disciples in the Upper Room on the night before He was crucified, Jesus gave a demonstration of this kind of love ... He washed each one of the disciples feet.

So when He had washed their feet, taken His garments, and sat down again, He said to them, "Do you know what I have done to you? You call me Teacher and Lord, and you say well, for so I am. If I then, your Lord and Teacher, have washed your feet, you also ought to wash one another's feet. For I have given you an example, that you should do as I have done to you" (John 13:12-15).

    3. Jesus prayed in the Garden of Gethsemane that we would be one as He and His Father are one.

Now I am no longer in the world, but these are in the world, and I come to You. Holy Father, keep through Your name those whom You have given Me, that they may be one as We are (John 17:11).

265

4. Jesus prayed that unity would be evidenced in His family throughout the generations, not just in His disciples that were with Him that day.

I do not pray for these alone, but also for those who will believe in Me through their word; that they all may be one, as You, Father, are in Me, and I in You; that they also may be one in Us, that the world may believe that You sent Me. And the glory which You gave Me I have given them, that they may be one just as We are one: I in them, and You in Me; that they may be made perfect in one, and that the world may know that You have sent Me, and have loved them as You have loved Me (John 17:20-23).

E. The Day of Pentecost ushered in this new community of faith: God's intentions were finally realized.

1. The people devoted themselves to fellowship; to ministry; and to meeting each others needs; as a result of their encounter with the Holy Spirit.

2. Living out their faith brought evangelistic success to all who saw their love for God and for each other.

Now the multitude of those who believed were of one heart and one soul; neither did anyone say that any of the things he possessed was his own, but they had all things in common. And with great power the apostles gave witness to the resurrection of the Lord Jesus. And great grace was upon them all (Acts 4:32-33).

F. There is coming a day when God will establish His ultimate, eternal community of faith.

Now I saw a new heaven and a new earth, for the first heaven and the first earth had passed away. Also there was no more sea. Then I, John, saw the holy city, New Jerusalem, coming down out of heaven from God, prepared as a bride adorned for her husband. And I heard a loud voice from heaven saying, "Behold, the tabernacle of God is with men, and He will dwell with them, and they shall be His people and God Himself will be with them and be their God" (Revelation 21:1-3).

II. Learning to Love Each Other.

A. **Living in the community of faith requires us to recognize that, as believers, we are all members of God's family and are expected to love one another.**

Beloved, let us love one another, for love is of God; and everyone who loves is born of God and knows God. He who does not love does not know God, for God is love. In this the love of God was manifested toward us, that God has sent His only begotten Son into the world, that we might live through Him. In this is love, not that we loved God, but that He loved us and sent His Son to be the propitiation for our sins. Beloved, if God so loved us, we also ought to love one another. No one has seen God at any time. If we love one another, God abides in us, and His love has been perfected in us (I John 4:7-12).

B. **Loving every member of God's family is not an option … it is a command.**

And this commandment we have from Him: that he who loves God must love his brother also (I John 4:21).

C. **Learning to love one another starts by recognizing that we are united by the bonds of the love of Christ.**

Now, therefore, you are no longer strangers and foreigners, but fellow citizens with the saints and members of the household of God, having been built on the foundation of the apostles and prophets, Jesus Christ Himself being the chief cornerstone, in whom the whole building, being joined together, grows into a holy temple in the Lord, in whom you also are being built together for a dwelling place of God in the Spirit (Ephesians 2:19-22).

   1. **Love means that we never show favoritism or esteem one above another.**

   If you really fulfill the royal law according to the Scripture, "You shall love your neighbor as yourself," you do well; but if you show partiality, you commit sin, and are convicted by the law as transgressors (James 2:8-9).

My brethren, do not hold the faith of our Lord Jesus Christ, the Lord of glory, with partiality. For if there should come into your assembly a man with gold rings, in fine apparel, and there should also come in a poor man in filthy clothes, and you pay attention to the one wearing the fine clothes and say to him, "You sit here in a good place," and say to the poor man, "You stand there," or, "Sit here at my footstool," have you not shown partiality among yourselves, and become judges with evil thoughts (James 2:1-4)?

2.   **Love means that we recognize the value of each member and their function within the Body of Christ.**

But now God has set the members, each one of them, in the body just as He pleased. And if they were all one member, where would the body be? But now indeed there are many members, yet one body. And the eye cannot say to the hand, "I have no need of you"; nor again the head to the feet, "I have no need of you." No, much rather, those members of the body which seem to be weaker are necessary. And those members of the body which we think to be less honorable, on these we bestow greater honor; and our un-presentable parts have greater modesty, but our presentable parts have no need. But God composed the body, having given greater honor to that part which lacks it, that there should be no schism in the body, but that the members should have the same care for one another (I Corinthians 12:18-25).

3.   **Love means that we care about what happens in the lives of others … we will comfort in times of sorrow and we will celebrate in times of victory.**

And if one member suffers, all the members suffer with it; or if one member is honored, all the members rejoice with it (I Corinthians 12:26).

D.   **We are members of God's family and are fellow-partners in the work of God. Our assignment is to build and advance His kingdom on earth.**

For we are God's fellow workers; you are God's field, you are God's building (I Corinthians 3:9).

1. **God is able to do His greatest work through His community of believers when we work together in unity for His common cause.**

From whom the whole body, joined and knit together by what every joint supplies, according to the effective working by which every part does its share, causes growth of the body for the edifying of itself in love (Ephesians 4:16).

2. **When we realize we are working together in a partnership with God to build His Kingdom, then no sacrifice will be too great for us to make.**

By this we know love, because He laid down His life for us. And we also ought to lay down our lives for the brethren (I John 3:16).

3. **We must have a proper attitude in our service to one another; our motivation will be pure if we do everything for Jesus and His Kingdom.**

Then the King will say to those on His right hand, "Come, you blessed of My Father, inherit the kingdom prepared for you from the foundation of the world: for I was hungry and you gave Me food; I was thirsty and you gave Me drink; I was a stranger and you took Me in; I was naked and you clothed Me; I was sick and you visited Me; I was in prison and you came to Me." Then the righteous will answer Him, saying, "Lord, when did we see You hungry and feed You, or thirsty and give You drink? When did we see You a stranger and take You in, or naked and clothe You? Or when did we see You sick, or in prison, and come to You?" And the King will answer and say to them, "Assuredly, I say to you, inasmuch as you did it to one of the least of these My brethren, you did it to Me" (Matthew 25:34-40).

4. **Our greatest witness to those who do not believe is our commitment and love for one another.**

A new commandment I give to you, that you love one another; as I have loved you, that you also love one another. By this all will know that you are My disciples, if you have love for one another (John 13:34-35).

269

E. **Jesus demonstrates how we are to love one another. He set the example when He proved His love for us.**

But God demonstrates His own love toward us, in that while we were still sinners, Christ died for us (Romans 5:8).

F. **The characteristics of the example of Jesus are to be modeled in the community of faith as we demonstrate our love for each other:**

1. **Our love for each other should be Godly and pure.**

As the Father loved Me, I also have loved you; abide in My love (John 15:9).

2. **Our love for each other should be unchangeable. Our unconditional love will become a consistent companion to those that are in the community of faith.**

Now before the feast of the Passover, when Jesus knew that His hour had come that He should depart from this world to the Father, having loved His own who were in the world, He loved them to the end (John 13:1).

3. **Our love for each other will make us inseparable. We will not allow ourselves to be affected by circumstances that confront us and seek to tear us apart.**

Who shall separate us from the love of Christ? Shall tribulation, or distress, or persecution, or famine, or nakedness, or peril, or sword? As it is written: "For Your sake we are killed all day long; We are accounted as sheep for the slaughter." Yet in all these things we are more than conquerors through Him who loved us. For I am persuaded that neither death nor life, nor angels nor principalities nor powers, nor things present nor things to come, nor height nor depth, nor any other created thing, shall be able to separate us from the love of God which is in Christ Jesus our Lord (Romans 8:35-39).

4. **Our love for each other should have the special quality of self-sacrifice.**

Greater love has no one than this, than to lay down one's life for his friends (John 15:13).

5. **Our love and concern for each other should bring about an earnest desire to cover the faults and the failures of another until that person can be restored.**

And above all things have fervent love for one another, for "love will cover a multitude of sins" (I Peter 4:8).

6. **Our love for each other should be expressed in our actions towards one another and not just in the words we speak.**

By this we know love, because He laid down His life for us. And we also ought to lay down our lives for the brethren. But whoever has this world's goods, and sees his brother in need, and shuts up his heart from him, how does the love of God abide in him? My little children, let us not love in word or in tongue, but in deed and in truth (I John 3:16-18).

G. **The Bible clearly defines the characteristics of the genuine love of God that should abound in our hearts towards one another.**

1. **This genuine love is to be consistently lived out on a daily basis.**

2. **This genuine love is to be freely expressed in our relationships with each other.**

Love suffers long and is kind; love does not envy; love does not parade itself, is not puffed up; does not behave rudely, does not seek its own, is not provoked, thinks no evil; does not rejoice in iniquity, but rejoices in the truth; bears all things, believes all things, hopes all things, endures all things. Love never fails. But whether there are prophecies, they will fail; whether there are tongues, they will cease; whether there is knowledge, it will vanish away (I Corinthians 13:4-8).

III. Living Free from a Judgmental Spirit.

A. **There is a tremendous difference in how we see people and how God sees them.**

1. **We look at a person's outward appearance and pass our judgment as to their worth.**

2. **However, God looks at a person's heart and weighs their worth.**

But the Lord said to Samuel, "Do not look at his appearance or at the height of his stature, because I have refused him. For the Lord does not see as man sees; for man looks at the outward appearance, but the Lord looks at the heart" (I Samuel 16:7).

B. **We have all failed to keep the laws of God; therefore, we are not qualified to pass judgment on anyone. Jesus is the only one qualified to judge because He lived a sinless life.**

Do not speak evil of one another, brethren. He who speaks evil of a brother and judges his brother, speaks evil of the law and judges the law. But if you judge the law, you are not a doer of the law but a judge. There is one Lawgiver, who is able to save and to destroy. Who are you to judge another (James 4:11-12)?

C. **Sitting in judgment brings negative consequences.**

1. **God will use the standard we have used in judging others to judge us.**

Therefore you are inexcusable, O man, whoever you are who judge, for in whatever you judge another you condemn yourself; for you who judge practice the same things. But we know that the judgment of God is according to truth against those who practice such things. And do you think this, O man, you who judge those practicing such things, and doing the same, that you will escape the judgment of God (Romans 2:1-3)?

272

Judge not, that you be not judged. For with what judgment you judge, you will be judged; and with the measure you use, it will be measured back to you (Matthew 7:1-2).

2. Our judgment of others will block our prayers from being answered.

Then you shall call, and the Lord will answer; you shall cry, and He will say, "Here I am." If you take away the yoke from your midst, the pointing of the finger, and speaking wickedness (Isaiah 58:9).

D. Our judgmental attitude and actions will cause others to stumble in their faith.

1. When we speak critically of someone to another person, we involve that person in our sin by spreading discord to their hearts.

Therefore let us not judge one another anymore, but rather resolve this, not to put a stumbling block or a cause to fall in our brother's way (Romans 14:13).

2. God specifically states in His Word that He hates the spreading of discord.

These six things the Lord hates, yes, seven are an abomination to Him: A proud look, a lying tongue, hands that shed innocent blood, a heart that devises wicked plans, feet that are swift in running to evil, a false witness who speaks lies, and one who sows discord among brethren (Proverbs 6:16-19).

E. When we pass judgment on others, we invalidate our witness and our ministry to the Lord is in vain.

If anyone among you thinks he is religious, and does not bridle his tongue but deceives his own heart, this one's religion is useless (James 1:26).

For all the law is fulfilled in one word, even in this: "You shall love your neighbor as yourself." But if you bite and devour one another, beware lest you be consumed by one another (Galatians 5:14-15)!

F. Passing judgment on others does a great deal of damage to the lives of those we judge.

1. The devil uses our words of judgment and condemnation to destroy the lives of others.

Even so the tongue is a little member and boasts great things. See how great a forest a little fire kindles! And the tongue is a fire, a world of iniquity. The tongue is so set among our members that it defiles the whole body, and sets on fire the course of nature; and it is set on fire by hell (James 3:5-6).

2. Judging another, while claiming to love God, exposes us as hypocrites.

But no man can tame the tongue. It is an unruly evil, full of deadly poison. With it we bless our God and Father, and with it we curse men, who have been made in the similitude of God. Out of the same mouth proceed blessing and cursing. My brethren, these things ought not to be so. Does a spring send forth fresh water and bitter from the same opening? Can a fig tree, my brethren, bear olives, or a grapevine bear figs? Thus no spring yields both salt water and fresh. Who is wise and understanding among you? Let him show by good conduct that his works are done in the meekness of wisdom (James 3:8-13).

G. The Scripture never gives us permission to sit in judgment of others; when we pass judgment, we anger and grieve the heart of God.

And why do you look at the speck in your brother's eye, but do not consider the plank in your own eye? Or how can you say to your brother, "Let me remove the speck from your eye"; and look, a plank is in your own eye? Hypocrite! First remove the plank from your own eye, and then you will see clearly to remove the speck from your brother's eye (Matthew 7:3-5).

He permitted no one to do them wrong; yes, He rebuked kings for their sakes, saying, "Do not touch My anointed ones, and do My prophets no harm" (Psalm 105:14-15).

Who are you to judge another's servant? To his own master he stands or falls. Indeed, he will be made to stand, for God is able to make him stand (Romans 14:4).

IV. Choosing to Forgive.

A. **The starting point for forgiving others is to have experienced God's forgiveness in our own lives.**

1. **Society seeks to lower the standard by which sin is determined, but God will never lower His standard. We have all missed the mark and are considered sinners in God's eyes.**

For all have sinned and fall short of the glory of God (Romans 3:23).

2. **No one can survive the penalty in the law of God for those guilty of sin ... eternal death.**

For the wages of sin is death, but the gift of God is eternal life in Christ Jesus our Lord (Romans 6:23).

3. **God is willing to forgive anyone who will acknowledge their sin and request His forgiveness.**

If You, Lord, should mark iniquities, O Lord, who could stand? But there is forgiveness with You, that You may be feared (Psalm 130:3-4).

But if we walk in the light as He is in the light, we have fellowship with one another, and the blood of Jesus Christ His Son cleanses us from all sin. If we say that we have no sin, we deceive ourselves, and the truth is not in us. If we confess our sins, He is faithful and just to forgive us our sins and to cleanse us from all unrighteousness (I John 1:7-9).

B. **Jesus set the standard by which we are to forgive others.**

1. **God's forgiveness is total and unconditional, and our forgiveness of others must be the same.**

2. **Our sin debt was canceled through the death of Christ on the cross. We are expected to extend the same forgiving grace to everyone in our lives.**

This is My commandment, that you love one another as I have loved you. Greater love has no one than this, than to lay down one's life for his friends (John 15:12-13).

Heal the sick, cleanse the lepers, raise the dead, cast out demons. Freely you have received, freely give (Matthew 10:8).

C. **Jesus taught that faith and forgiveness are tied together. If we fail to forgive others, we negate the operation of our faith and forfeit our own forgiveness.**

So Jesus answered and said to them, "Have faith in God. For assuredly, I say to you, whoever says to this mountain, 'Be removed and be cast into the sea,' and does not doubt in his heart, but believes that those things he says will come to pass, he will have whatever he says. Therefore I say to you, whatever things you ask when you pray, believe that you receive them, and you will have them. And whenever you stand praying, if you have anything against anyone, forgive him, that your Father in heaven may also forgive you your trespasses. But if you do not forgive, neither will your Father in heaven forgive your trespasses" (Mark 11:22-26).

D. **Peter believed that he was making a gracious offer when he asked Jesus if he should forgive someone seven times.**

Then Peter came to Him and said, "Lord, how often shall my brother sin against me, and I forgive him? Up to seven times" (Matthew 18:21)?

   1. **The school of thought in Peter's day was that even God did not forgive more than three times. This belief came from the writings of Amos, the Old Testament prophet.**

Thus says the Lord: "For three transgressions of Tyre, and for four, I will not turn away its punishment, because they delivered up the whole captivity to Edom, and did not remember the covenant of brotherhood. But I will send a fire upon the wall of Tyre, which shall devour its palaces" (Amos 1:9-10).

2. **The answer Jesus gave to Peter must have shocked him ... forgive seventy times seven.**

Jesus said to him, "I do not say to you, up to seven times, but up to seventy times seven" (Matthew 18:22).

3. **Jesus wasn't suggesting that we are only responsible to forgive someone up to 490 times and then we are free to condemn them.**

4. **Jesus was stating a truth that the Apostle Paul would later affirm in his letter to the Corinthian church ... love doesn't keep score.**

Love suffers long and is kind; love does not envy; love does not parade itself, is not puffed up; does not behave rudely, does not seek its own, is not provoked, thinks no evil; does not rejoice in iniquity, but rejoices in the truth; bears all things, believes all things, hopes all things, endures all things. Love never fails. But whether there are prophecies, they will fail; whether there are tongues, they will cease; whether there is knowledge, it will vanish away (I Corinthians 13:4-8).

E. **Jesus tells a parable in Matthew 18 that illustrates how we are to live with an unending and unrelenting forgiveness. He reminds us that the forgiveness we freely received is to be the motivating force in our forgiving others.**

1. **Consider the plight of the first servant in the parable in Matthew 18:**

Therefore the kingdom of heaven is like a certain king who wanted to settle accounts with his servants. And when he had begun to settle accounts, one was brought to him who owed him ten thousand talents. But as he was not able to pay, his master commanded that he be sold, with his wife and children and all that he had, and that payment be made (Matthew 18:23-25).

a. The first servant was helpless to repay his debt and had absolutely no appeal to excuse himself from his debt.

b. His debt in today's monetary value would be close to one-hundred million dollars.

c. He was a man without hope. The custom of his day was for a debtor, along with his family, to be sold into slavery for cash. Often, families were scattered among slave owners and separated for the rest of their lives.

d. However, the master extended mercy and forgave the servant releasing him from his debt.

The servant therefore fell down before him, saying, "Master, have patience with me, and I will pay you all." Then the master of that servant was moved with compassion, released him, and forgave him the debt (Matthew 18:26-27).

(1) We can see ourselves in this indebted servant ... helpless and hopeless; because of a sin debt we cannot pay. However, Jesus, in His mercy, forgave us and paid our sin debt in full.

(2) We will be inclined to forget the grace of God shown to us, if we fail to remember our own helplessness and hopelessness.

(3) We will fail to extend the forgiving grace of Christ to others if we forget God's grace that was extended to us to cancel our debt of sin.

2. Consider the plight of the second servant in the parable in Matthew 18:

But that servant went out and found one of his fellow servants who owed him a hundred denarii; and he laid hands on him and took him by the throat, saying, "Pay me what you owe!" So his fellow servant fell down at his feet and begged him, saying, "Have patience with me, and I will pay you all." And he would not, but went and threw him into prison till he should pay the debt (Matthew 18:28-30).

    a. The debt of the second servant was only about forty dollars in today's economy which was an amount that was easily payable over time.

    b. Even though the first servant was forgiven for his massive debt, he refused to forgive the second servant for his small debt and had him thrown into a debtor's prison.

        (1) Again, we can see ourselves in this unforgiving first servant. We enjoy unconditional forgiveness from God, and yet we are only willing to extend conditional forgiveness to those who have offended us.

        (2) God will not overrule our will in matters of forgiveness. If we choose to forgive, it will be an action of our wills.

3. The pivotal point in the parable takes place in the confrontation between the forgiving master and the unforgiving servant.

So when his fellow servants saw what had been done, they were very grieved, and came and told their master all that had been done. Then his master, after he had called him, said to him, "You wicked servant! I forgave you all that debt because you begged me. Should you not also have had compassion on your fellow servant, just as I had pity on you" (Matthew 18:31-33)?

a. **The unforgiving servant re-incurred his debts. He suffered the loss of his peace of mind that would have been his, knowing his debts were forgiven.**

And his master was angry, and delivered him to the torturers until he should pay all that was due to him (Matthew 18:34).

b. **The torturers were not bullies who went around torturing debtors; they were bill collectors who regularly appeared at the debtor's door demanding repayment of the debt owed.**

4. **If we choose not to forgive, we will retain our sins; lose our peace of mind; and forfeit the joy of knowing that we are forgiven.**

So My heavenly Father also will do to you if each of you, from his heart, does not forgive his brother his trespasses (Matthew 18:35).

Chapter Sixteen

Life after Death
Part One

I. God's Divine Appointments.

A. God has a divine order and a purpose for everything He created.

To everything there is a season, a time for every purpose under heaven (Ecclesiastes 3:1).

B. God has established five divine appointments which everyone of us, without exception, will keep.

1. Our first divine appointment is to be born.

A time to be born, and a time to die (Ecclesiastes 3:2).

a. God is the author of our lives: He knit us together in our mother's womb.

For You formed my inward parts; You have covered me in my mother's womb. I will praise You, for I am fearfully and wonderfully made; Marvelous are Your works, and that my soul knows very well. My frame was not hidden from You, when I was made in secret, and skillfully wrought in the lowest parts of the earth (Psalm 139:13-15).

b. God knew us and purposed our lives even before we were born.

Your eyes saw my substance, being yet unformed. And in Your book they all were written, the days fashioned for me, when as yet there were none of them (Psalm 139:16).

Then the word of the Lord came to me, saying: "Before I formed you in the womb I knew you; before you were born I sanctified you; and I ordained you a prophet to the nations" (Jeremiah 1:4-5).

Listen, O coastlands, to Me, and take heed, you peoples from afar! The Lord has called Me from the womb; from the matrix of My mother He has made mention of My name (Isaiah 49:1).

2. **Our second divine appointment is to live out our lives in a probationary period called "time."**

    a. **The span of time, between our birth and our death, is regarded as a probationary period.**

Lord, make me to know my end, and what is the measure of my days, that I may know how frail I am. Indeed, You have made my days as handbreadths, and my age is as nothing before You; certainly every man at his best state is but vapor (Psalm 39:4-5).

Whereas you do not know what will happen tomorrow. For what is your life? It is even a vapor that appears for a little time and then vanishes away (James 4:14).

    b. **During this probationary period we are given the freedom to make a choice that will determine our eternal destiny.**

        (1) **We can repent of our sins and receive God's gift of eternal life in heaven;**

        (2) **Or, we can choose not to repent and suffer the consequences of sin's penalty.**

I call heaven and earth as witnesses today against you, that I have set before you life and death, blessing and cursing; therefore choose life, that both you and your descendants may live (Deuteronomy 30:19).

    c. **The probationary period of our life is over when we die. The decisions we made concerning our eternal destiny will be settled.**

    d. **God has given us a "knowing" in our hearts that we will live forever; therefore, it is critical that we choose our eternal destiny.**

He has made everything beautiful in its time. Also He has put eternity in their hearts, except that no one can find out the work that God does from beginning to end (Ecclesiastes 3:11).

3.   Our third divine appointment is to physically die.

   a.   Every one has an appointed time to die, but only God knows when this appointment will be kept.

   And as it is appointed for men to die once, but after this the judgment (Hebrews 9:27).

   b.   When we experience death as a believer, our spirit is ushered immediately into the very presence of God.

   And they stoned Stephen as he was calling on God and saying, "Lord Jesus, receive my spirit" (Acts 7:59).

   Therefore we are always confident, knowing that while we are at home in the body we are absent from the Lord. For we walk by faith, not by sight. We are confident, yes, well pleased rather to be absent from the body and to be present with the Lord (II Corinthians 5:6-8).

   c.   When an unbeliever dies, they find themselves within the region of the damned; there they will wait in torment for their day of judgment.

   So it was that the beggar died, and was carried by the angels to Abraham's bosom. The rich man also died and was buried. And being in torments in Hades, he lifted up his eyes and saw Abraham afar off, and Lazarus in his bosom (Luke 16:22-23).

   d.   Jesus has forever removed the sting and fear of death from those who have placed their faith in Him for salvation.

   So when this corruptible has put on incorruption, and this mortal has put on immortality, then shall be brought to pass the saying that is written: "Death is swallowed up in victory. O Death, where is your sting? O Hades, where is your victory?" The sting of death is sin, and the strength of sin is the law. But thanks be to God, who gives us the victory through our Lord Jesus Christ (I Corinthians 15:54-57).

Inasmuch then as the children have partaken of flesh and blood, He Himself likewise shared in the same, that through death He might destroy him who had the power of death, that is, the devil, and release those who through fear of death were all their lifetime subject to bondage (Hebrews 2:14-15).

4. **Our fourth divine appointment is to be resurrected from the dead.**

   a. **Believers, and unbelievers alike, will be resurrected from the dead.**

   Do not marvel at this; for the hour is coming in which all who are in the graves will hear His voice and come forth—those who have done good, to the resurrection of life, and those who have done evil, to the resurrection of condemnation (John 5:28-29).

      (1) **Believers will be resurrected to enjoy the rewards of their eternal home in heaven with Christ;**

      (2) **However, unbelievers will be resurrected to face the consequences of their rejection of Jesus Christ.**

   b. **The resurrection of the dead is the central theme of Christ's gospel, and the ultimate hope of Christianity.**

   Jesus said to her, "I am the resurrection and the life. He who believes in Me, though he may die, he shall live" (John 11:25).

   c. **The resurrection of Jesus is proof of God's power over death; it holds the promise that every believer will be raised from the dead.**

   For if we have been united together in the likeness of His death, certainly we also shall be in the likeness of His resurrection (Romans 6:5).

*But if there is no resurrection of the dead, then Christ is
not risen. And if Christ is not risen, then our preaching is
vain and your faith is also vain. Yes, and we are found
false witnesses of God, because we have testified of God
that He raised up Christ, whom He did not raise up—if in
fact the dead do not rise. For if the dead do not rise, then
Christ is not risen. And if Christ is not risen, your faith is
futile; you are still in your sins! Then also those who have
fallen asleep in Christ have perished. If in this life only we
have hope in Christ, we are of all men the most pitiable.
But now Christ is risen from the dead, and has become the
firstfruits of those who have fallen asleep*
(I Corinthians 15:13-20).

d. At the resurrection of the dead, the believers will receive a new glorified body that will be fitted to enjoy all that heaven offers.

*There are also celestial bodies and terrestrial bodies; but
the glory of the celestial is one, and the glory of the
terrestrial is another. There is one glory of the sun,
another glory of the moon, and another glory of the stars;
for one star differs from another star in glory. So also is
the resurrection of the dead. The body is sown in
corruption, it is raised in incorruption. It is sown in
dishonor, it is raised in glory. It is sown in weakness, it is
raised in power. It is sown a natural body, it is raised a
spiritual body. There is a natural body, and there is a
spiritual body* (I Corinthians 15:40-44).

e. At the resurrection of the dead, the unbelievers will receive a body that is fitted for suffering the torments of hell.

*What if God, wanting to show His wrath and to make His
power known, endured with much longsuffering the
vessels of wrath prepared for destruction* (Romans 9:22).

5. Our fifth divine appointment is to stand before God in judgment.

a.	**Every one who has ever lived will stand before the Lord at one of two seats of judgment.**

I said in my heart, "God shall judge the righteous and the wicked, for there is a time there for every purpose and for every work" (Ecclesiastes 3:17).

(1)	**Believers will appear before the Judgment Seat of Christ.**

(2)	**Unbelievers will appear at the Great White Throne Judgment.**

b.	**Jesus will be the appointed judge at both of these judgment seats.**

I charge you therefore before God and the Lord Jesus Christ, who will judge the living and the dead at His appearing and His kingdom (II Timothy 4:1).

For the Father judges no one, but has committed all judgment to the Son (John 5:22).

c.	**Jesus will judge everything according to the standard set forth in His Word.**

He who rejects Me, and does not receive My words, has that which judges him—the word that I have spoken will judge him in the last day (John 12:48).

But I say to you that for every idle word men may speak, they will give account of it in the day of judgment. For by your words you will be justified, and by your words you will be condemned (Matthew 12:36-37).

"Behold, the Lord comes with ten thousands of His saints, to execute judgment on all, to convict all who are ungodly among them of all their ungodly deeds which they have committed in an ungodly way, and of all the harsh things which ungodly sinners have spoken against Him (Jude 14-15).

For God will bring every work into judgment, including every secret thing, whether it is good or whether it is evil (Ecclesiastes 12:14).

II. The Judgment Seat of Christ.

A. **Every believer will stand before the Judgment Seat of Christ.**

   1. **At the Judgment Seat of Christ believers will not be judged to determine their salvation; the issue of the believer's salvation was settled when they received Christ as their Savior and received His forgiveness for their sins.**

   2. **At the Judgment Seat of Christ believers will personally give an account for how they used their time; their talents; and their resources; in service to the Lord.**

      For we must all appear before the judgment seat of Christ, that each one may receive the things done in the body, according to what he has done, whether good or bad (II Corinthians 5:10).

      But why do you judge your brother? Or why do you show contempt for your brother? For we shall all stand before the judgment seat of Christ. For it is written: "As I live, says the Lord, every knee shall bow to Me, and every tongue shall confess to God." So then each of us shall give account of himself to God (Romans 14:10-12).

   3. **At the Judgment Seat of Christ the Lord will test our works; our words; and our motives; in the fire of His holiness.**

      a. **Works that were done through God's power, and for His glory, will survive the test and be as gold, silver, and precious stones.**

      b. **Works that were done in our own strength, and for our own glory, will not survive the test; they will be destroyed as though they were wood, hay, and straw.**

289

For no other foundation can anyone lay than that which is laid, which is Jesus Christ. Now if anyone builds on this foundation with gold, silver, precious stones, wood, hay, straw, each one's work will become manifest; for the Day will declare it, because it will be revealed by fire; and the fire will test each one's work, of what sort it is. If anyone's work which he has built on it endures, he will receive a reward. If anyone's work is burned, he will suffer loss; but he himself will be saved, yet so as through fire (I Corinthians 3:11-15).

B. At the Judgment Seat of Christ rewards will be given to those who served the Lord faithfully. The Bible speaks of five crowns to be awarded to the faithful:

1. The Crown of Righteousness;

   a. This crown is sometimes referred to as the Victor's Crown.

   b. The recipients of this crown mastered their carnal natures and disciplined themselves to live according to the precepts of the Bible.

   Do you not know that those who run in a race all run, but one receives the prize? Run in such a way that you may obtain it. And everyone who competes for the prize is temperate in all things. Now they do it to obtain a perishable crown, but we for an imperishable crown. Therefore I run thus: not with uncertainty. Thus I fight: not as one who beats the air. But I discipline my body and bring it into subjection, lest, when I have preached to others, I myself should become disqualified (I Corinthians 9:24-27).

2. The Crown of Life;

   a. This crown is sometimes referred to as the Martyr's Crown.

   b. The recipients of this crown remained faithful as they endured hardship, even unto death.

290

Blessed is the man who endures temptation; for when he has been proved, he will receive the crown of life which the Lord has promised to those who love Him (James 1:12).

Do not fear any of those things which you are about to suffer. Indeed, the devil is about to throw some of you into prison, that you may be tested, and you will have tribulation ten days. Be faithful until death, and I will give you the crown of life (Revelation 2:10).

3. **The Crown of Glory;**

   a. **This crown is sometimes referred to as the Elder's Crown.**

   b. **This crown will be given to ministers for their faithfulness to the work of God; it will also be awarded to those who encourage and faithfully support their ministers.**

Shepherd the flock of God which is among you, serving as overseers, not by constraint but willingly, not for dishonest gain but eagerly; nor as being lords over those entrusted to you, but being examples to the flock; and when the Chief Shepherd appears, you will receive the crown of glory that does not fade away (I Peter 5:2-4).

He who receives a prophet in the name of a prophet shall receive a prophet's reward. And he who receives a righteous man in the name of a righteous man shall receive a righteous man's reward (Matthew 10:41).

4. **The Crown of Righteousness;**

   a. **This crown will be given to those who remained faithful to the Lord as they conquered the trials of life.**

   b. **The recipients of this crown have lived with anticipation for the Lord's return.**

I have fought the good fight, I have finished the race, I have kept the faith. Finally, there is laid up for me the crown of righteousness, which the Lord, the righteous Judge, will give to me on that Day, and not to me only but also to all who have loved His appearing (II Timothy 4:7-8).

5.   **The Crown of Rejoicing.**

     a.   **This crown is sometimes referred to as the Soul Winners Crown.**

     b.   **This crown will be awarded to those who lead people to a saving knowledge of Jesus Christ; they will see them enjoying heaven.**

The fruit of the righteous is a tree of life, and he who wins souls is wise (Proverbs 11:30).

Those who are wise shall shine like the brightness of the firmament, and those who turn many to righteousness like the stars forever and ever (Daniel 12:3).

For what is our hope, or joy, or crown of rejoicing? Is it not even you in the presence of our Lord Jesus Christ at His coming (I Thessalonians 2:19)?

C.   **Immediately after the examination and distribution of rewards at the Judgment Seat of Christ, believers will participate in the Marriage Supper of the Lamb.**

Then a voice came from the throne, saying, "Praise our God, all you His servants and those who fear Him, both small and great!" And I heard, as it were, the voice of a great multitude, as the sound of many waters and as the sound of mighty thunderings, saying, "Alleluia! For the Lord God Omnipotent reigns! Let us be glad and rejoice and give Him glory, for the marriage of the Lamb has come, and His wife has made herself ready." And to her it was granted to be arrayed in fine linen, clean and bright, for the fine linen is the righteous acts of the saints. Then he said to me, "Write: 'Blessed are those who are called to the marriage supper of the Lamb!'" And he said to me, "These are the true sayings of God" (Revelation 19:5-9).

1. **This event is called the Marriage Supper of the Lamb because Jesus is referred to in the Scriptures as the "Lamb of God."**

The next day John saw Jesus coming toward him, and said, "Behold! The Lamb of God who takes away the sin of the world" (John 1:29)!

But one of the elders said to me, "Do not weep. Behold, the Lion of the tribe of Judah, the Root of David, has prevailed to open the scroll and to loose its seven seals." And I looked, and behold, in the midst of the throne and of the four living creatures, and in the midst of the elders, stood a Lamb as though it had been slain, having seven horns and seven eyes, which are the seven Spirits of God sent out into all the earth (Revelation 5:5-6).

"You are worthy to take the scroll, and to open its seals; for You were slain, and have redeemed us to God by Your blood out of every tribe and tongue and people and nation, and have made us kings and priests to our God; and we shall reign on the earth." Then I looked, and I heard the voice of many angels around the throne, the living creatures, and the elders; and the number of them was ten thousand times ten thousand, and thousands of thousands, saying with a loud voice: "Worthy is the Lamb who was slain to receive power and riches and wisdom, and strength and honor and glory and blessing!" And every creature which is in heaven and on the earth and under the earth and such as are in the sea, and all that are in them, I heard saying: "Blessing and honor and glory and power be to Him who sits on the throne, and to the Lamb, forever and ever" (Revelation 5:9-13)!

2. **The church is referred to as the "Bride of Christ."**

He who has the bride is the bridegroom; but the friend of the bridegroom, who stands and hears him, rejoices greatly because of the bridegroom's voice. Therefore this joy of mine is fulfilled (John 3:29).

"Let us be glad and rejoice and give Him glory, for the marriage of the Lamb has come, and His wife has made herself ready." And to her it was granted to be arrayed in fine linen, clean and bright, for the fine linen is the righteous acts of the saints (Revelation 19:7-8).

III. The Great White Throne Judgment.

A. At the end of the millennium (which is the thousand year reign of Jesus Christ on earth), those who did not receive Jesus as their Lord and Savior throughout the corridors of time will receive their final judgment at the Great White Throne Judgment.

Then I saw a great white throne and Him who sat on it, from whose face the earth and the heaven fled away. And there was found no place for them. And I saw the dead, small and great, standing before God, and books were opened. And another book was opened, which is the Book of Life. And the dead were judged according to their works, by the things which were written in the books. The sea gave up the dead who were in it, and Death and Hades delivered up the dead who were in them. And they were judged, each one according to his works. Then Death and Hades were cast into the lake of fire. This is the second death. And anyone not found written in the Book of Life was cast into the lake of fire (Revelation 20:11-14).

1. All the unbelieving dead will be resurrected to stand in this judgment.

And as it is appointed for men to die once, but after this the judgment (Hebrews 9:27).

But the rest of the dead did not live again until the thousand years were finished. This is the first resurrection (Revelation 20:5).

Do not marvel at this; for the hour is coming in which all who are in the graves will hear His voice and come forth—those who have done good, to the resurrection of life, and those who have done evil, to the resurrection of condemnation (John 5:28-29).

2. Believers will not stand in the Great White Throne Judgment for they have already been judged and have given an account for their lives at the Judgment Seat of Christ.

B. Jesus will be the judge at the Great White Throne.

For the Father judges no one, but has committed all judgment to the Son, that all should honor the Son just as they honor the Father. He who does not honor the Son does not honor the Father who sent Him. Most assuredly, I say to you, he who hears My word and believes in Him who sent Me has everlasting life, and shall not come into judgment, but has passed from death into life. Most assuredly, I say to you, the hour is coming, and now is, when the dead will hear the voice of the Son of God; and those who hear will live. For as the Father has life in Himself, so He has granted the Son to have life in Himself, and has given Him authority to execute judgment also, because He is the Son of Man (John 5:22-27).

C. The Bible states that unbelievers will be judged according to the things which are written in the books.

And I saw the dead, small and great, standing before God, and books were opened. And another book was opened, which is the Book of Life. And the dead were judged according to their works, by the things which were written in the books. The sea gave up the dead who were in it, and Death and Hades delivered up the dead who were in them. And they were judged, each one according to his works (Revelation 20:12-13).

A fiery stream issued and came forth from before Him. A thousand thousands ministered to Him; Ten thousand times ten thousand stood before Him. The court was seated, and the books were opened (Daniel 7:10).

1. The Bible repeatedly warns us about what this judgment will be like as unbelievers are judged according to their works.

For God will bring every work into judgment, including every secret thing, whether it is good or whether it is evil (Ecclesiastes 12:14).

For there is nothing covered that will not be revealed, nor hidden that will not be known. Therefore whatever you have spoken in the dark will be heard in the light, and what you have spoken in the ear in inner rooms will be proclaimed on the housetops (Luke 12:2-3).

But in accordance with your hardness and your impenitent heart you are treasuring up for yourself wrath in the day of wrath and revelation of the righteous judgment of God, who "will render to each one according to his deeds" (Romans 2:5-6).

2. **This will be a fearful moment for all unbelievers when they finally face Jesus; even the heavens and earth will flee from His awesome presence.**

Then I saw a great white throne and Him who sat on it, from whose face the earth and the heaven fled away. And there was found no place for them (Revelation 20:11).

3. **Unbelievers will be utterly defenseless and without an appeal as they stand before the Lord with only their evil works to show for their time on earth.**

Now we know that whatever the law says, it says to those who are under the law, that every mouth may be stopped, and all the world may become guilty before God (Romans 3:19).

D. **After the unbelievers are judged according to their works that have been recorded in the books another book is opened—the Book of Life.**

And I saw the dead, small and great, standing before God, and books were opened. And another book was opened, which is the Book of Life. And the dead were judged according to their works, by the things which were written in the books (Revelation 20:12).

1. **Everyone whose name is not recorded in this Book of Life will be cast into the lake of fire to be in torment for all of eternity.**

And anyone not found written in the Book of Life was cast into the lake of fire (Revelation 20:15).

2. **After this sobering event there will be one final action from the Great White Throne: Death and Hades are cast into the lake of fire.**

Then Death and Hades were cast into the lake of fire. This is the second death (Revelation 20:14).

3.   **This fulfills the promise of God recorded by the Apostle Paul in his letter to the Corinthian church.**

The last enemy that will be destroyed is death (I Corinthians 15:26).

E.   **When judgment is passed, and the eternal sentence is carried out on all unbelievers, no one will be able to accuse the Lord of being unjust.**

1.   **Jesus warned us that the Day of Judgment would come unexpectedly.**

2.   **Jesus also warned us that we should be in right relationship with Him when we find ourselves standing before Him.**

But take heed to yourselves, lest your hearts be weighed down with carousing, drunkenness, and cares of this life, and that Day come on you unexpectedly. For it will come as a snare on all those who dwell on the face of the whole earth. Watch therefore, and pray always that you may be counted worthy to escape all these things that will come to pass, and to stand before the Son of Man (Luke 21:34-36).

Chapter Seventeen

Life after Death
Part Two

I. The Horror of Hell.

A. God created man in His own image; eternal in existence and sovereign in the exercise of his will. It is by divine decree that man has a free will and therefore, his eternal choices are irrevocable.

Then God said, "Let Us make man in Our image, according to Our likeness; let them have dominion over the fish of the sea, over the birds of the air, and over the cattle, over all the earth and over every creeping thing that creeps on the earth." So God created man in His own image; in the image of God He created him; male and female He created them (Genesis 1:26-27).

B. The most important question that can be asked of anyone is, "Where will you spend eternity?"

   1. It is a fact that we will all spend eternity in one of two places: heaven or hell.

Do not marvel at this; for the hour is coming in which all who are in the graves will hear His voice and come forth—those who have done good, to the resurrection of life, and those who have done evil, to the resurrection of condemnation (John 5:28-29).

   2. Our eternal destination is determined by the choice we make regarding our acceptance, or rejection, of God's offer of salvation.

C. When choosing our eternal home, there are only two options given to us and the choice we make is a declaration of our will.

   1. It is an amazing trait of human nature that when we insist on our way, especially if our way is contrary to God's way, we assume we can do as we please with impunity of penalty or punishment.

2. **We can choose God's will and His way of salvation through His Son; or we can choose our will and way and suffer the consequences of eternity.**

I call heaven and earth as witnesses today against you, that I have set before you life and death, blessing and cursing; therefore choose life, that both you and your descendants may live (Deuteronomy 30:19).

Unless you are converted and become as little children, you will by no means enter the kingdom of heaven (Matthew 18:3).

Jesus said to him, "I am the way, the truth, and the life. No one comes to the Father except through Me" (John 14:6).

Let it be known to you all, and to all the people of Israel, that by the name of Jesus Christ of Nazareth, whom you crucified, whom God raised from the dead, by Him this man stands here before you whole. This is the "stone which was rejected by you builders, which has become the chief cornerstone." Nor is there salvation in any other, for there is no other name under heaven given among men by which we must be saved (Acts 4:10-12).

D. **It has never been God's will, nor His desire, that anyone should go to hell. Anyone who goes to hell will do so as a sovereign act of their own will.**

The Lord is not slack concerning His promise, as some count slackness, but is longsuffering toward us, not willing that any should perish but that all should come to repentance (II Peter 3:9).

1. **Jesus declared that His mission was to rescue us from suffering the loss of God's plan for mankind.**

For the Son of Man has come to save that which was lost. What do you think? If a man has a hundred sheep, and one of them goes astray, does he not leave the ninety-nine and go to the mountains to seek the one that is straying? And if he should find it, assuredly, I say to you, he rejoices more over that sheep than over the ninety-nine that did not go astray. Even so it is not the will of your Father who is in heaven that one of these little ones should perish (Matthew 18:11-14).

302

2. **God has made every effort to make His love known to us and encourage us not to choose hell as our eternal home.**

    For God so loved the world that He gave His only begotten Son, that whoever believes in Him should not perish but have everlasting life. For God did not send His Son into the world to condemn the world, but that the world through Him might be saved. He who believes in Him is not condemned; but he who does not believe is condemned already, because he has not believed in the name of the only begotten Son of God. And this is the condemnation, that the light has come into the world, and men loved darkness rather than light, because their deeds were evil (John 3:16-19).

E. **Man's persistent argument against the reality of hell has always been, "How can a loving God send anyone to such a horrible place as hell?"**

    1. **A pertinent counter question would be, "How can an intelligent person reject a God who offers such forgiving grace and unconditional love?"**

        Anyone who has rejected Moses' law dies without mercy on the testimony of two or three witnesses. Of how much worse punishment, do you suppose, will he be thought worthy who has trampled the Son of God underfoot, counted the blood of the covenant by which he was sanctified a common thing, and insulted the Spirit of grace (Hebrews 10:28-29)?

    2. **Our time would be better spent considering the great sacrifice God made to provide a way of escape from the judgment of our sin.**

        Therefore we must give the more earnest heed to the things we have heard, lest we drift away. For if the word spoken through angels proved steadfast, and every transgression and disobedience received a just reward, how shall we escape if we neglect so great a salvation, which at the first began to be spoken by the Lord, and was confirmed to us by those who heard Him, God also bearing witness both with signs and wonders, with various miracles, and gifts of the Holy Spirit, according to His own will (Hebrews 2:1-4)?

F. It is important to remember that hell was not in God's original design for mankind.

1. Hell was prepared for the devil and his angels.

Then He will also say to those on the left hand, "Depart from Me, you cursed, into the everlasting fire prepared for the devil and his angels" (Matthew 25:41).

2. Hell was enlarged to accommodate all who deny and defy their Creator; thereby, they reject His offer of saving grace.

Therefore Sheol has enlarged itself and opened its mouth beyond measure; their glory and their multitude and their pomp, and he who is jubilant, shall descend into it (Isaiah 5:14).

G. Consider the horrors of hell:

1. Hell is a place where the conscience never dies and the lusts of the flesh can never be satisfied.

And if your eye causes you to sin, pluck it out. It is better for you to enter the kingdom of God with one eye, rather than having two eyes, to be cast into hell fire—where "Their worm does not die, and the fire is not quenched" (Mark 9:47-48).

a. The word "worm" used in this text is the same word for maggot.

b. The picture is that of one whose conscience will continuously play the events of their life. The memory of their rejection of God's offer of grace will be unbearable.

c. It will be as though a maggot were continually eating away at them, yet never consuming them.

2. Hell is a place of outer darkness and isolation.

Then the king said to the servants, "Bind him hand and foot, take him away, and cast him into outer darkness; there will be weeping and gnashing of teeth" (Matthew 22:13).

And cast the unprofitable servant into the outer darkness. There will be weeping and gnashing of teeth (Matthew 25:30).

    a.   **The words "outer darkness," signify a total disassociation with everyone and everything.**

    b.   **The picture is of one who is totally alone as they increasingly become distanced from God and from all other expressions of life.**

There will be weeping and gnashing of teeth, when you see Abraham and Isaac and Jacob and all the prophets in the kingdom of God, and yourselves thrust out (Luke 13:28).

    c.   **Their sorrow will be vented in unrelenting weeping. Their emotions will be so troubled that they will gnash their teeth in agony.**

3.   **Hell is the eternal habitation and place of torment for the wicked.**

    a.   **Every unbelieving, wicked, and vile person who ever lived will suffer in the fires of hell.**

But the cowardly, unbelieving, abominable, murderers, sexually immoral, sorcerers, idolaters, and all liars shall have their part in the lake which burns with fire and brimstone, which is the second death (Revelation 21:8).

And anyone not found written in the Book of Life was cast into the lake of fire (Revelation 20:15).

    b.   **The devil, the false prophet, and the beast will be forever tormented in the fires of hell.**

And the devil, who deceived them, was cast into the lake of fire and brimstone where the beast and the false prophet are. And they will be tormented day and night forever and ever (Revelation 20:10).

c. **The angels who followed Lucifer's rebellion, and served his kingdom of darkness, will forever be tormented in the fires of hell.**

For if God did not spare the angels who sinned, but cast them down to hell and delivered them into chains of darkness, to be reserved for judgment (II Peter 2:4).

4. Hell is a place of fire and brimstone.

Then the beast was captured, and with him the false prophet who worked signs in his presence, by which he deceived those who received the mark of the beast and those who worshiped his image. These two were cast alive into the lake of fire burning with brimstone (Revelation 19:20).

The Son of Man will send out His angels, and they will gather out of His kingdom all things that offend, and those who practice lawlessness, and will cast them into the furnace of fire. There will be wailing and gnashing of teeth (Matthew 13:41-42).

Then He will also say to those on the left hand, "Depart from Me, you cursed, into the everlasting fire prepared for the devil and his angels" (Matthew 25:41).

a. **The suffering that is experienced by those in the fires of hell is unrelenting and unending.**

b. **There will never be a moment's rest from the flames of torment in hell.**

Then a third angel followed them, saying with a loud voice, "If anyone worships the beast and his image, and receives his mark on his forehead or on his hand, he himself shall also drink of the wine of the wrath of God, which is poured out full strength into the cup of His indignation and he shall be tormented with fire and brimstone in the presence of the holy angels and in the presence of the Lamb. And the smoke of their torment ascends forever and ever; and they have no rest day or night, who worship the beast and his image, and whoever receives the mark of his name" (Revelation 14:9-11).

II. The Glories of Heaven.

A. The Scripture speaks a great deal about heaven.

    1. The Bible begins with God creating the heavens and the earth. It culminates with a description of God's new earth; new heavens; and His eternal city, the New Jerusalem.

    2. Fifty-three of the sixty-six books of the Bible contain a specific mention of heaven.

    3. The remaining books (six in the Old Testament and seven in the New Testament), carry themes compatible with heaven and life lived there.

B. There are seven dominate facts about heaven.

    1. Heaven is a place of beauty beyond our earthly comprehension.

But as it is written: "Eye has not seen, nor ear heard, nor have entered into the heart of man the things which God has prepared for those who love Him" (I Corinthians 2:9).

    2. Heaven is a place of complete rest. We will be forever free from our fears; our anxieties; our tears; our pains; our strife; and our grief.

Then I heard a voice from heaven saying to me, "Write: 'Blessed are the dead who die in the Lord from now on.'" "Yes," says the Spirit, "that they may rest from their labors, and their works follow them" (Revelation 14:13).

Therefore they are before the throne of God, and serve Him day and night in His temple. And He who sits on the throne will dwell among them. They shall neither hunger anymore nor thirst anymore; the sun shall not strike them, nor any heat; for the Lamb who is in the midst of the throne will shepherd them and lead them to living fountains of waters. And God will wipe away every tear from their eyes (Revelation 7:15-17).

3. Heaven is a place where our knowledge and understanding will be complete.

For now we see in a mirror, dimly, but then face to face. Now I know in part, but then I shall know just as I also am known (I Corinthians 13:12).

4. Heaven is a place of continual service to the Lord.

Therefore they are before the throne of God, and serve Him day and night in His temple. And He who sits on the throne will dwell among them (Revelation 7:15).

And there shall be no more curse, but the throne of God and of the Lamb shall be in it, and His servants shall serve Him (Revelation 22:3).

5. Heaven is a place of incredible joy.

His lord said to him, "Well done, good and faithful servant; you have been faithful over a few things, I will make you ruler over many things. Enter into the joy of your lord" (Matthew 25:23).

These things I have spoken to you, that My joy may remain in you, and that your joy may be full (John 15:11).

And God will wipe away every tear from their eyes; there shall be no more death, nor sorrow, nor crying. And there shall be no more pain, for the former things have passed away (Revelation 21:4).

6. Heaven will be a place where we will never say goodbye again. We will enjoy fellowship with the redeemed of all the ages; the angels; and God the Father; Jesus; and the Holy Spirit.

But you have come to Mount Zion and to the city of the living God, the heavenly Jerusalem, to an innumerable company of angels, to the general assembly and church of the firstborn who are registered in heaven, to God the Judge of all, to the spirits of just men made perfect, to Jesus the Mediator of the new covenant, and to the blood of sprinkling that speaks better things than that of Abel (Hebrews 12:22-24).

Now I saw a new heaven and a new earth, for the first heaven and the first earth had passed away. Also there was no more sea. Then I, John, saw the holy city, New Jerusalem, coming down out of heaven from God, prepared as a bride adorned for her husband. And I heard a loud voice from heaven saying, "Behold, the tabernacle of God is with men, and He will dwell with them, and they shall be His people. God Himself will be with them and be their God. And God will wipe away every tear from their eyes; there shall be no more death, nor sorrow, nor crying. There shall be no more pain, for the former things have passed away." Then He who sat on the throne said, "Behold, I make all things new." And He said to me, "Write, for these words are true and faithful." And He said to me, "It is done! I am the Alpha and the Omega, the Beginning and the End. I will give of the fountain of the water of life freely to him who thirsts. He who overcomes shall inherit all things, and I will be his God and he shall be My son" (Revelation 21:1-7).

7. **Heaven is a place of perpetual permanence and stability; nothing will ever change there or be taken from us.**

And he showed me a pure river of water of life, clear as crystal, proceeding from the throne of God and of the Lamb. In the middle of its street, and on either side of the river, was the tree of life, which bore twelve fruits, each tree yielding its fruit every month. The leaves of the tree were for the healing of the nations. And there shall be no more curse, but the throne of God and of the Lamb shall be in it, and His servants shall serve Him. They shall see His face, and His name shall be on their foreheads. There shall be no night there: They need no lamp nor light of the sun, for the Lord God gives them light. And they shall reign forever and ever (Revelation 22:1-5).

C. **The Bible refers to heaven as Paradise.**

1. **Jesus promised the dying thief on the cross that they would be together in Paradise that very day.**

And Jesus said to him, "Assuredly, I say to you, today you will be with Me in Paradise" (Luke 23:43).

2. **The Apostle Paul spoke of Paradise when he told of his experience of being caught up into the third heaven.**

I know a man in Christ who fourteen years ago—whether in the body I do not know, or whether out of the body I do not know, God knows—such a one was caught up to the third heaven. And I know such a man—whether in the body or out of the body I do not know, God knows— how he was caught up into Paradise and heard inexpressible words, which it is not lawful for a man to utter (II Corinthians 12:2-4).

3. **Jesus spoke of Paradise in His promise to the church of Ephesus.**

He who has an ear, let him hear what the Spirit says to the churches. To him who overcomes I will give to eat from the tree of life, which is in the midst of the Paradise of God (Revelation 2:7).

4. **The Bible first introduces us to Paradise in the Garden of Eden.**

    a. **We are tempted to believe that Paradise had its beginnings here on earth, but that is not what the Scriptures teach.**

    b. **The Scriptures teach that God ... "planted a garden."**

    This is the history of the heavens and the earth when they were created, in the day that the Lord God made the earth and the heavens, before any plant of the field was in the earth and before any herb of the field had grown. For the Lord God had not caused it to rain on the earth, and there was no man to till the ground. The Lord God planted a garden eastward in Eden, and there He put the man whom He had formed (Genesis 2:4-5, 8).

    c. **Hebrew scholars tell us that the word we have translated as "planted" literally means "transplanted."**

    d.   **God already had all the plants, herbs and trees ... He merely transplanted a portion of Paradise to earth to share with His highest creation, mankind.**

5.   Paradise was located within the heart of the earth in the days of Christ; it was sometimes referred to as "Abraham's Bosom."

So it was that the beggar died, and was carried by the angels into Abraham's bosom. The rich man also died and was buried (Luke 16:22).

6.   Christ not only walked out of the tomb victorious at the resurrection, He also led all the inhabitants of Paradise out of captivity and moved Paradise back into the very presence of God.

And the graves were opened; and many bodies of the saints who had fallen asleep were raised; and coming out of the graves after His resurrection, they went into the holy city and appeared to many (Matthew 27:52-53).

Therefore He says: "When He ascended on high, He led captivity captive, and gave gifts to men." (Now this, "He ascended"—what does it mean but that He also first descended into the lower parts of the earth? He who descended is also the One who ascended far above all the heavens, that He might fill all things.)" (Ephesians 4:8-10).

7.   Paradise is God's garden. When a believer dies, they are instantly taken to God's presence in Paradise; therein, they await their ultimate home in the New Jerusalem.

We are confident, yes, well pleased rather to be absent from the body and to be present with the Lord (II Corinthians 5:8).

D.   The Bible also refers to heaven as Father's House.

1.   Jesus taught us that what belonged to Him, as a result of His gift of salvation, now belongs to us.

Jesus said to her, "Do not cling to Me, for I have not yet ascended to My Father; but go to My brethren and say to them, 'I am ascending to My Father and your Father, and to My God and your God'" (John 20:17).

2. On the night before He was crucified, Jesus told His disciples that His Father's House has many mansions.

In My Father's house are many mansions; if it were not so, I would have told you. I go to prepare a place for you (John 14:2).

3. By virtue of our life span, our places of dwelling on earth are temporary; whether we rent, or own. However, in heaven, we will have a permanent address for all of eternity.

And if I go and prepare a place for you, I will come again and receive you to Myself; that where I am, there you may be also (John 14:3).

E. Our ultimate and eternal dwelling place in heaven will be the New Jerusalem.

1. The New Jerusalem is a celestial city whose designer and builder is God.

For he waited for the city which has foundations, whose builder and maker is God (Hebrews 11:10).

2. John saw this city come down from heaven.

Now I saw a new heaven and a new earth, for the first heaven and the first earth had passed away. Also there was no more sea (Revelation 21:1).

3. The New Jerusalem will not rest on the earth. This city will be suspended above the earth and will be the source of light for the earth.

But the Jerusalem above is free which is the mother of us all (Galatians 4:26).

The city had no need of the sun or of the moon to shine in it, for the glory of God illuminated it and the Lamb is its light. And the nations of those who are saved shall walk in its light, and the kings of the earth bring their glory and honor into it (Revelation 21:23-24).

4.   The New Jerusalem is colossal and beyond description in its dimensions.

    a.   The New Jerusalem is a city that is built layer upon layer and is in the shape of a perfect cube.

    b.   The measurements of this cubed city are 1,500 miles in every direction.

The city is laid out as a square; its length is as great as its breadth. And he measured the city with the reed: twelve thousand furlongs. Its length, breadth, and height are equal (Revelation 21:16).

5.   The New Jerusalem is aglow with the glory of God.

And he carried me away in the Spirit to a great and high mountain, and showed me the great city, the holy Jerusalem, descending out of heaven from God, having the glory of God. Her light was like a most precious stone, like a jasper stone, clear as crystal (Revelation 21:10-11).

6.   The throne of God will take its permanent residence in the New Jerusalem.

Immediately I was in the Spirit; and behold, a throne set in heaven, and One sat on the throne. And He who sat there was like a jasper and a sardius stone in appearance; and there was a rainbow around the throne, in appearance like an emerald (Revelation 4:2-3).

7.   The walls of this heavenly city are so immense, they almost are beyond description.

a. The walls of the city are 6,000 miles in length and height.

b. The walls of the city are approximately 216 to 240 feet wide.

Also she had a great and high wall with twelve gates, and twelve angels at the gates, and names written on them, which are the names of the twelve tribes of the children of Israel (Revelation 21:12).

And the city is laid out as a square, and its length is as great as its breadth. And he measured the city with the reed: twelve thousand furlongs. Its length, breadth, and height are equal. Then he measured its wall: one hundred and forty-four cubits, according to the measure of a man, that is, of an angel (Revelation 21:16-17).

c. The walls are made of jasper so pure, that it has the appearance of crystal.

And the construction of its wall was of jasper, and the city was pure gold, like clear glass (Revelation 21:18).

8. The foundation upon which the walls of the city rest is made of precious stones.

a. They are each 500 miles in length.

b. These stones are like all of the other building materials in heaven, they are pure and transparent:

And the foundations of the wall of the city were adorned with all kinds of precious stones: the first foundation was jasper, the second sapphire, the third chalcedony, the fourth emerald, the fifth sardonyx, the sixth sardius, the seventh chrysolite, the eighth beryl, the ninth topaz, the tenth chrysoprase, the eleventh jacinth, and the twelfth amethyst (Revelation 21:19-20).

(1) The first stone is jasper, which is a combination of purple, blue, green, and brass in color;

(2) The second stone is sapphire, which is dark blue in color;

(3) The third stone is chalcedony, which is a combination of grey, blue, and yellow in color;

(4) The fourth stone is emerald, which is green in color;

(5) The fifth stone is sardonyx, which is pale blue in color;

(6) The sixth stone is sardis, which is blood red in color;

(7) The seventh stone is chrysolite, which is a combination of purple and green;

(8) The eighth stone is beryl, which is a combination of blue and green in color;

(9) The ninth stone is topaz, which is a golden, pale green in color;

(10) The tenth stone is chrysoprasus, which is a combination of blue, green, and yellow in color;

(11) The eleventh stone is jacinth, which is a combination of red, violet, and yellow in color;

(12) The twelfth stone is amethyst, which is purple in color.

9. **The walls of the New Jerusalem have twelve gates—three in each wall.**

Three gates on the east, three gates on the north, three gates on the south, and three gates on the west (Revelation 21:13).

10. **The gates in the walls of the New Jerusalem are made of twelve giant pearls and they are positioned 375 miles apart in the walls.**

And the twelve gates were twelve pearls: each individual gate was of one pearl and the street of the city was pure gold, like transparent glass (Revelation 21:21).

   a. **Each gate is perpetually open.**

   Its gates shall not be shut at all by day (there shall be no night there) (Revelation 21:25).

   b. **Each gate has an angel as its sentry.**

   Also she had a great and high wall with twelve gates, and twelve angels at the gates (Revelation 21:12).

11. **The New Jerusalem is made of pure gold and is like transparent glass. The streets are also of pure gold and they are like clear glass.**

And the street of the city was pure gold, like transparent glass (Revelation 21:21).

The city was pure gold, like clear glass (Revelation 21:18).

   a. **The construction materials used in the New Jerusalem are pure and transparent: There is nothing in heaven that will restrict the flow of the light of the city; the glory of God.**

   b. **All the materials used are heavenly in nature, and are eternal in durability … nothing will ever decay, rot, mold, rust, or fade in color.**

F. **There are seven defining characteristics about the New Jerusalem.**

1. **There is no temple in the New Jerusalem.**

But I saw no temple in it, for the Lord God Almighty and the Lamb are its temple (Revelation 21:22).

    a. **In the New Jerusalem we will enjoy unlimited access and fellowship with God.**

    b. **We will not need a designated place or building for the church to meet with God; the entire city will be filled with God's glory and presence.**

    c. **Literally, the New Jerusalem will be God's temple.**

2. **There is no need of the sun or of the moon in the New Jerusalem.**

And the city had no need of the sun or of the moon to shine in it, for the glory of God illuminated it, and the Lamb is its light (Revelation 21:23).

    a. **The glory of God will replace the created light of the sun and moon.**

    This is the message which we have heard from Him and declare to you, that God is light and in Him is no darkness at all (I John 1:5).

    b. **The light of God's glory will illuminate the New Jerusalem. His light is life-giving and therefore, will rejuvenate its inhabitants.**

    For in Him we live and move and have our being (Acts 17:28).

    In Him was life, and the life was the light of men (John 1:4).

3.   There are no locked gates in the New Jerusalem.

Its gates shall not be shut at all by day (Revelation 21:25).

a.   **While we lived on earth, closed doors were a necessity for the preservation of life and property.**

b.   **However, in the New Jerusalem the angels will stand guard at the twelve gates and will be a constant reminder of the safety and security of this great city.**

4.   There is no night in the New Jerusalem.

There shall be no night there (Revelation 21:25).

a.   **We will continually bask in the light of God's presence in the New Jerusalem. Our activities will not have to cease by virtue of darkness or from our mere exhaustion.**

And there shall be no night there: They need no lamp nor light of the sun, for the Lord God gives them light. And they shall reign forever and ever (Revelation 22:5).

b.   **One of the benefits of our new, glorified body will be that we will never grow tired and need periods of rest to recuperate.**

5.   There will be no defiling factors in the New Jerusalem.

But there shall by no means enter it anything that defiles, or causes an abomination or a lie, but only those who are written in the Lamb's Book of Life (Revelation 21:27).

a.   **There will be nothing out of place; nothing will be un-kept or unsightly; colors will never clash; and the air will never be polluted.**

    b.   **We will be never be subjected to an impure thought; an impure action; or an impure motive.**

6.   **There are no abominations in the New Jerusalem.**

But there shall by no means enter it anything that defiles, or causes an abomination or a lie, but only those who are written in the Lamb's Book of Life (Revelation 21:27).

    a.   **When Jesus used the term, "abomination of desolation," He was making reference to that which defiles the sacred holy place.**

Therefore when you see the "abomination of desolation," spoken of by Daniel the prophet, standing in the holy place (Matthew 24:15).

    b.   **There will be no more religious pride which causes us to exalt ourselves above others.**

Now the Pharisees, who were lovers of money, also heard all these things, and they derided Him. And He said to them, "You are those who justify yourselves before men, but God knows your hearts. For what is highly esteemed among men is an abomination in the sight of God" (Luke 16:14-15).

7.   **There will be no more lies in the New Jerusalem. On earth we constantly have to judge between what is true and what is false.**

But there shall by no means enter it anything that defiles, or causes an abomination or a lie, but only those who are written in the Lamb's Book of Life (Revelation 21:27).

Beloved, do not believe every spirit, but test the spirits, whether they are of God; because many false prophets have gone out into the world (I John 4:1).

Test all things; hold fast what is good (I Thessalonians 5:21).

G. Our emotional experiences will be limited in the New Jerusalem.

"And God will wipe away every tear from their eyes; there shall be no more death, nor sorrow, nor crying and there shall be no more pain, for the former things have passed away." Then He who sat on the throne said, "Behold, I make all things new." And He said to me, "Write, for these words are true and faithful" (Revelation 21:4-5).

1. **The New Jerusalem will be a place of abundant joy and happiness. Absolutely nothing will be permitted that will diminish the joy we will find within the gates.**

2. **The New Jerusalem will be a place where sorrow is replaced with joy; laughter; and love; for all of eternity.**

3. **The New Jerusalem will be a place that we live free from pain, sickness, disease, and death—we will live eternally in Christ's victory!**

So when this corruptible has put on incorruption, and this mortal has put on immortality, then shall be brought to pass the saying that is written: "Death is swallowed up in victory. O Death, where is your sting? O Hades, where is your victory?" The sting of death is sin, and the strength of sin is the law. But thanks be to God, who gives us the victory through our Lord Jesus Christ (I Corinthians 15:54-57).

Other Books by Dr. Elliott

My Daily Appointment

is the perfect companion for the development of a daily devotional habit. Dr. Elliott speaks from his heart as he gives insight into the Scriptures in a way that can be applied to your everyday life experiences. Discover the fulfilling joy of spending time each day with Jesus…draw from His wisdom and allow Him to lead you into His eternal purposes for your life.

ISBN 1-931178-72-0 ~ $15.00 (paperback)

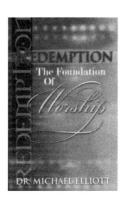

Redemption: The Foundation of Worship

takes the reader on a journey of discovery about man's ultimate purpose in life. In this book, Dr. Elliott explains why worship flows out of our redemption; why it is important for us to know the patterns of worship set forth in the Tabernacle of Moses; and why understanding God's redemptive names expands our worship.

ISBN 1-931178-75-5 ~ $10.00 (paperback)